*Thank you for y[our]
contribution t[o]
Ukrainian*

Lydia's Child

by

Valentine Kirychenko

Val Kirychenko
4/7/22

STRATEGIC BOOK GROUP

Strategic Book Group
P.O. Box 333
Durham CT 06422
www.StrategicBookClub.com

ISBN: 978-1-60976-471-5

Book Design: Bonita S. Watson

Acknowledgments

I would like to thank my children and all the friends who helped and encouraged me in this project by reading the early versions and providing valuable suggestions. My friend Betty Gray did the typing from scratch and sometimes inaudible dictation tapes. Her enthusiasm made me persevere with the project.

Siobhan and Pat Campbell provided valuable suggestions in the later versions of the drafts. John Hollows had valuable input, supplied some historical details, did some editing, and reorganized some of the narrative.

Dedications

I dedicate this book to the memory of my parents, Lydia and Ivan, and Ludmilla, my sister, whose constant love assured my survival. I also dedicate it to my four children, Peter, Natalie, Louise, and Sara. The children are the conduit of our immortality.

Contents

Chapter 1

Something Happened on the Way

Everything that ever went seriously wrong for my family was somehow connected with a train journey. Even in Russia, where travel is generally an endurance feat anyway, that seemed just a little unusual. I wasn't even born then, of course, but I know what happened and I also feel I know the individuals, from the accounts my family told and re-told one another. To them, what they endured was just a part of living in Central Europe when the twentieth century was destroying itself. They seemed to think it was almost to be expected given the circumstances, whereas to me, looking back from the peace of life in Australia, it is more like a nightmarish nadir of human existence. And we were not even Jews, the century's most persecuted people. We were German/Ukrainian.

It all began because we were living in Lvov, in western Ukraine, then part of Austro-Hungary, in the years before World War One. And we tried to leave too late. The long saga began one sunny spring morning when my mother, then four years old, heard the postman's ring at the front door and went to answer. It was her house-task to pick up the letters that were dropped through the letter-slot. Lydia was a chubby little girl, with strong legs and a round face. Her eyes were round and dark brown, with dark hair cut short, as was the fashion then. Her family loved her smile: it would break out at the least provocation and light up her whole face. That's not to say that she was not a determined little puss when she felt like it, and sometimes even obstinate. When she set her mind on something, she would put her whole heart into it and overcome anything in her path.

She picked up the letter and took it to her father, breakfasting in the dining room with the rest of the family.

"I've got a letter, I've got a letter," she told him. "Look, lovely stamps on it." She gave it to her father, Alexander. He looked at it closely to see who it was from.

"Must be your brother Heinrich, Louiza," he told her mother. "It's from Canada." He opened up the envelope and a photograph fell out. Lydia picked it up: she had never seen anything like this picture before. It showed a locomotive of the Trans-Canadian Railway, in the middle of winter, with falling snow thick on the ground. But in front of the engine was a huge bear, which stood on his hind legs, leaning his paws on the locomotive so he appeared to be stopping the train in its tracks. Lydia would remember that picture for the rest of her life. Her father began laughing.

"Look at this, Louiza, Heinrich must have been stopped by one of the bears."

Heinrich Bauer had gone to live in Canada several years before, and found a job as a train driver for the Canadian Pacific Railways. He was always trying to encourage the rest of the family to join him.

"What's he say in the letter?" asked Louiza.

"Oh, as usual, just to hurry up and come over. He says there's plenty of work there, and according to him, with our experience we shouldn't have any worries at all."

Alexander Goltz did not sound too impressed. He was the manager of a plant processing sugar beets in Lvov. The Goltz family was Volksdeutsch, descendants of the Germans brought to Russia by Catherine the Great almost two hundred years before, to spearhead her attempt to foster a Russian Industrial Revolution. Most of them still had either technical or some kind of scientific expertise, or managed factories.

Underneath, though, Alexander was increasingly tempted by his brother-in-law's suggestion. He'd certainly been reluctant initially—after all, he was approaching middle age, held a secure job, and had five children to consider—but he was beginning to feel a growing hostility in the local people. It didn't matter that western Ukraine had been part of Austria Hungary for over a century and Polish before that; most of the locals were ethnic Poles, around a quarter saw themselves as Ukrainians, and that was it. This large group had no residual loyalty for Poland and considered the Austrian Emperor a foreign annoyance, Russia an irrelevance. Both Poles and Ukrainians were for the most part workers, who saw their Volksdeutsch managers as unwelcome impositions, an alien middle class exploiting a Ukraine that belonged to them. For their part, the Volksdeutsch in Poland, Ukraine, or Russia all faced the same problem. Anti-German sentiment was rising and, with encouragement filtering down from the government, workers and hooligans alike were starting to perform acts of violence and vandalism on Volksdeutsch people and property.

"You know, Louiza," Alexander told his wife after a second or two, "maybe we might think about it after all if things keep getting worse. The hooligans broke three windows last week. Who knows what they will do next?"

Louiza was not instantly taken with this idea. She always loved ancient Lvov—the narrow streets of tall houses, the wealth of three-hundred-year-old churches, both Catholic and Orthodox that graced the squares, the old opera house, and the graceful panorama of history you gazed over from heights such as the Zamkova Hill above the city. On the other hand, she knew as well as her husband how the Ukrainians felt about them. "Well, I certainly don't want to," she said, "but you may be right. The children are starting to suffer at school."

"I'm getting less and less cooperation from my staff," said Alexander. "Some of them are even getting aggressive and obstructive towards me. I'm seriously beginning to think we might take your brother's advice and move. At least in Canada there would be some peace and freedom for the children, even though we will have to start a new life."

"Well, I'm certainly getting more nervous." Louiza conceded. "I'm even frightened to walk down the street to the shops. At this stage, they're only calling me names from a distance, like 'German swine,' but you never know. Sooner or later they could get bolder and attack us physically. But going to Canada will create so much trouble. We have been here for twenty years, we had all our five children here, we've made friends. It will be a dreadful wrench."

"It's better to move voluntarily than be thrown out on a heap. I think if things don't settle down soon, we will make plans to emigrate."

Alexander wasted little time after that. Within a few days, he came to a final decision, formed a plan of action, and then began to implement it.

By mid-summer they had sold their house, all the furniture, and a lot of their clothing. They were going to Canada: they made certain they were well prepared. They packed as lightly as they could but wisely. They made sure they had very warm clothing, with every member fitted out with lambskin jackets, warm hats, gloves, and a good supply of warm boots, fur-lined. They took good notice of Uncle Heinrich's description of Canada's winter extremes, with 20 degrees below zero a commonplace in the northern part. Alexander and Louiza weren't going to leave anything to chance.

Alexander also realized that they might be heading into the wilderness and they had to be prepared to eke out a living in what would be harsh conditions. He bought tools and equipment: a large cross-saw to cut timber, axes of different variety and sizes, sharpening instruments, woodworking tools with plenty of hammers, chisels, planes, and plenty of nails and bolts. If he had to, he was even ready to build a sturdy cabin. He had two strong boys to help him, and he ensured that they were properly fitted out with everything they needed to be safe and comfortable. He even bought a set of rubber boots for each member of the family. They were novelties at the time, a recent innovation advertised as the ideal answer to snow and melting slush.

The family finally left their home, saying good-bye to neighbors and friends, and the fond memories they left behind in the house. Even Louiza, a tall, strong woman who thought she could cope with any situation, shed a few tears. She was saying good-bye to the little family nest where she had all her five children, two boys and three girls, and she knew life would never be quite the same again. Twenty years of happy marriage in this house had come to an end: all hopes aside, she knew she and her family faced a totally new future, and one that was not necessarily certain.

She looked at her family. There was Karlov, aged sixteen, physically strong and handsome with a ready eye for the girls. He was already showing his rebellious spirit to his father, objecting to the autocratic control by the parents of that time.

His younger brother Ludwig was much different. He was shy, studious, and dependable, always ready to help his father around the home and the older girls with their homework.

Olga and Marie, aged twelve and ten, were inseparable. They played happily together and whispered and laughed all the day long. They were, however, very clever, and Louiza knew they would be able to cope in a crisis.

The person she worried about most was Lydia. At the moment, everybody loved her, but she was very young. If something should happen to Alexander and herself, Louiza was fearful for Lydia's welfare.

Louiza's family made her life worth living, and she felt she would do anything to provide for and protect them. But while she was glad in the end that they were leaving Lvov for a safer place without the age-old divisions of Ukraine, she had to be a little nervous.

The family took all their belongings, including their individual suitcases of clothing and boxes of gear and equipment, to the railway station. The big stuff was packed away in the luggage wagon, while the family took up their reserved compartment in the train to Odessa. It was sparse, but comfortable, with upholstered seats and wooden paneling. They put their bags on the brass luggage shelves above and made themselves comfortable. The children were excited. It was going to be a great adventure to go somewhere new and exotic, like Canada, where the large polar bears stopped trains and the settlers lived by hunting. At the same time, the older children were rather sad to leave their friends. The two boys in particular were slightly regretful. They had started seeing one or two young girls more often after school.

It was going to be a two-day trip to Odessa. The train initially wound its way through the mountains of western Ukraine to the vast flat plains of the Dnieper River and on to Kiev. The train would then change direction, heading nearly due south for long periods along the same route as the river, meandering down to the Black Sea. Once at Odessa, they were to embark on a passenger ship to take them over the Black Sea, through the Dardanelles, the narrow passageway into the Mediterranean Sea, then heading west over the North Atlantic to Canada.

Louiza began telling the younger children all the stories she could think of about sailing on the ocean and all the exciting things to do on a passenger ship. Since none of them had even seen an ocean in their lives, this was something new to the entire family, but Louiza had been reading up. The older children read, or played card games to pass the time. Little Lydia spent a lot of time talking to her mother, with Louiza reading and telling her stories that she remembered from her own childhood.

She had brought enough food for the family, with white crispy bread, butter, salami sausage, tomatoes, and green cucumbers. Alexander brought hot water from the samovar set up in one of the carriages, to make tea. They drank it with plenty of sugar and lemon; milk was not their custom. They slept as best they could when night came, propped up at odd angles against each other's bodies. At long last, the train crept into Odessa's Central Station.

And it was July 28, 1914. The Austrian artillery had begun bombarding Belgrade a few hours before. Austria had declared war.

* * *

Of course, the Goltzes and probably everyone else on the train were well aware of the international crisis that had been building for a month. The newspapers had been full of it from the moment of Archduke Franz Ferdinand's assassination at Sarajevo in Serbia. It ran on, a saga of threat and counter-threat; partial ultimatum from the tsar to Austria, the tsar's retraction, followed by a new ultimatum; cautious backing for Vienna from the new Prussian-led Germany; a groveling backdown from the Serbs, rejected by Austria. But apart from a few scattered madmen, no one in government anywhere actually seemed to want war, so it hardly seemed to most people that such horror would really begin. They all underestimated Austrian stupidity.

The entire implications were not immediately clear on the twenty-eighth, when they got to Odessa. At the Central Railway Station, Alexander got his baggage together with the help of porters and the young boys, and had it loaded onto a cart. A whole row of them were lined up outside to serve the travelers. The family was taken to the dock area with other groups and families, ready to embark onto the passenger ship, already docked.

But when they got there, no one was ready to start loading luggage. No boarding was going on either; instead the dock was barred with heavy wrought-iron gates, locked and guarded by soldiers. It looked more like a jail than a harbor—the gates were reinforced with thick wire netting so that no one would be tempted to climb over.

There was nothing that could be done. The bags and other luggage were unloaded, and the family took up their positions, hoping to get onto the boat as soon as possible. A crowd of families and single people sat around the area ready to embark, their luggage packed in untidy piles. People were getting more impatient and agitated as time went by. No one could understand the delay and why they could not get onto the boat. They'd made plans and arrangements so long ago.

Finally a uniformed official came to the gate and made the announcement Alexander was dreading. Once the fighting began in Serbia, the Russian government had closed all frontiers. No one would be allowed to leave for the foreseeable future. It might never be possible at all.

Of course, the reasoning was pretty obvious. With Turkey widely known to be in the Germanic camp, it would be lunacy for a Russian passenger ship to risk the passage out of the Black Sea through the narrow Bosphorous, the Sea of Marmara, and the Dardanelles. The ship definitely wasn't leaving for Canada. And for Alexander there was a second, huge complication. Since that morning, he and his family were now enemy aliens in tsarist Russia. And that was ominous.

The reasoning wasn't immediately obvious to the growing crowd on the quay. They had planned their own emigrations for many months, sometimes years. They had sold homes and belongings and often bought themselves new equipment: they were committed to make a new life in a new and better world. To be told that all of that had been for nothing, that they had nowhere to go after they had spent most of their resources, was beyond acceptance. The frustration was explosive. The mob became angry. They started shouting and marching towards the officers at the docks, demanding to be let in to join their ships.

In the circumstances, Alexander felt it wiser to hang back with the family, and watch. Mounting a mass protest was not a particularly good move in tsarist Russia at any time. The police and the army loved this sort of thing. The troops were immediately called and an attachment of Cossacks on horseback, swords drawn, swept down to confront the marchers. The would-be emigrants had no weapons, apart from their anger and bare hands. They were helpless against the Cossacks, and they were quickly rounded up, to be taken to the detention center.

Then, just to make a neat job of it, the police came in and arrested the bystanders as well.

There was no court, no judge, and no jury. Each individual man was interviewed at the police station and told bluntly that they were citizens of "no fixed abode," contributing to a dangerous revolutionary situation with a country on the brink of war. This would not be tolerated, and they were to be sent to Siberia, forthwith.

Alexander, after spending the night in a cell, was hauled into an office the following morning to sit across a table from a row of stern-faced officials. The leader gave him a blunt lecture.

"We are entitled to send you to Siberia as a convict for taking part in, or at least contributing, to the rebellious riot yesterday. That has some unpleasant consequences. You might be sent to the mines, which is not a good prospect—it means working long hours in backbreaking conditions. Miners in Siberia tend not to last long. And, of course, you would have to leave your family here: there would be no one to look after them in Odessa, they will have no housing, nowhere to go, and no means of support. Your family's chances would be fairly dismal.

"On the other hand," he said, softening, "you could go to Siberia as a free settler." He looked at Alexander expectantly. This was part of a relatively new policy by the State. After centuries of regarding Siberia as a terminal rubbish dump for undesirables, it had dawned on Moscow with the rise of the Industrial Revolution that there were actually untold quantities of raw materials lying untapped there. The idea now was to populate it, something that became much easier once the Trans-Siberian Railway was built. It was now a relatively safe journey of no more than ten days, depending on the final destination. Public servants were told to sell the possibilities to people willing to become free settlers there, cementing the Russian claim to Siberia and blocking any intentions Japan and China might develop. The settlers were welcomed by the government with up to 160 acres of free land per family, much more than peasants had in Ukraine and Russia, and other help in equipment and capital was provided as well. The normal military service liability was waived. On the face of things, it wasn't a bad offer. And by 1914 almost seven million peasants had voluntarily moved to Siberia.

"You have some money to pay for the railway wagon," said the official, "and you can take your whole family, equipment, and even some farm animals to start a new life there. You'll get a grant of land, and as a settler you will participate in expanding the economy of the Siberian province. The lifestyle can be good. The farmers and peasants are industrious, producing good crops. It can be a happy life. At least it will save your family from starvation."

Alexander tried to look neutral, but underneath he was crestfallen. This represented a totally catastrophic reversal of the wonderful hopes of only a day before. The name "Siberia" itself sent a shiver of fear down most people's spines; but he had no option, no escape. There would be no way home to Lvov.

"Alright," he said slowly. "I agree to go as a settler, with my wife and children."

"A wise move, a very wise move, Mr. Goltz," said the official with a novel burst of something close to politeness. "I'm sure you will not regret it. Of course, you have to pay for your transport. This usually takes the form of hiring a whole railway box car for the family. That's so you can carry your chattels as well as some farm animals if you want to, for the new life in Siberia."

The family was taken back to the railway station with some other groups, in a team of horse-drawn carts. They were not the only ones to make the forced decision, and quite a few families who had originally planned to take the same boat to emigrate to Canada went together to a reluctant exile in Siberia. A train was eventually arranged for them to travel north, and during the wait, they survived sleeping in the railway yard with their luggage and equipment. The area was a disorganized muddle with family groups together with their belongings, making camp with crowded sleeping areas.

While waiting for the train to become available, Louiza hunted through the markets to buy as much food as possible. She managed to lay in such things as a small keg of herrings, dark rye bread, flour, potatoes, some rice, and smoked fat pork belly, the most concentrated energy available in food. She also obtained staples such as dried peas, lentils, sunflower seeds, and as much tea and sugar as possible. Things were in very short supply then, as everybody was scared and worried about the flood of international ultimatums and counter-ultimatums, and the declarations of war that were now following. People were stocking up against the eventual shortages they knew would come. Louiza was putting the money they had set aside to start in Canada to good use. She knew what she was buying had to last more than the journey, and might have to help them carry over the winter in Siberia.

After a few days, a train was ready. It was a stark change from the train to Odessa: each family hired a seatless boxcar used for carrying horses or other goods, and settled down in the spartan interior. They packed all their gear in one corner and made the other end into living/sleeping quarters for the family, with pillows and eiderdowns on the floor. Happily, the weather was warm in early August. One of the larger packing boxes was used as a table, with a few smaller ones serving as chairs. Louiza unpacked some plates, drinking mugs, spoons, and knives.

At last, slowly and with long, sad wheezes from the old locomotive, the train got under way and eased out of the Odessa station.

Germany, committed to the Austrians, had already declared war on Russia when the tsar finally mobilized against Austria. Two days after that, Germany moved to attack France, and invaded Belgium on the way. Then the British claimed they were compelled to defend Belgium. Almost overnight, the world was in flames.

The Goltzes didn't agree at the time, but under the circumstances, Siberia wasn't a bad place to be heading.

* * * *

Chapter 2

Siberia

The trip would take a crawling ten days, first heading north from Odessa, then turning to go through the whole of Ukraine into Russia, and on to the main East/West rail line, which eventually became the Trans-Siberian Railway.

The line had been running for less than eleven years, but it had already proved its worth during the war with Japan in 1904: it couldn't stop the Russians badly losing the war, but the reinforcements it brought at least delayed the result. But its real purpose was Siberia's settlement, and to assist the passengers Moscow hoped to attract, there were government-built hospitals, laundries, bath houses, and catering facilities at the major stations *en route,* which eased their ordeal considerably.

Slowly the train lumbered eastward, halting for long periods to let scheduled services through, as the landscape seen from the

boxcar slowly grew stranger to their eyes. The last stop in European Russia was Perm, just west of the Ural Mountains, a prosperous, very Russian city. Then the scenery began to change: the
train slowly wound its way into the mountains through tunnels
and steep grades. As the train descended the southern side of the
range, they saw a large white obelisk—the official boundary of
Asia. Now they were truly in alien territory.

After the Urals, the next city was Yekatarinburg, which then,
did not yet carry the sinister reputation it won after the revolution. It also felt slightly European, with streets built of brick, and
equipped with tramways and electric lighting. But from there the
railway stretched for ever further into the unknown. The mountains were behind them now and the next thousand kilometers
were flat, monotonous steppe country, taiga forests, swamps,
bogs, and jungles of nettle. Finally they reached the great stone-
piered steel bridge across the Irtysh River.

Then they came to Omsk, on the central Asian steppes. This
place had a mixed population, with Muslims outnumbering the
Jews and Christians, giving it a largely oriental flavor. Kirghiz
horsemen and camels could be seen at the outskirts of the town
where the native tribes still lived in their age-old portable yurts,
large round tents made of wood and hides.

The passengers were allowed to disembark and take on fresh
supplies of water, wash their dirty clothing and have the pleasure
of hot bath facilities, provided by the government at nominal
cost to help maintain the hygiene and health of the hoped-for
settlers. The death rate had plummeted from the days when the
settlers and convicts had to walk all the way on the Great Siberian Post Road in dirty conditions, with poor sanitation and
little food. Then it was as high as thirty percent. With the new
railroad and the new facilities, the travelers' health was so much
improved that deaths were down to only one percent, not much
more than in the general population at that time.

The next stretch of railway from Omsk to Irkutsk was mainly forested taiga, with little human habitation. There was a great
bridge spanning the Yenaseysk River consisting of seven steel

spans and stone piers, and then, on the last section before Irkutsk, the train slowed to cope with sharp gradients and curves.
Irkutsk, which liked to call itself "the Paris of Siberia," was built
on the Angora River, not far from the shore of the huge Lake
Baikal. During the tsars' time it was a center for better-off exiles.
Only four years before, they had hosted what was advertised as
the Siberian Exhibition, designed to follow the pattern of the
period's famous World Fairs.

It was certainly the most cosmopolitan of the Siberian cities,
looking prosperous with its sparkling modern brick and stone
buildings. The Goltz family disembarked, used the facilities for
washing and cleaning, and felt considerably refreshed.

They were now about ten days into their journey, and they
were tired and weary of the constant travelling, although their
routine had been established with the allocation of different jobs
for every person. Louiza tried to keep the children occupied with
reading and playing cards and games, but they were as bored as
the others in the end. The boxcar's only ventilation was through
a sliding door on the side, left partly open to let in fresh air and
allow a view of the countryside. Alexander set a semicircle of
boxes around the door to keep the smaller children clear.

The family rejoined the train after a good wash, and travelled
on to Udinskoe, their final destination, now known as Ulan-Ude
since the Bolshevik period. This was only a short trip of about
450 km, but the journey was slowed down by the host of bridges to cross over the Angora River and its tributaries. The line
twisted around the tip of Lake Baikal, through tunnels or with
huge overhanging cliffs soaring above the railway line on one
side and the water's edge on the other. It was majestic, but wild
and unfriendly-looking countryside. The crystal clear waters of
the lake reflected a distant forest shore with majestic mountain
ranges blue in the beyond and covered with perpetual snow in
the far distance.

It took a full day to reach Udinskoe on the eastern side of
Lake Baikal, where they disembarked and unloaded all their
luggage and supplies. This settlement in southern Siberia, about

350 kilometers north of the Mongolian border, was still a wild colonial town. The roads were not surfaced and turned into mud when the snow melted. Here the permafrost melts sometime in June, and in winter the whole area becomes frozen with some two meters of permafrost penetrating the ground. Now they knew they were in Siberia: most of the people on the streets were native Buryat tribesmen with long, thin almond-shaped eyes and distinctly Asian faces.

There was no time to waste. They had to select their land and quickly build shelter before the start of winter, as the frosts would start for real in late November. This was the end of August: they had only two and a half to three months to prepare themselves to survive some of the harshest living conditions on the planet.

Alexander was allocated a 140-acre plot with the special features he desired. He had visions of running a piggery, so proximity to the main city was important since he needed to be close to the market and the railway line. It didn't have to be very fertile ground, but it would be best if there was some forest still standing so that wood for fuel and buildings was available and they were self-sufficient. The plot he chose was about half-timbered with a small hill, which was cleared, and then it graduated to a higher level, covered by thick fir forest common to the area. A stream flowed fast from the steeper slopes, shallow with a stony bottom with some deeper waterholes. Alexander hoped to test its fishing potential when the urgent task of building shelter had been completed.

He hired a cart and transported all their goods to the location. They set up camp, and the older boys and Alexander started to fell timber for a small cabin to see them through the winter. They cut lengths of pine lumber, which was fairly soft, using the large, two-man cross-saw that they brought with them, with Alexander and Karlov on each end. The work was hard and slow, but they progressed steadily. The insects around their sweating faces were unbearable, and in the end, Louiza had to make up protective headgear from very light muslin to protect them. It worked well. They could breathe and see through it, but it stopped the insects from attacking their faces.

Painfully they built a notched log cabin with corners wedged into place, a little like the American frontier cabins of the previous century. At one end of the cabin, Alexander constructed a huge fireplace out of rock for cooking and warming. Two small windows were left for light, and a double sheet of mica was used for the windowpanes. Mica was locally mined, and plentiful.

The equipment Alexander brought with him for his Canadian settlement had turned out to be invaluable in Siberia. He was using the same techniques, and hand-drilled and bolted the logs to tie the main logs together. It made a very strong simple construction. On the outside, he built an earthen embankment for extra insulation and protection against the wind. At the same time, like most men in early middle age, the physical work for the first time since his twenties was forcefully making him aware that the strength he remembered from his youth was now diminished. He had two strong young men to do the heavy lifting, but all the same, the concentrated effort building the cabin was taking its toll.

While the men worked feverishly to finish the cabin before winter arrived, Louiza and her three daughters were also busy. Olga and Maria did everything together. They would skip along, hand in hand, playing their games of hopscotch, skipping, and ball throwing. Sometimes they fought and bickered among themselves, but if anyone else confronted them, they instantly resumed the alliance and automatically protected each other. Lydia, much younger, was too small to join the older girls' games. She felt left out, following them around with her thumb in her mouth, looking on. She would try to emulate them as best she could, but they whispered to each other with their little stories and jokes, and Lydia would be frustrated, unable to understand what they were on about.

Louiza realized they had no time for games. Like the animals and the plants in this harsh world of Siberia, the short summer months had to be utilized to build up resources for the long cold winter. In this part of the world, the ground was covered by snow for seven to eight months of the year, so that the short summer months were a period of feverish activity for every living thing. The blossoms bloomed more quickly, the grass grew faster, and the berries ripened quicker. It was now late August, and the snow would start as early as October.

Louiza organized foraging parties of herself and the three girls into the woods. They found many types of edible berries to be picked, and mushrooms growing in profusion in the decomposing plant material at the base of trees. Only Louiza, however, would pick the mushrooms, as she couldn't take the risk of the girls mistaking a poisonous mushroom for an edible one. She had long talks with some of the neighboring women to make sure which types were safe and which were dangerous. But picking berries of any kind was one task the girls could do well. They could eat them as they picked them to their hearts' content, and Louiza was pleased, as they were full of vitamins. The accumulated supply slowly increased after each day of foraging. Every few days Louiza cooked them with sugar to make a thick, sweet jam. She packed it in glass jars that she had bought when she thought she was going to the wilderness of Canada. The mushrooms were placed on wooden trays in the sun. After two or three days in the summer temperatures of 25 degrees, they shriveled up and dried. Then she would pack them away in calico bags for storage.

Altogether, the family was now well provided with the essential equipment and stores to survive in the wild winter, and their frantic activity on the house was starting to show some progress. It had only one large room, with the fireplace at one end and alcoves on each side with bunks built in. The boys had two bunks on one side and the girls three on the other, so that the children could sleep close to the fire, the warmest part of the house during the winter.

The fireplace was large. There was plenty of wood to burn, and in a Siberian winter, keeping the house warm would obviously be a priority. Alexander designed the fireplace with a section above the main grate, like a small cave. When this heated up as the fire was burning, it became an oven. He also set up an area higher above the grate with a steel bar and hooks attached to be used as a smoking oven. A whole carcass of pig or other animal could be butchered into the appropriate pieces and hung there while the fire burned the right type of wood, to smoke and preserve it. Fish could be treated the same way.

Cracks and crevices in the cabin walls were plastered up with wet clay. The split logs that formed the floor were leveled as far as possible and set straight onto the earth. This half-log floor was to serve as insulation. The roof had to be very strong and steep, to withstand the weight of the snow that would fall over the winter, and the strong, cold wind that would roar from the Arctic Circle. They used half logs again, but this time smaller so they were less heavy. These were placed with the flat side facing out, and bolted down with large bolts as each one was fitted into position. Clay filled the cracks between to waterproof it. Then wooden shingles were nailed to the logs on the top.

For furniture they used the boxes that they brought with them, holding all their goods, and built a few long trestle seats out of logs. The bed, also made out of logs, stood on the other side of the cabin away from the fire and the children's bunks. After six weeks or so the task was complete, very rough and small, but cozy, safe, and warm for the coming winter. They knew that they would be able to survive.

"Well, now we must go and buy some more supplies from the local markets at Udinskoye," Alexander told Louiza as he admired his handiwork.

He left Karlov behind, and told him to get the rifle ready and loaded in case any danger presented. He knew that the boy was an able marksman. The settlers in these wild parts were allowed firearms, something that would never have been permitted in Russia. Here they were exposed to wild beasts, and in addition hunting for fur was one of the main industries and source of wealth in Siberia. Consequently, every settler had a trusty rifle and most were experienced users. Karlov had been very keen to learn, and he had been practicing every few days since their arrival to improve his skills. Alexander took Ludwig with him, and they set off for the main town, which was some twenty kilometers away, more than a full day's walk. As yet they had no horses.

Udinskoe was different from most of the other towns in Siberia, towns like Tomsk, Omsk, or Irkutsk. Those had been built during the expansion of the tsarist regime as river-crossing points, and then grew tremendously after the Trans-Siberian Railway was built. They were now becoming busy centers of trade, manufacture, communication, and transport. Udinskoe was a much older settlement. It had originally been one of the main centers on the trade routes on the Great Silk Road from China to the west, and settled by an exotic mixture of ethnic groups. Mongols and Chinese mingled with the more recent Russian, Ukrainian, and Polish arrivals. The faith was also a mixture. There was the Orthodox religion of the Russians and the Ukrainians, and all the different sects that had escaped persecution in Russia by fleeing to Siberia, such as the "Old Believers." The influence from China and Tibet was strong, and many practiced Buddhism. There was still a strong oriental feel to this city, different from the others.

Alexander and Ludwig paused at the end of their long walk to survey Udinskoe from a distance. They saw a number of Orthodox churches with large bulbous, onion-shaped turrets, covered with tin and painted green. The rest of these buildings were constructed from wood. Houses were mainly one or two stories, and also made of dressed wooden logs. Structurally they were plain and simply designed, but decorated fretwork on the windows and doors gave them a distinctive style. There were also Buddhist temples, and occasionally Muslim minarets punctuated the skyline.

Outside the town, groups of nomadic families camped with their camels and horses tethered together, living in yurts made from animal hides. Most of their clothing was also made from hides for warmth and protection from the harsh winds. Once they replenished their needs in town, the nomads moved back to the empty steppes. Their caravans made an exotic sight, with each camel carrying a large skin vessel containing mares' milk slung under its belly, the contents fermenting as the caravan walked leisurely on its way. The milk swayed from side to side, sloshing and splashing in the containers as it turned into a fermented drink. It was actually mildly alcoholic, and much favored by the nomads when they could not get vodka. Vodka, with its forty percent alcohol content, was a much quicker way to inebriation compared to the gentle fermented mares' milk—albeit harsher and much more destructive.

Alexander and his son headed for the market. It was a very busy place. All sorts of stock, wheat, and other commodities were being sold. Shopkeepers and traders were buying goods and loading them onto wagons to take to the outer parts of the area to further trade with other settlers and the indigenous people.

The pair walked around in the bedlam of noise and the bustling activity surveying the stalls and the prices on offer. Alexander noted that the pigs were cheap at this time—with the coming winter, most of the farmers wanted to get rid of their stock in order not to have to feed them over winter. This would be a good time to buy some. The smell was foul, as the pigs trod in the mud and excrement, squealing and snorting as people poked them in the ribs to see how fat they were.

After making a study of what was available, and the prices, Alexander made up his mind. He bought bags of flour, buckwheat, onions in large bags, and potatoes, or anything that would keep. He then bought two large pigs.

"You wait here, Ludwig, and guard the supplies while I arrange transport."

He went quickly to the edge of the market where there were some carts waiting to transport goods and made a short bargain with one of the drivers. Together they returned and loaded the goods: the pigs were a problem. They squealed and resisted, and before they finished, Alexander and Ludwig had pig shit all over their clothes. But Alexander was happy. He had enough food, together with what they had already brought with them. As an afterthought, he purchased a large keg of salted herrings, big, fat juicy herrings, which had always been his favorite at home. Then he found ammunition for the rifles. It was expensive, but he wanted to take the opportunity of doing some hunting when all the building tasks were complete, to try to build up their larder further.

Snow came in late October and the winds started to howl from the Arctic, freezing everything in their path, but the family was comfortable. They had a good supply of wood just outside the cabin; every corner was crammed with supplies, bags of flour, onions, lentils, potatoes. Alexander butchered the pigs, cut them into manageable portions and smoked them in his new chimney. The whole cabin was filled with the comforting smell of smoked meat. Louiza was getting quite adept in using the baking oven, and every two or three days she would bake thick heavy rye bread, filled with seeds.

The family settled in their little warm cocoon of survival. The fire burned all day and for most of the night, keeping the place warm and providing a warm glow throughout the cabin. They felt safe and were beginning to think that coming to Siberia may not have been so tragic. They were living in a similar situation to what they would have been in Canada had they managed to get there, and at least the war was far behind them. They had a block of land, a sturdy little house that was warm, safe, and well-stocked for the winter. Through the winter, the girls read books, sang, danced, and often put on little plays for the whole family. The boys went out skiing and tobogganing, but the activities they liked most were hunting and fishing. They would go through the woods and try to hunt the game in the area. Although there were deer in the woods, they had not seen one, but they managed to shoot some smaller game. The fur provided them with warm mittens, and Louiza made hats for the boys, round with a flat top and side flaps to put over the ears and tie under the chin—the Russian design to keep the head, face, and ears warm from the icy winds. There was some schoolwork done in the light of the fire. The older girls would read their lessons, and the boys continued with some of the subjects they had done at school. Alexander valued his own scientific training, and made sure that the boys did their practice and homework, managing to help them understand the more complex concepts.

The problem was Lydia. Being the youngest, she had never even started school, and although Louiza would read her books and tell her stories whenever their busy life allowed, it was hardly enough to start her education. She still had not started reading.

Louiza was a strong Lutheran, and she made sure that the family had some prayer time and Bible reading together. She reminded them to give thanks for what they now saw as their deliverance, and for the safe haven they had come to enjoy.

Through the long winter months, Alexander planned his future activities. He was so pleased with the pig meat that he now thought he could process the meat from his planned piggery himself. He would slaughter his own pigs, smoke the meat, and transport it west. Food was in short supply in European Russia because of the war.

When the weather was not too severe, Alexander and the boys took the opportunity to go out and cut some more logs. Over the months, they built up quite a supply in readiness for springtime, when they could start building the piggery. Alexander, precisely analytical as ever, planned the whole project. He worked out the shed sizes required for the pigs, the flow of food into the piggery to feed them, and the best way to keep the place clean.

He would build a storage building for the wheat and feed as an extension of the cabin, and at the end of that he planned to build the quarters for the pigs. They needed to be housed in a warm protective environment, especially the breeding sows, which would be preserved from slaughter to produce replacement stock for the following season.

One day when he could get into town, he bought two horses and a cart, as he needed to pick up wheat and grain for the pigs direct from the local farmers, cheaper than going to the markets.

Karlov was thrilled when the two horses arrived. He had grown into a tall, strong, and able young man. The hard physical work of cutting wood, building, and hunting had honed his skills, and developed his strength and endurance. There would be few people who could shoot as well, and he could move quickly and quietly through the forest on the trail of some unsuspecting animal. He had no fear. He would coax the horses up the steepest incline and jump over streams and gullies. He practiced shooting as he was riding at full gallop. He had a natural ability to ride, shoot, and hunt, and it was his greatest joy.

Ludwig was a different character. He was a thoughtful young man, and he stayed with his father and helped him in running the business. He enjoyed making up charts of the production that was achieved. He would weigh the pigs and compare that to the usage of food stocks, and would try to work out what would be the most efficient feeding method, and which litters provided the best results. He could sit down, calculate, and analyze, just like his father.

In springtime the work of building the piggery began, and within a month or two, Alexander's first tiny herd of pigs was squealing in their shelter at the end the complex. Cleaning them out proved to be rather more difficult than he had bargained for, but the first sales in the Odinskoe market showed a satisfactory profit. Alexander had now worked out the best methods and procedures to get optimal results out of his piggery. He knew how much to feed the animals, what to feed them, which litters to get rid of, and which litters to breed from to produce better meat production. He was starting to prosper as the demand for food increased because of the war, with so many millions of men fighting rather than contributing to production in Russia and Ukraine. The effect on the whole country was beginning to be catastrophic. Food was so scarce that famine made its first, ominous appearance. Siberia, where the food was more plentiful, was fortunate. The wartime dislocation had not reached there, and the province was able to send some food supplies west to the front and to European Russia.

But even before the end of their first year in Siberia, the news from the west was getting worse. Russian retreats had already begun: food shortages and industrial pressure were building resentment in the civilian population. None of this mattered much to the Goltzes, who could hardly care less who won the war, but according to Karlov, whose occasional trips to town for supplies once the horses became available were their principal source of news, it created a good deal of joy among the exiles. They had no love for the tsarist regime that expelled them, and they welcomed the news of the occasional revolutionary eruptions that were now breaking out back home. Strikes were starting up in the factories. People were beginning to talk about the philosophy of Karl Marx, already the idol of the core of revolutionaries exiled in Siberia. When Karlov was having a drink in the tavern, he would listen to the philosophical exuberance of the revolutionaries. He himself believed in freedom and independence and sometimes challenged their views, mockingly criticizing the stupidity of their workers' "utopia." He was soon noted as a "German upstart," especially among the Bolshevik ringleaders. Sometimes he got into fights, but he managed to acquit himself well and people were not keen to take him on. Still, he became a marked man, and as the years passed, he became more and more unpopular with the communists.

Alexander's piggery did well the first year, better than he had dared hope, and he made plans to expand with time. The price of food was rocketing now, as the war news got even worse the following year: the tsar had lost Poland altogether now, and the Germans re-established it as the independent state it had been in ancient times. Obviously the war would end one day, and regardless of who won, food would not always hold its present price as conditions improved. But Alexander would make the most of it in the meantime. He hoped to be able to afford a laborer by the time the boys decided to leave home. He knew in his heart that the work would be too much for his sole efforts by then.

By 1917 Russia's war was falling apart. Losses became enormous. Tsar Nicolas had neither the military training nor the organizational skills to hold things together. The aristocracy was not prepared to support him after Rasputin's period of malign influence. Ordinary people were also suffering severely, living in grinding poverty as food got scarcer and the economy tumbled towards collapse. Bread marches were now common, and the Imperial Guard's mutiny in February 1917 led to violent clashes in the streets of St. Petersburg and throughout the realm.

Tsar Nicolas was forced to abdicate on March 2. After a few months of near chaos, Kerensky managed to form a provisional government, and tried to carry on the war, but the country was unstable. In what seemed at the time a masterstroke, later regretted, the Germans smuggled Lenin into the country to foment more instability. Revolutionary fervor erupted throughout the country.

Kerensky, largely because he had insisted on trying to keep the war going, lost power on October 25 after the Bolsheviks stormed the Winter Palace and seized all strategic points. Lenin gained control of the new government, on the slogan "Bread, not war." Starting from St. Petersburg—patriotically renamed Petrograd for the war—small independent "Soviet People's Republics" began coming to life all across the map.

Later that year, Alexander was working hard to drag some bags of wheat to a large pot, where the wheat was boiled to soften it before feeding it to the pigs. He usually found this job easy, but today he was somehow very tired and breathless, and as the day went on, it became harder and harder for him to manhandle the wheat, even with Ludwig's help. Suddenly, as he tried to lift a bag and drag it along, he felt a crushing pain in his chest and down his left arm. He became dizzy and sick, and he started to perspire and became pale. He collapsed beside the sacks of wheat. Ludwig noticed something was wrong when he went towards him. He ran urgently into the house and called Louiza.

"Mum, Mum," he called out. "Dad is very sick—come and help him." Louiza rushed out of the cabin and into the storeroom. She was frightened. She saw Alexander on the floor and quickly lifted up his head and undid his collar and shirt to allow him to breathe. He was in severe pain and breathing short quick breaths. His lips were blue, and his skin was white, drained of blood, with beads of sweat on his brow. She lifted his head and held it to assist his breathing.

"Go and get a bottle of vodka, quickly, Ludwig, we'll give him a drink. It might help."

She knew it would not, but she had to do something, and all she could do was wipe the perspiration off his brow. He looked up at her and whispered, "Louiza, I'm sorry I've left you in this position. Things happened the way they did. None of this was my doing, it was just fate. Louiza, look after the children." He closed his eyes, and his breathing became more irregular and labored, and she knew that there was little she could do. She tried to massage his chest, and massaged his neck and hands. She tried to give him some vodka, but he just spluttered and coughed, and it interfered with his breathing.

After an hour, he stopped breathing altogether. His eyes were closed, and his face muscles became relaxed.

Louiza was crying softly. He was her companion of twenty-five years and, although he was autocratic and ruled the family strictly, he still loved them all and worked for the welfare of the family.

His death devastated her, but she knew her task was now to look after the children, and to assure the safety and survival of her family. She had three young girls and two boys to care for. The boys were nearly grown up, headstrong Karlov and studious, supporting Ludwig. She could depend on them and if things went right, they would survive. She could run the piggery with their help. Everything was in order, well developed. During the busy times, they could always use Alexander's plan and hire some laborer to help out.

* * * *

Chapter 3

Strange Dawn

It didn't work out quite the way Louiza expected. Early in 1918, Lenin signed a peace treaty with the Germans, exchanging most of Poland and western Ukraine for what the Soviets expected to be a period of security. In that they were disappointed because with the encouragement of the Allies, the counter-revolutionary White Army was formed in parts of Siberia and Ukraine. These counter-revolutionaries started to advance westward. The whole area fell into turmoil, with revolutionaries fighting from armed trains and forts, and their opponents ranging around on horseback as a kind of semi-organized cavalry.

Siberia was turning into a vulnerable place to be. Obviously Karlov was now a marked man. He had been completely outspoken on his rowdier nights out in Odinskoe: the revolutionaries who were running the town remembered him from those taverns. Now that they had control, they were well able to deal with anyone they considered a threat, and clearly Karlov was in that category. Louiza was well aware of the situation and though she hated the idea, she soon decided there was no choice but for Karlov to leave immediately. He was reluctant. He told her it felt completely wrong to leave the family just when their father had died. They faced huge difficulties—they needed to be able to rely on their older brother to help.

"Don't be stupid, Karlov," Louiza told him. "What good would you be to me or any of us dead? Go and save yourself. Things will settle down later and you can come back, but we'll survive. We are well provided for. There's plenty of money, even if we don't run the piggery for a year or two. We'll get by one way or another—no one thinks the rest of us are reactionary."

Karlov hoped she was right: he realized in his heart he had to get away. He hugged Ludwig good-bye, and kissed him on the cheeks. He kissed his mother and hugged her, and then he said good-bye to his three sisters, Olga, Maria, and last of all, Lydia, his baby sister, who was now seven. She didn't understand what was happening when she was saying good-bye to him, and she gave him a kiss on the cheek and a hug. He held her closely to him, and then he put her down and said, "Good-bye my little button, I will see you soon."

Karlov jumped on his horse, and with a rifle strapped to his back and a cavalry saber by his side, he rode off into the forest. He knew the woods and the area well. Louiza knew he was an expert marksman and a great horseman. She prayed that God would protect him from the turmoil and carnage that were developing.

The rest of the family went into their cabin again—Ludwig, the three girls, and Louiza. She looked around her diminished group. Despite the brave face she'd shown Karlov, Louiza was nervous and unsure of what to do. In her heart, she feared that things might well not improve as she had pretended. And there, she was entirely correct.

According to reports from town, gangs of hungry marauders, both anti-government activists and simple thieves, were increasing as time went by. Revolutionary loyalists prowled the country searching for them, and neither side was exactly meticulous about looting. A poorly-defended farm occupied by four women and a teenage boy would be easy pickings.

But amazingly, there was also a bright side to the situation. Early in 1918, the Lenin government, flush with early success, had come to the reasonable assumption that anyone the tsars had exiled to Siberia was bound to be a Soviet supporter today. Accordingly, Lenin decreed that everyone was now free to leave Siberia and return home, if they chose to. The trains began to fill with joyously returning exiles.

One morning Louiza heard that the formerly Austrian section of Ukraine had declared its independence as the Western Ukrainian People's Republic—and some of the departing trains were now going there as well. Her mind was made up in a second. "Ludwig," she told her son, "we're going home."

"We'll have to get rid of all our stock as soon as possible and turn it into money, gold if we can. Go to the market tomorrow and talk to the merchants. See if they will take our remaining pigs, together with the wheat and other pig food. We only need to keep the food we will need for ourselves."

Hurriedly she packed some belongings that she wanted to take with her, clothing and some of the necessities of life. She packed the wagon and sadly went through her little cabin, which had protected them and given them so much joy for three years. She also went to Alexander's grave and said good-bye to her husband. She knew she would never come back again. She took a handful of soil from the top of his grave and put it into a little bag, and she whispered quietly, "At least, Alexander, when I die I will be covered with some of the earth that you are covered with. We will share the soil in our graves, even if I cannot be buried here with you." She turned away and walked to the wagon with her arm around little Lydia, and holding Olga's hand. They all traveled slowly down the track to Odinskoe to join the hordes of deportees on the journey home.

As they entered the town, they could see that the streets were congested with carts and horses and people moving their goods on trolleys and even wheelbarrows. They were all heading for the station. There was a grand exodus of a vast number of people wanting to go back home. They were all the deportees sent to Siberia at the whim of the tsar or his officials, many without trial or even a charge. As they neared the station, they could see the crowds waiting with their goods for the next train.

A number of trains came, but they were full and did not even stop. They were not going to west Ukraine, but to various parts of Russia. The whole system was in chaos. There were no train schedules and trains stopped if they were empty, but just continued if they were too full, with people hanging on precariously. After two days of waiting, they finally were told that the next train would be going to the western Ukraine and it was not full. Louiza purchased the tickets for herself and the children, although there was no one to check or collect the paperwork.

When the train arrived, everybody rushed on. Louiza and Ludwig managed to force their way on board with some of the luggage, and quickly appropriated a space in one of the carriages. "Now you stay here with this luggage, Ludwig, and I'll go and get the girls and the rest of the luggage. Keep this space for us." As she struggled back to the door, more and more people were rushing in to take up positions and the stream of humanity was preventing her getting to the exit. At that moment, the train emitted a loud whistle, and started moving. The driver decided that the train was full enough for him and decided to take off. Louiza froze. She realized the children were still on the platform, and she fought her way desperately to the open door to try to jump out. She had no chance against the solid wall of people who were now hanging onto the train, even on the outside. She raced to the window, and opened it and put her head out and called out loudly to the girls.

"Take the next train, take the next train, for God's sake. I'll meet the next train at the station, and I'll meet you there. It will go to the same place. God look after you."

She worked her way back to the seat where Ludwig was waiting for her in shock. All she could repeat to herself was, "I've lost my children. I've lost my children." Her mind was numb, but over the next few hours the reality sunk in. She just sat there with Ludwig and wailed her sorrow. She was inconsolable.

Poor Ludwig did not know what to do. He kept repeating, "They'll be all right, Mum. Don't worry. They'll catch the next train and they will be behind us by a day or so, so don't worry."

In the end, the sorrow exhausted her and she fell into a fitful sleep. It was two o'clock in the morning, and most people around her were crushed together, snoring, sleeping quietly, or turning around to get more comfortable. She felt the crush of humanity on her. She felt she was being squeezed and she had difficulty breathing. She had a headache from her crying and grief, and her eyes were swollen and gritty. There was an all-pervading heaviness that engulfed her whole body, with a sinking feeling in the pit of her stomach. She slept fitfully, waking up from terrifying dreams. As soon as she woke up, her heaviness returned. She'd had nothing to eat or drink all day, and although she was thirsty, she did not care about food. For most of the time, she was in a state of deep depression, unable to think and move.

The train continued on its long journey, stopping at the main towns along the way back to Russia. It slowly travelled west along the Trans-Siberian Railway. It passed the vast expanse of steppes with forests covering most of the land, although some areas were cleared and there were small cabins, similar to their own, with some signs of farming. They stopped at Irkutsk the next day and got off the train to buy some food. There was a large supply of boiling water to make tea. She was interested only in a glass of tea and didn't want to eat. The train then continued through Krasnoyarsk where they again stopped before the wide Yenisey River was crossed using the long iron bridge. They continued on to Novosibrisk, Omsk, Yekaterinburg, the last major town before the Ural Mountains, and then Perm, which was the first city in European Russia. Then they made their way slowly across Russia itself and on into Ukraine.

Finally the train got back to Lvov, four years after Louiza and the family had left. Things had changed considerably. Signs of war were everywhere. The city was cold and barren with the wind blowing through it at the start of winter. The people that were left stayed inside, and there was no one there to welcome her—no one even knew she was back.

The whole episode seemed like a bad dream. She remembered leaving her beautiful home with a healthy happy family. Four years later, after struggling and surviving the hardship of Siberia, she was back. Her husband had died; Karlov, her elder son, was somewhere in Siberia fighting the communists; and her three daughters were all gone, Maria, Olga, and little Lydia, lost in the middle of Siberia. The only person she had left was Ludwig, her younger son. She had now lost everybody else in the world.

With Ludwig and her meager belongings, Louiza made her way to an old school friend, Rosa, who was still living in Lvov. She explained to Rosa that she was desolate, with little money left and no home. Rosa, too, knew the misery the war had created: she threw her arms around Louiza and assured her there was room for her and the boy in her little house.

For the next month, Louiza hung about the station. She met every train and as the passengers went by with their luggage and equipment, she scrutinized every face, looking for her three daughters.

At first she hoped they would soon arrive following her train, but as the weeks dragged by optimism faded. Finally she was beside herself: she didn't know what could have happened. Were the children in captivity somewhere? Did they catch another train, and get taken to another part of Russia, or Ukraine, or Poland? The whole place was still in post-war turmoil, which was actually getting worse by the day, as the skirmishes mounted into set battles between the Red and White Armies.

Summary executions continued in that climate of crisis, perpetrated by whichever side was prevailing in the area at the time. This was not a time to search for three lost little girls.

Poor Ludwig could do very little to comfort his mother. He

tried to find work. He was good with figures and was sharp. He managed to obtain work in one of the large shops, although it was not very profitable at this stage. They were struggling for the supply of merchandise to sell, as a lot of factories had converted to production of war materials. And, of course, no one had much money to spend.

Rosa looked after Louiza for six months. Most of that time, Louiza was incapacitated with deep depression, walking around each day like a somnambulist, a faraway look in her eyes. She was totally distracted by the central problem of the children: she took no notice of the world around her. She ate only when Rosa insisted. She dressed in any clothes that were available—Rosa had to wash them for her.

Rosa had been her best friend at school. She too married and had children, although Rosa had only one boy, and at this stage, she also did not know where he was. He had been called up into the German army, and now he was one of the anonymous millions who had been lost, wounded, or killed on the Eastern front, and whose families never knew their fate.

As Louiza gradually recovered, she came to understand she had to go on living for Ludwig's sake. She would have to leave the awesome task of trying to find the children in the hope that one distant day things might become more settled.

She and Ludwig slept in one small room at the back of Rosa's house, and she started working in Rosa's small drapery shop, selling materials, threads, and buttons.

With the disruption of the economy, many women who would not previously have considered sewing clothing for themselves or the children had started doing so. With the invention and manufacture of the new Singer sewing machine, sewing became a popular occupation. The shops therefore began to do a brisk business, for these depressed times.

Talking to the customers and their children also distracted Louiza, and she started taking an interest in the world around her again, but she was never happy. Her thoughts were elsewhere.

* * *

The train that doomed the family had pulled out of Odinskoe in a storm of loud shrill whistles while people were still trying to get on and hang onto every possible foothold outside the carriages. The three girls still on the platform were petrified. They could see the train slowly gaining speed, and they could not see their mother. Suddenly Louiza's face and half of her shoulders squeezed out a window, and they heard her call urgently to them, "Catch the next train. Catch the next train!"

They felt very alone—three girls aged only eight, twelve, and fifteen. They were all used to having people around to look after them. Not so long ago there had been two big brothers, a father, and a mother, and suddenly there were only the three of them. They felt very afraid. People crowded around, looking sideways at them and their belongings as they walked past. No one offered to help, too busy looking after their own affairs and trying to get out of Siberia. The girls stayed the night on the platform surrounded by the remaining crowd, hoping they would be safe. They placed their luggage around them to protect themselves.

For two days they waited like this. They still had plenty of food that Louiza had prepared for the whole family, for the long journey. It sustained them, and there was plenty left.

For hours Olga and Maria discussed what to do. They had to move, as obviously Mother was not going to come back for them, and in any case, she had told them to catch the next train. The girls decided that they could take only as much luggage as each person could carry by themselves. The luggage was repacked, one case per head, as much as they could carry. A smaller bag or sack was packed with as much food as they could manage for the journey home. Once they got back, their mother would look after them and all of the luggage they left behind could be replaced. They picked out anything that was valuable and not too heavy to carry. They treasured things like a picture frame with a picture of the family, a favorite book, and for Lydia, a little teddy bear and an amber necklace that belonged to Mother.

Olga was not silly, and the luggage that they could not cope with she started to sell. She started calling out, "Who wants to buy some women's clothing, hardly ever used, lovely beautiful warm coats, etc." She did not care what price she got as long as she could sell it and get rid of it and they would have some money for the trip. It was surprising, but they collected quite a lot of cash by this means. All the people had their own luggage they were carrying with them. However, some of Olga's sale items were very pretty, and unusual in Siberia: Louiza had brought some of her best things from Lvov, items such as a silver mirror, hair brushes, and combs that out here were considered quite luxurious.

After the majority of the luggage was disposed of and they felt more in control of the new situation, they moved as near as they could to the edge of the platform, thinking that if a train did come they would be the first to get on. There were only three of them, with little luggage, and they could worm their way through the crowd waiting for the train. Nobody took too much notice of them, assuming they were just children wandering around and their parents would be somewhere in the vicinity.

On the second day, a train that was not completely filled to overflowing finally stopped. As it came to a halt the doors opened, and the children squeezed their way closer. Then the force of the people behind them just propelled them into the carriage. They took over a little corner with Lydia between them, Olga and Maria protecting her on each side. The cases were underneath their feet, safe from any pilfering. The carriage was soon overcrowded, filled to capacity, to the extent that they could hardly breathe, but because they were near a window they could open, they had a little relief. By this time, Lydia was crying; although she was between her two sisters, she still felt very alone and lost, and yearned for her mother to comfort her and protect her.

Then the journey back from Siberia began. The three girls kept together, sometimes just crying in the corner, sometimes sleeping. The only time they left their corner was to go to the toilet, which was very soon a filthy mess. Nothing there was working, and there was no running water. They still had plenty of food. The bread had turned to a hard crust, but the sausage was still quite edible. It was made to last without refrigeration, with plenty of peppers and spices to preserve the meat.

Stopping at the major towns allowed the people time to buy food at the station. Olga would sneak out quickly, get some tea, and replenish their bottles with boiled water. Mother had always insisted that water had to be boiled before drinking to avoid cholera, dysentery, and other diseases, but there was always plenty at the stations, provided with large samovars.

They gradually left the forests and the steppes of Siberia behind them and passed the large white obelisk marking the start of European Russia. The train climbed slowly over the Ural Mountains, and made its slow way through Russia before turning south into Ukraine. The journey was slower than ever because, with the turmoil of the revolution and war, the railway maintenance had virtually ceased. The fighting had damaged some of the line, so the train had to crawl through several sections and wait, sometimes for hours, for some breakdown or malfunction to be repaired. It didn't worry the girls, for it felt now that this was their whole life—just constant moving, the noise of the train chugging along, stopping, starting. Days consisted of sleeping and looking out the window at the changing countryside. From time to time they cried. Lydia would be the first one to start, particularly when she got tired and wanted to sleep. She would start weeping and calling out, "I want Mummy, Mummy." Olga put her arm around her and gently reassured her with "Now, now, don't cry too much, we will see Mum soon. We're nearly home and she will be waiting for us, so don't worry." In her heart, however, she was not so sure. She didn't know where they were, she didn't know where Mum was, whether she was alive or dead, or even where they were going. They would only know when the train finally stopped, and they had to get off.

Olga was still only fifteen years old, and the responsibility of the children weighed heavily on her. She tried to stay positive, keeping up the spirits of the other two children, and she continued telling them stories, playing word games, and sometimes softly

singing them lullabies. She was increasingly worried that they
might not be found, and end up separated from her mother and
brothers forever. The eight-year-old Lydia was not old enough to
understand. All she wanted was to have her mother there.

Early on the tenth morning, they were woken up by the train
slowing down. It seemed to be stopping and starting, and then
finally they came to a complete stop. They were in some town or
city. They could see other railway lines around, and other trains,
some stopped. Houses could be seen beyond the railway lines.
Only a few people were out this early in the morning, as it was
just about sunrise. The people around them started to wake up
and look around inquisitively, and quickly a sense of excitement
spread. Some of the passengers seemed to recognize the place.
They had arrived at Kharkov, the biggest city in Ukraine, and
the final destination of the train. Shortly after it stopped, a railway official walked along shouting, "Everybody out, everybody
out," as he hit the side of the wagons with a stick.

Lydia started calling out, "Mummy, Mummy, she will be
here waiting for us." Olga put a reassuring arm around her. "Yes,
she will be waiting, but don't worry, we'll find her soon. We just
have to get out and find our way around." They took their bags
and dragged them out of the train and followed the rest of the
crowd to the station. Some people were carrying their bags over
their shoulders, some with their cases on their heads. They were
all happy to be out of Siberia at last, with big smiles and waving
of arms to friends as they called out greetings enthusiastically.

The three girls wandered to the station where they looked
over the whole station and all the platforms. Olga noted the station's name. She had never heard of it. But certainly it was nowhere near their hoped-for Lvov.

She asked the railway official, who was busy doing something, "Are we far from Lvov?" He looked at her quizzically.
"Lvov, you are nowhere near there. Trains don't run from here
to Lvov anymore—they're fighting in that area again. The
border's closed now and there is no way they will let anyone
through, in or out of Russia. You've no chance of getting to

Lvov from here, my dear."

What had happened, which, even if the railway man was entirely aware of it, the girls would not have understood, was that the proclamation of the Western Ukrainian Republic had immediately inflamed the newly independent Poles—who weren't going to put up with that situation for a minute. As far they were concerned, the west section of Ukraine, which had been ruled by Austria for a century, should now return to the Poles, its historic owners before the Austrian takeover. Consequently, the newly-reorganized Polish army was now battling to get it back. They were doing particularly well, since the Poles had always been expert cavalrymen and Eastern Europe was still technology-deficient in most areas; cavalry retained the dominance on eastern battlefields it had lost one thousand years earlier. The new republic lasted hardly a year, and a second attempt to bring the Lvov area under the new Ukrainian Soviet Socialist Republic at Kharkov also failed in 1921. Lvov would remain in Poland until World War Two.

Understood or not, the news about Lvov was a thunderbolt to the children. Lydia started crying, carrying on about her mother again. Olga and Maria could not contain themselves, and also started weeping. Here they were in Kharkov in Ukraine, nowhere near to where they wanted to be, still lost, and with no way of getting in touch with anyone who knew their mother. Olga, the oldest, felt very responsible for her sisters. The Russian Empire was crumbling with the start of the battle raging between two major philosophies, which would convulse the world for the rest of the twentieth century. The rest of the world was in complete disarray, with the old European empires that controlled the world in their death throes, destroyed and never to recover, after the end of the homicidal bloodletting of World War One. The girls were caught in these titanic struggles, and there was no one to help them. They did not know of these events. No one fully understood them. People could only struggle to survive on a day-to-day basis.

Finally, the girls decided to be positive and try to work

out how they could survive in this strange place. They left the station and headed towards the center of the town where the markets were, in a large area paved with cobblestones. Stalls were set up selling a sparse selection of goods. At this time, there was not much available, with the dislocation of war and constant fighting between the Red and White Army. Nothing could be imported, and very little was being made in Russia and Ukraine at that time. Still, people sold second-hand goods, and peasants brought in meager items of food from the farms. The collectivization program had not yet begun, and many peasants still controlled their own land.

"I know what we'll do," said Maria. "Let's sell ourselves. We can put a sign on us saying "Lost children," and somebody might be kind enough to want us. At least we may get food and a bed for the night. I don't know where we're going to stay now that we've left the train."

So, with spirits heightened by this positive idea, Olga and Maria got a pencil out of their bag and tore a piece of paper out of a book. Olga wrote in large-printed lettering, "LOST CHILDREN, PLEASE HELP." She brushed the hair of the other two children and made them as tidy as she could, and then they set themselves up near a stall and put the sign in front of them. They tried to look as pleasant as possible, thinking that if they looked cross nobody would want them.

It certainly drew the attention of the crowd as they passed. They would point at them and say, "That's a novel idea. There is now nothing to buy at the markets, except children!" Some of the women felt deeply sorry for them and stopped to talk to them, asking them where they were from and the name of their mother. But not many were keen to take extra children into the household. They were extra mouths to feed, at a time when hardly any households could afford the luxury, sorry as they might be. However, Olga at fifteen and Maria at thirteen were now quite big and would be very useful in the household if they could afford to keep them. Eventually a woman did stop and started talking to Olga, asking her pertinent questions. Could they cook and wash and clean? She offered a position to Olga or Maria in her home, as they had two young children. Her husband was a well-placed official in the new regime, so feeding them was not a problem. She, however, could not take all the sisters.

"Thank you so very much, madam. I would love to come and stay and work in your house, but I also have to think of the younger children, and I would have to be sure that they have also found a home before I could take up your offer. Please, could you give me your address? When I have found a home for the other two children, I will then come and work for you." The lady agreed to this and gave Olga her address and instructions on how to get there.

Before long Maria too had an offer of a position. She didn't hesitate, as they were now desperate; they had been sitting for hours in the marketplace, and apart from a few giggles from younger girls, and a few jokes from the older people, no one else had come forward to help them. They still had to look after poor Lydia, who was only eight at the time. Although she looked quite robust and well built, she could hardly be expected to perform a day's productive work.

Towards the end of the day, a couple in their forties walked by and stopped and read the sign. They looked at each other and talked for a few minutes. They then enquired of the details of why they were here and where their parents were, and they realized that these were lost children and they did need some help.

"We'll take the youngest one then. She will be able to help around the house. We don't have any children, and it will be nice to have a little child around the house to amuse us." So by the end of the day, everybody was "sold."

As it turned out, the various homes where they were taken in were not far from each other, and Olga, to her relief, could keep in touch with her two sisters, and support them as necessary. She hoped that this was only a temporary solution and they would soon be reunited with their mother.

Lydia went to live with the childless couple. They were both teachers, and their whole time was spent teaching at school. They did not invite Lydia to school, but she remained at home, and she acted as an unpaid housekeeper. Although they were reasonably kind to her and fed her, if she angered them, she would get a beating. At first she did simple things like sweep and wash the floors, but with their training and insistence, she gradually took over more and more of the tasks in the house. She prepared the vegetables and food to be cooked for the evening. She cleaned up after the meals and kept the floors clean. As she grew older, she even did the washing. She was an unpaid housekeeper, underage, and used as a child slave. For her efforts, she was given food and a little room, a cupboard big enough only for a bed. She was at least safe and had something to eat, which is probably more than she could have expected. However, at night, when she went to bed, she would fall asleep crying, thinking of her loving mother and pray that she would be reunited with her soon. That was not to occur for another twenty-four years in the middle of another Great War.

Chapter 4

Lost in Ukraine

It was around June 1920 before Louiza could really settle
into her restored life in Lvov. She cooked for Ludwig, washed
and cared for him as an only child—which, of course, was what
he had become, at least for the moment. He was busy working
as a junior accountant in one of the large shops, and she was also
fully occupied, now as a partner, in the drapery shop. One day,
as she was serving some customers in the shop, she happened to
glance out the window. There in the distance, walking towards
her, was a tall, strong, young man. Somehow his gait and bearing seemed familiar. He was too far away for her to make out his
face, but she could not stop looking.

Suddenly her heart missed a beat. "It couldn't be," she
thought, "my son Karlov." In the middle of serving a customer,

she dropped everything and ran outside towards the figure, and as she came closer, she realized that it *was* Karlov. He also saw her and came running towards her. He picked her up and swung her around in his arms.

"Karlov, Karlov, where have you been all this time?" she cried through her choking throat, "it's two years since I've heard from you."

"I was fighting with the White Army, Mum. I've been all this time in Siberia, up and down the railway lines, attacking and counter-attacking, and retreating. We were winning for a while, because the Bolshies were disorganized. Then it all fell apart, and I had to get out."

"Where were you? We never heard."

"I was at Omsk when it was taken by the Red Army. That's when I knew it was a downhill battle. Our officers were abandoning the troops and fleeing to the rear. I managed to escape because I knew the woods so well, and for a time I could live on my own, hunting in the wild. Couldn't contact anyone I saw, in case they might be Reds."

All Louiza could think of saying was "Thank God, thank God," and it was heartfelt.

But Karlov seemed almost apologetic. "It was all right at the beginning because the Allies were helping us. They'd landed at Vladivostok and brought us arms and equipment. But in the end, our resolve just broke. There was no real choice but go."

"Thank God you did," Louiza breathed again, "thank God you managed it."

"Once I was out of Omsk, I just worked my way further east, because I realized that Russia itself would be in the control of the Reds, and I couldn't risk going there. I tried to get to the railway line again, hoping it was under Allied control, but by this time everything was terrible, completely in disarray. Hundreds and thousands of our soldiers were taken prisoner, and the rest were jammed onto the railways and roads, starving and dying from wounds and disease, and, of course, it was winter. People were dying from pneumonia and frostbite.

"So I went back into the forest and kept going east. I overtook the retreating White Army remnants, and tried to join the railway at Chita, right out near the Chinese border. There were still Allied troops there, behind good defensive lines. But they knew it was all lost, too, and I retreated back with them as far as Vladivostok. From there I got to Japan on one of the allied steamers.

"So I just switched from being a soldier to being a sailor."

"You've never even seen the sea in your life," exclaimed Louiza.

"Maybe not, but they always need people to haul ropes and lift weights. I was fit and strong enough for it, and they took me on without even a question. With the little experience I had from the steamer to Japan, I was able to get a berth on a trading ship to America. Then I travelled right across America, walking and catching lifts on freight trains, until I reached the East Coast, turned sailor again and then caught another ship to Europe, and here I am. And how are the children?"

At this Louiza's face drained of joy, and she started crying.

"Karlov, Karlov, I've lost the girls. I don't know where they are. Ludwig and I were in the train and the girls were waiting on the platform to join us, when suddenly the train left the station and the girls were left behind. I've written to everybody I can, the Russian Embassy, the Red Cross, and there is no way I can find them. Russia is in such a mess that the fate of three girls is not worth anyone bothering about, and no one has done a thing."

Karlov was shattered. "Oh, my God," he cried illogically, "*It's all my fault*. I should have been there with you to help, and then they wouldn't have been lost."

The joy of seeing his mother again was suddenly submerged in the chilling discovery that his three sisters were lost in the chaos of post-revolution Russia.

"But Ludwig's well," Louiza told him quickly. "He's with me. He looks after me, and he is actually working as a junior accounting clerk in one of the large shops in town. I'm working in this drapery shop, so we are comfortable, but, of course, desolate because of what has happened to the girls. Let me close up the shop, and I'll take you to him."

The reunion left no one dry-eyed. Ludwig was overwhelmed to see his older brother again, and Karlov felt huge waves of emotional relief. The next few days were joyous—but Karlov's sense of guilt at his sisters' fate kept gnawing in the back of his mind.

Finally, he told his mother, "I am going to find them. I'm sure I can. It's understandable that they couldn't get here, because the trains were stopped soon after you got here, but logic says they would have gone somewhere in Ukraine, which narrows it down a bit.

"I speak Russian well, and I know my way around in the woods. I'll cross the border, and start making inquiries."

For a moment, Louiza's spirit lifted. Perhaps Karlov could find the girls again. With luck they would still be alive in the turmoil, and somehow by a miracle, they could be brought back.

But it was too hard to even think about the possibility, for what would happen if Karlov failed, and was also lost? The thought of losing Karlov a second time after his return from the dead was too much to bear. She felt a pain in her heart.

"No, Karlov," she told him reluctantly. "Don't go. We don't know where they are, and you will be captured and killed. Remember that the Soviets probably know you, they'll have records that you fought against them, and they will not forgive you. Stay with us, stay with Ludwig and me and we'll make a life together, and still find them by the official route or through the Red Cross. Things will settle down again once the civil war is over."

But Karlov would not be persuaded. Ludwig was not happy with the idea either, when Louiza told him about that night, and he did his best to change his brother's mind. But he couldn't move him.

"Well," Ludwig told his mother next day, "you know Karlov. Once he's made up his mind, there's no shifting him. You can't tell him about the danger, because he went through two years of it. Going back across the Russian border looks like child's play to him as a result. And combing Ukraine looking for three children will be a piece of cake, apparently."

Over the next month or so, Karlov stayed with them, resting. He bought some new clothing, and started hanging out in taverns, talking to people who might have heard something about the conditions in Russia.

And then Karlov went back, telling his mother, "Don't worry, they couldn't catch me in the last two years, and they won't catch me now, so don't think about it." Once more, Louiza was left in tears.

* * *

Karlov's first move was to get close to the border so he could observe different localities and check his maps, memorizing the topography of various areas. He was trying to find the best place to cross. He needed a rugged area with lots of forests that he could easily negotiate, which would probably be poorly manned by border guards. Finally, he was able to choose a likely crossing point.

In late October, as autumn was approaching, with a cold wind blowing the dead leaves, Karlov decided to make his move. He was friendly with the Polish guards by this time, and they had no qualms about letting him through after he told them the tragic circumstances of losing his sisters. His loss and sorrow were discussed at length in the tavern over a bottle or two of vodka, and by then they were crying with him and singing patriotic songs. Their usual trouble was the other way round, people wanting to get out of Russia, and they were less concerned about anyone trying to get in. As for the guards on the other side, he hoped the cold weather would encourage them to stay inside, rather than move outside monitoring the border, as no one wanted to get into Russia.

He picked a dark night with no moon. It was cloudy and drizzling, most unpleasant weather, but it seemed like an ideal time. He crawled slowly to the wire barrier, and quietly cut a few strands with pliers. He could hear footsteps walking up and down. Looking above the grass, he saw two soldiers walking along the fence line inspecting the border.

Karlov crouched in the shadows of the grass until the sounds of footsteps faded. Gently he crawled away from the fence line until he passed through a clearing some hundred meters away and came to a sparsely wooded area. He was more confident now that he was across the border that he would have no further problems. He was comfortable in the woods, and would be able to get quickly away from the frontier zone.

But suddenly, as he moved through the forest, there was a sound to his right. He froze, uneasy. He tried to reassure himself that it was dark, there was no moon in the forest, and he could easily hide even if some guards were patrolling the area. The noise grew louder, a few cracks of twigs and a swishing noise as branches were pushed aside, and then to his horror he heard a dog bark. Quickly he turned and ran in the opposite direction away from the noise as quietly as he could, hoping to get far enough upwind so that the dogs would not catch his scent.

He failed. The dogs picked up his scent and were soon running, barking, and yelping behind him on the trail. There must have been three or four of them, judging by the noise and commotion they were creating, and he realized that if they caught up with him, they would tear him apart. Fear permeated his body. He looked around and saw a tree with low branches, so he climbed up as quickly as possible. As he went up the first few branches, he could see the shadowy forms of a number of large animals running towards him baying and barking. The handlers must have been some distance behind as he could not see them, but he heard the crackling and rushing in the undergrowth as they followed the dogs. The dogs at last stopped underneath the tree where he was trying to hide. They could not see him but they could smell him. He was trapped. He could not get down as he would be torn to pieces, and he knew that this was where he had to stay until the handlers called them off.

He didn't have long to wait. Two burly soldiers came hurrying up to the dog pack. They had their rifles in their hands on the ready, wary of intruders. The communists at this stage were paranoid about the Allies, and were on full alert for any border intrusions. The war in Siberia was still dragging on, and they were suspicious of the Allies' intentions in the West, and particularly about Britain and France.

The guards realized their quarry was up in the tree. They couldn't see anyone through the darkness and the foliage, but they looked up and shouted, "Come down at once whoever you are, or we'll shoot you."

Karlov was quiet and still, hoping that perhaps they might think they were mistaken and go on their way. Without any more warning, however, the two men started shooting up into the tree.

"Stop, stop, I'm unarmed." Karlov screamed. "I'll come down if you stop shooting."

The shooting halted. "Come now," they ordered. Slowly Karlov climbed down, fearful for his life. To think that he had managed to avoid Russian soldiers and capture and death for two years in Siberia, only to be caught in that quiet desolate place, where there was not even any fighting. And it hadn't happened because of any special skills of the guards', but just by the dogs' inborn ability to follow a scent.

The hounds were now secure on their leashes, but they still strained and lunged to get at him, to tear their quarry apart. They were well trained for their job.

"Well, what have we here, Ivan? That's a big bird to be nesting in the trees," one soldier joked as he inspected Karlov closely, hoping to identify him. He frisked him to ensure he was not carrying a weapon. But Karlov had none with him. He was dressed lightly, but warmly, and he had brought only money with him, to help him search for the girls.

"Who are you and what are you doing here? Do you realize you are in the frontier zone, and you could be shot instantly without any questions as an infiltrating spy or as a traitor trying to run away from his responsibilities? We won't shoot you until we know who you are and what you are doing here. Then I rather imagine we will."

"I'm not a spy, and I'm not a fugitive trying to escape. I'm looking for my sisters," explained Karlov quietly.

"Well, that's a new one," said the leading guard.

"This is a funny place to lose your sisters. What, have you been collecting mushrooms and got lost or something? A likely story," retorted the soldier.

"No, they've been lost for a long time," said Karlov glumly. "It's very complicated." After that they did not speak. They made their way as quickly as possible to the frontier outpost to report to the officer in charge.

The post was no more than a large hut with a main room with a pot-bellied stove, a small table and chairs, with maps on the walls showing patrol routes of the area and stationary guards in observation posts. A notice board was hanging on one wall with sheets of papers attached with curled up corners, no doubt instructions from the local headquarters.

Karlov quickly assessed the room and the senior soldier, who had the rank of a sergeant. He was thin and had dark lanky hair, dirty and greasy, obviously not washed for many weeks, and a pockmarked face with a four-day stubble.

"What have we here?" asked the sergeant.

"Man we caught not far from the frontier line," the senior guard told him. "He was obviously either trying to get in or trying to get out."

"Why didn't you just shoot him, and save me the trouble?" the sergeant said grumpily, "whether he's a spy or an escapee, he'll end up that way anyway."

"He's got some story of looking for his three sisters, so we thought we'd better bring him back in case there was some useful information he can give us."

"Well, we don't need to bother further, then. I will just hand him over to the NKVD. The secret police will straighten him out and find out his true story, and God help him if they find out he's lying."

That gave Karlov a small flash of hope. After all, he had told them the truth. He stayed in the main room, guarded by the two soldiers, while the sergeant went to a desk and wrote a report of the incident to be sent down with him to the NKVD. The room was warm and Karlov was sitting thinking of his fate. He was thinking to himself that he better get his story right and correct, as any inconsistency would be regarded as intentional lying and torture would be applied. At all costs, he needed to hide his true activities during the civil war. That revelation would be a death sentence. Hard as the seat was, he was tired and eventually he drifted off to sleep, lulled out of his concerns by the warmth in the room.

For breakfast he was given a cup of black tea with no milk or sugar, and a piece of bread. Before long the regular truck arrived with some supplies and instructions. He was put in the truck under guard. After a time, they drove to the NKVD headquarters in the nearest town, where the officers locked him in a cell.

After a boiled potato, a piece of dark rye bread, and a mug of tea for lunch, he was called up for his first interrogation.

Karlov was hauled into an office with a desk and two chairs, one of them a hard wooden design, which looked uncomfortable, and another one more executive in style. An officer dressed neatly in a uniform with the NKVD insignia was looking out the window with his back to him. The soldier who brought him in briskly saluted, and then turned around and closed the door behind him.

The officer didn't say a word and kept looking out the window, ignoring him completely. Karlov didn't say anything either; in fact, the silence continued and appeared to be lasting forever, although it was no more than about eight minutes. The officer then turned around, motioned him to sit and looked at him intently, and started his interrogation.

He warned Karlov that his fate would probably be death, but to save himself further suffering and perhaps even torture, he should reveal his whole story, omitting no details. He particularly wanted to hear of any accomplices who might have been involved in his activities, whatever they might be.

Karlov was frightened despite himself. He was unnerved by the cold, efficient behavior of this man. The officer was looking at him intently with burning brown eyes that seemed to be looking right through him. He was not very tall, perhaps less than average height, but very strong, all muscle, and he could easily have been a weightlifter or wrestler, with strong arms and shoulders. But his appearance was not European: he had the slanting eyes and flat nose of Asian descent, with facial features of the ethnic Mongol race. Karlov was familiar with that look from his time in Siberia. Intermarriage between the western colonists and the Siberian natives was commonplace, because there were few Russian or Ukrainian women there. This man was probably of mixed blood.

Now perhaps that offered a chance. There might be a thread of common interest if he played his cards right.

Karlov started at the beginning, explaining how the autocratic dictatorial tsarist regime had banished his family to Siberia as a result of his father participating in a demonstration. He did not let on that the demonstration was because people could not board their ship to leave for Canada, but indicated that it was a demonstration against the regime in general for the down-trodden peasants and proletariat. As a result of his father's revolutionary zeal, they were sent to Siberia, and in particular to Odinskoe. He then explained how the family settled there, despite the severe adverse conditions, and his father had died as a result of the labor and deprivation he was subjected to by the regime.

At this story, the interrogator's face softened. If this was true, obviously this was an honest, patriotic family, which had suffered in their determination to fight against the tsar for the people.

Karlov was questioned on some of the features around Odinskoe, the type of trees and hills, bushes and animals. His interrogator obviously knew the area well, and in fact, he had also grown up in the area of Lake Baikal. He indicated later that he knew Odinskoe extremely well, going there quite often as a boy for supplies and to sell the products of their own farm.

He then asked Karlov, "What is the biggest feature as you enter the town near the river?"

"What feature do you mean—man-made or natural?"

"Well, man-made," answered the interrogator.

"Let's see. As you enter the town after crossing the Ude River and heading north, the most striking thing is the very large, old Hodigitria Cathedral situated on the right side," Karlov replied thoughtfully. "You then pass an area of old wooden log houses. Further on, if you turn right at the next corner and keep on walking, you would reach a large pink house."

"Ah, tell me something about this large mansion. What's its history?" said the interrogator slowly. He knew that this would only be local knowledge, and anyone who did not come from that area, or know that area well, would not have known this particular story.

Karlov had to think only for a moment. He knew the story of the pink mansion well. It was often talked about in the taverns that he frequented, and the story was well known in the area.

"Well, the mansion was owned by a rich American merchant, a Colonel Morrow. He was caught embezzling from the natives and stealing gold. He was eventually thrown out of town by the people during the revolution because he had robbed so many, and everyone was disgusted."

"That's right, that's correct! Only a true son of Siberia who grew up in the area would have known that story. I think you are probably telling the truth, as I can't find any discrepancies in your story and all the details of your life in Siberia I can vouch for as I come from the same place." The officer felt a warm rapport with this young stranger as the memories of his childhood flooded back. He felt more at ease than with his fellow officers who despised him behind his back because of his ethnic background. He could imagine the pangs of loss, and he would act the same to find his sisters. "I'll tell you what—I will try to find your sisters.

"You know the date when you and your mother left Siberia. We also should have a record of the trains that left that area in that period, and their destinations. We'll check those towns through the NKVD network, and if your sisters are found, we will believe your story.

"Of course, if they are not found, you will be shot."

Karlov sighed with relief. At least there was the possibility of surviving this ordeal. The girls could be found and he would not be shot or hanged.

After many weeks of investigation, the girls were found in Kharkov, and Karlov was off the hook and dispatched to the same place. Nevertheless, he was placed under regional arrest: essentially free to move around the city, to work and participate in all activities. But he had to report regularly to the authorities and was warned he was not allowed to move out of the area.

Karlov-Fighting against the Red Army along Trans Siberian Railway-1919.

Chapter Five

A Kind of Reunion

The girls were delighted to find Karlov again. The reunion was moist-eyed on both sides. Seeing them brought him a sense of time passing that he'd not expected. Olga and Marie were young women now, beginning to think about their futures. Lydia, the child of the family he'd left, was a fast-developing teenager.

But there were other thoughts deep beneath his relief at finding them. At least they were reunited and reasonably secure, but this was hardly the liberty he'd set out to bring them when he left Lvov to find his sisters. Both he and they were now deep in the grip of the Soviet state. They couldn't return home together. He knew he could never now escape his constant watchers, and there was no point in bringing the girls further into the attention zone of the NKVD. Altogether it was distinctly not the result

Karlov had hoped to achieve. Materially, things for the girls remained as they always had been since Siberia, and Karlov's position was diminished.

Over time he came almost to accept things. He managed to find a job and eventually got married, producing a son he called Markov. Old talents surfaced and he became noted as a horseman in the Kharkov shows. All the same, a piece of sour knowledge lurked at the back of his mind down the years. Essentially, he had thrown away his life.

Still, Kharkov was not a bad place to be, if you had to be trapped somewhere. Ukraine was enjoying a brief golden era in those early years after the revolution. To win support from the people and stop further fighting until they were in a much stronger position, the Communist Party had promised self-rule to all the different republics, which proclaimed themselves across Russia when the tsar fell.

And in the cities at least, there was an early air of confidence as a result. People there were better educated than the rural class. They were mainly the administrators, government officials, traders, and artisans. Just after the revolution, the towns boasted a forty percent literacy rate compared to around ten in rural Ukraine. The ethnic mix was also different here as well, with a high percentage of Russians who had originally been sent there by the tsars to administer the countryside. They had been followed by Russian Communist officials, who were now slowly taking over ultimate control. Stalin, like the tsar before him, trusted only Russians in positions of power. The artisans and shopkeepers tended to be Jewish, and they were also reasonably educated. This group had always treasured literacy as an asset, with the advantage of being portable. So, in those early years, the cities in general and Kharkov in particular were relatively vibrant.

It wasn't quite the same in the countryside, where the majority of the Ukrainian population lived. They followed their traditional way of village life, continuing their close bond with the land. They saw little need for education or literacy there. Fathers taught sons the practical skills they believed sufficient: how to till the land and tend the animals. Mothers taught their daughters how to run an efficient household, the art of sewing, embroidering, and supporting the family on subsistence farming.

But in that early time of optimism, one of the Soviets' first goals was to Ukrainianize the republic's political and educational establishments. The Commission for Education was headed by a Ukrainian, and he sought to fortify the Ukrainian language the tsars had discouraged. Within a few years, there was a surge of Ukrainian education to the extent that ninety percent of the republic's children had the opportunity to learn their native language in school. Even the Russian and Jewish minorities had to take some course in Ukrainian. Before the revolution, there had been no Ukrainian schools at all.

Carla and Boris, the couple Lydia lived with, prospered as a result of the education blitz. They both became head teachers in Kharkov high schools.

Lydia was now a valuable addition to their home and more than a charity, since she was now quite capable of running the household, conveniently looking after their needs in return for a very meager outlay in food and accommodation. Whereas, under the communists, it was possible but dangerous to have servants in one's home, no one would question or criticize a couple who from the kindness of their hearts had picked up a lost child and looked after her. The fact that she was being used as a servant was just her way of contributing. So Lydia gave them the leisure time for professional development and intellectual pursuits as they became part of the new "intelligentsia," enthusiastically attending night meetings that basked in the fresh nationalistic flowering of Ukrainian culture. Unfortunately, the one thing they overlooked was the need to undertake a little education work at home. Lydia was never taught to read or write.

Lydia still saw Olga and Maria regularly, but they were very busy with their own activities, working in various households, helping busy housewives with children and the house, and it was difficult to meet them more than once every week or two. They would try to get away on Sunday afternoon after lunch, when Carla and Boris were having their afternoon nap, and they could walk arm in arm in the older part of the town, with its wide tree-lined roads. The outskirts of town were covered with shanty dwellings, which had been springing up like mushrooms to house a huge influx of workers to serve the labor requirements of rapid industrialization.

The girls also managed to see Karlov fairly frequently, and in time communications with Louiza opened up. Every few weeks, they got a letter from their mother and they could also write back.

As far as Lydia was concerned, though, it was a fairly empty life. By the time she turned fifteen, she was a dissatisfied, bored young girl. Existence consisted of nothing more than being an unpaid servant. Although Carla and Boris were tolerable guardians as far as safety and food were concerned, they gave her no love or understanding. She had few cultural or emotional outlets, and apart from seeing her sisters and receiving the regular letters from her mother, which she could not even read, she had little emotional support.

She managed to make friends with a local girl about the same age, who was also a rebellious spirit like Lydia. Both wanted to escape their stifling, barren surrounds. They met in the street when they had some free time and walked to the shops arm in arm, eyeing the young men and boys on the way, and then running off and giggling together whenever someone showed an interest. Lydia was now developing into full womanhood. She had attractive brown eyes and thick dark hair, cut by her sisters in the fashionable short pageboy style. Both Olga and Maria already had relationships with young men, which were taking more and more of their time.

Lydia looked older than her age. Her skin was clear, and she topped off her bright appearance with makeup she "borrowed" from Carla.

One night she fell victim to the international teenage phenomenon of the age. She and Lisa decided to go to the movies for the first time—and Lydia found a new ambition. The movies were a new experience in those days, and suddenly everybody was talking about films and film stars. Lydia and Lisa had no idea what this was all about and decided to investigate. They saved a little money and, though the price seemed quite exorbitant, ventured into the new dimension.

The girls stood in line waiting to buy their tickets and listened to the other young people talking about the films that they had previously seen. This was all strange to Lydia and Lisa, who did not know what to expect as they made their way to their seats. There was a piano at the edge of the stage with someone playing a selection of songs. They tried to act grown-up and sophisticated, as if slightly bored with the whole event, but inside they were excited. Soon the lights were dimmed and went out altogether, with the piano player playing a romantic tune. The film then started. Lydia couldn't believe it. There were people moving around on the flat white screen, and soon she was completely absorbed in the experience.

The movie lifted her out of herself. She imagined she was the heroine, experiencing the tragedy and the exhilaration, the dangers and the seduction in the story. The piano player tried to play appropriate music, with dramatic tunes when the heroine faced danger, and then emotional, soft music during the romantic interludes. Lydia was enthralled, experiencing every moment as if she were part of the story. She had never experienced anything like this.

After the film, both girls were flushed with excitement and talked rapidly on the walk home.

"Wasn't that wonderful?" Lydia said. "I could live in that movie all my life. It was just me. Now that's what I want to be, I've decided! That woman who is so sophisticated, in control of her life, and loved by the handsome hero."

Lydia had been lifted out of her dull, drab life for an hour, and in that time she experienced more emotions and thrills than she ever had before. Lisa was just as enthusiastic.

"That's what I'm going to do with my life," said Lydia. "I want to be a film star. I'm going to run away from this hole of a place, from these horrible people, and be like that woman in the film. I'm going to experience all her life and emotions and thrills. My mind's made up."

Determined as she might be, Lydia was still naïve and unsure how to achieve this sudden ambition. Nevertheless she was going to try.

"Are you going to come with me Lisa, or shall I go by myself?"

"But where will you go?"

"Well, obviously there's no movie-making here in Kharkov. We'll have to go to another city. I suppose the best would be Kiev. That's the republic's capital, where all the books and plays are written, and I expect there's a filmmaking industry centered there as well. They still have all the universities there—I've heard Carla and Boris talk about the wonderful facilities in Kiev, and how they would love to move there."

"Well, I'll think about it, but I am tempted, Lydia. I really loved that film and I would love to become a glamorous movie star, too."

The girls were so smitten they never realized in their innocence that the whole project was just a dream. It was not a wish to be achieved, lived, or even sought, particularly in Ukraine under communist rule. But they believed it was a reality, and they wanted nothing more.

Over the weeks, they met as often as possible and conspired over the project. Lydia gradually picked out the best of the clothing that she had, meager as it was, and packed it in the suitcase under her bed, which she had kept from her trip from Siberia. Now she had a positive use for it. She also "borrowed" a few pieces of make-up, such as lipstick and eyeliners that she had seen Carla use, and packed the precious few pieces of jewelry that she still had from her mother. Her favorite piece was a brown amber necklace, which she actually treasured the whole of her life. She took all the money that she saved over the years, not that it was very much, and on Friday morning, after everybody went to their work, the girls dressed in their best clothing, made up their faces to appear as old as possible, and snuck out of their houses.

Lydia wanted to leave a note saying good-bye to Boris and Carla, but since she could not write, she had to ask Lisa to scribble a quick farewell. It said simply, "Dear Boris and Carla, I have to leave to make a new life for myself. Thank you for what you have done for me over the years. I will miss you both. Love, Lydia."

They carefully omitted any mention of what she was going to do or where she was going, in case they came after her and brought her back. She never realized that she could have left anytime without their permission—they were the ones breaking the law by keeping her as an unpaid servant.

The girls lugged their suitcases to the railway station, and excitedly bought tickets for Kiev. They were excited but scared. Even though they didn't know what lay ahead of them or how to achieve it, they were certainly doing something decisive, and they hoped their whole lives would be changed for the better.

Eventually they got to Kiev late in the afternoon. It was early summer and the sun was shining. The city was beautiful: a profusion of trees and parks, and streets tree-lined and wide. Ancient churches stood majestically among grand stone structures, government buildings, and private homes that had been built across the centuries. Many Russian noblemen kept homes in Kiev, and the cultural life that it offered had attracted rich Jewish traders.

The grandeur of the city overwhelmed the girls, but that did not help them to survive. They knew no one, had nowhere to go, and had very limited funds. That night they ate whatever food was left over from their trip, and slept on a seat in the railway station. The next day, they had to make a critical plan of how to survive while they tried to fulfill their ambitions.

"Well, there is very little I can do except cook and clean house," said Lydia, "and I suppose you are the same. We don't have any other training."

"Yes, you're right, Lydia, we will just have to try to find housework with someone. I bet the Jews have more money than anyone. Let's start looking for jobs in the Jewish neighborhood."

The next day, they tidied themselves up, and while one looked after the luggage, the other girl would walk up the road and ask at every shop to see if they wanted a housekeeper. Lydia was lucky after some hours of trying. She managed to interest the owner of a large bakery. He was indeed Jewish, and his wife had some young children. They needed help urgently in the home because she was also working in the bakery supervising staff selling the bread. The owner had to get up very early in the morning to start baking the bread for the day, and he went home in the afternoon to sleep and rest while his wife took control of the bakery after lunch. They were keen to find someone to help care for the house and the three young children. One child had started school already, but there were two still at home and they needed supervision, feeding, and dressing. Lydia was again offered board and lodging for her efforts, but this time the deal included a little pay and some time off for herself. That was much better than her previous situation as an unpaid housekeeper.

Lisa, too, managed to obtain a position in the household of a communist bureaucrat.

At last Lydia felt she was a person in her own right and could do what she liked in her spare time. She felt an immense sense of freedom. She spent her money on make-up, perfume, clothing, and, of course, cigarettes. Her first film had depicted the heroine smoking a cigarette in a long holder, and she tried to emulate this. Every spare moment in the evening, she would go to the taverns near the university, the favorite gathering places for the students, actors, playwrights, and painters of Kiev. They were all highly optimistic, talking and planning the new republican nationalism, when Ukraine was still looking forward to being self-governing as an independent communist republic, where people would be equal, well educated, and cared for.

Everybody was optimistic about the future. The yoke of the tsar had at last been lifted, and the hammer of the communist regime had not yet struck.

Lydia and Lisa were spellbound by this atmosphere, the company, and the ambience. They were smoking like everybody else, drinking only a little bit, and joining in with the laughter and singing. The taverns echoed with nationalistic songs of Ukrainian past greatness and the heroes, myths, and culture. It was all uplifting and joyous to the girls, who had never experienced anything like this before. They felt they were free, grown-up, and experiencing life at a higher level than they had thought possible.

Nothing pleased Lydia more than the singing and dancing that developed towards the end of the night as people became tipsier. She met many young men and formed attachments, but only superficial. The casual relationships would initially blossom and then fade away. Although she was a very bright, intelligent girl, it was difficult for her to hide her lack of education in a group that valued learning and culture above all else. Nevertheless she didn't mind: she was gaining experience, poise, and confidence. She still wanted to become an actress, but she had no training or background, she was competing against young people who were more gifted, skilled, and trained, and there were few acting jobs available. Besides, all the plays had central Ukrainian nationalistic themes that were always emphasizing the Ukrainian culture, myths, and heroes. With her German background and her lack of any education, she knew nothing of this. She was illiterate not only in writing and reading, but also in the traditions of Ukraine. Most children absorbed at least some cultural familiarity from their parents in stories and fairy tales. Lydia had no such parenting.

One evening while sitting in a favorite tavern with Lisa and some friends, listening to the "high-level" philosophy and theoretical sociology promulgated by some of the half-drunk students, Lydia noticed a group of people engaged in similar pursuits. There was one young man, however, who was sitting quietly on the edge and was not as boisterous and pushy. He was sitting quietly having a few sips of vodka and smoking a cigarette. He was listening, but had very little to say. Lydia was impressed with that, as she herself was very much in the same position on the edge. She listened quietly, laughed, sang, but spoke rarely because she was too often ridiculed by those around her. She got up and sat beside him.

"Hello there, you're very quiet and thoughtful sitting by

yourself, not having much to say," she told him in a friendly, playful manner. He smiled back and said, "I noticed you've been very quiet, too. I saw you sitting with that other group."

"I just listen, hoping to pick up and absorb all their knowledge. I'd rather sing and dance than talk about philosophy and all that rubbish, as I know very little about it. What do you do? Are you a student, too?"

"No, I'm not a student, I'm a painter," said the young man, explaining that his name was Ivan.

"You mean a picture painter or a house painter?" Lydia looked at him mischievously.

"No, I paint pictures." He went on to explain that he had found a good income painting pictures to order for the kulags, Ukraine's independent landowners since the revolution. They had money to spend on luxuries, and they liked to buy paintings of their most treasured possession, their house and properties. "I've been doing this for a few years, and I've become well known in this area, so most of my work is obtained by word of mouth. You must come around one day and I will show you my paintings, if you are interested."

"I would love to," said Lydia. "Why don't we make a time?" They arranged to meet early the next week.

Lydia felt very comfortable with Ivan. He was a dreamy young man, thin in build, with kind brown eyes and a faraway look. His speech was different from the others, and he was more down-to-earth. There was no nationalistic zeal or pretense of super intelligence, as most of the other young men seemed to have. He didn't look at her with disdain when her speech was not articulate in the high-culture manner of the new intelligentsia.

She started meeting him near the river and walking together in the gardens of Kiev, along the wide, wooded paths secluded from the crowds and the bustle of the town. As they got to know one another, they quickly became close friends, and Lydia discovered the youthful feeling that long predated the ambition to get into movies. She fell romantically in love with Ivan, and they became lovers.

Ivan was also studying electronics and electrical technology, as well as painting. He was not allowed to go to university since his father had been a member of the Tsarist Imperial Guards, killed during the revolution, and considered an enemy of the people. He was permitted a technical education, nevertheless, because his skills as an electrical technician would be useful to the Socialist Republic's planned accelerated industrialization.

Lydia and Ivan spent every possible moment together. They stopped going to the taverns, as there was really nothing to draw them. They had no real friends there, but they grew closer and warmer to each other. Ivan could play the balalaika, and he would often sit and play for her on picnics in the public gardens. They walked hand-in-hand through the streets, looking at the shops, and walked in the parks, talking about things more meaningful to them, such as what they would do in the future, where they were going to live and how they would survive. He read books to her, both romantic and historical narratives, and it reminded her of her mother reading to her so many years ago. It gave her as much peace and comfort as a caress.

After six months, they decided to get married. This was no big thing. Lydia put on her best dress and Ivan borrowed a suit, and they went to the local courthouse with a few friends. Birth certificates were produced and necessary papers filled in, and a chamber magistrate matter-of-factly pronounced them man and wife. At last Lydia had someone who was close to her heart that she could depend on, now joined together as her partner in the difficult passage of life.

Ivan was a sincere, kind man. He was, however, very proud and also just about as obstinate as Lydia. He was proud of what he had achieved as a painter, but he also loved his electrical work, and he felt almost as fulfilled in that. He was a born artisan, who loved doing anything with his hands, to the extent he could build or repair anything and make it work. Ivan did not tell Lydia until fifteen years later that he had started work as a cobbler's apprentice. When his father died in the revolution, he was apprenticed to a cobbler, and for years he was confined in a black smelly hole, repairing and making shoes and boots. He had to sit in cramped conditions, continually hammering, sewing, and cutting leather. It was boring, unrewarding work, but as his mother had three younger children to care for, there was little chance of him getting any education. He was only thirteen years old when he started work. When the revolution ended, he took the opportunity to attend school, and with his natural scientific gifts, he had been readily accepted to study electrical science, then the most advanced technical subject. When he discovered his skill in painting and a ready market for his work, he very quickly dropped his cobbler's job and started his professional painting career, at the same time continuing with his electrical studies.

From the money he earned painting, he was able to provide for his family and his sisters, who were now growing up and also starting to work, reducing the stress on the family finances. He had also managed to put a considerable amount of money away, hidden around his house—there were no banks at that time and money could not be trusted with anyone else.

As soon as Lydia and Ivan were married, they started planning to use some of it and build a house. They managed to buy a small block of land at the edge of a village outside Kiev's city boundary, out in the countryside. Small as it was, it was big enough for the home that they had dreamed about. In six months, Ivan finished it, using the best materials he was able to buy, scrounge, or find. It consisted of a large main room that served as the kitchen, sitting and dining room, and two small bedrooms, with a small outhouse for chickens and the occasional pig that they hoped to fatten. It was built expertly, with all the corners square and straight, windows well-fitted without any chance of leaks, and double-glazed for the cold, harsh winter. The chimney was large and incorporated a baking area for bread and other food. They lived there even before it was finished, and finished it together, whitewashing the outside walls, with Lydia helping to thatch the roof. The house was built in the traditional style, with thick earthenware walls and a thatched roof.

But soon after they moved in, they were visited by a local communist functionary. It seemed that Ivan had not sought his permission before building the house. The official considered that he was in charge of every activity in his area, and so he should have been consulted and an appropriate permission sought from him, with, of course, some sort of under-the-table payment for his trouble.

As the bureaucrat walked in, he looked around admiringly at the well-built structure and said, "You certainly did a good job, even though you didn't get my permission."

"I didn't know you had to have permission to do with your land as you pleased. I paid for it and I built this house with the money I saved, so whose business is it anyway?" retorted Ivan very angrily. Lydia tried to quiet him down gently so as not to cause trouble.

"You don't own anything anymore, comrade!" bellowed the official. He was a short, fat man of Russian descent, one of the thousands of Russians who had been sent to Ukraine to start taking over the country. "This property and every centimeter of land in our glorious country belong to the great proletariat of the workers. Whatever is good for the workers will be done, and scum like you who have been feeding off their sweat will be thrown out where you belong," he shouted. He turned on his heel, walked out of the house and slammed the door behind him.

Lydia and Ivan were dumbfounded, and felt the cold hand of fear rising up to their necks. They realized that things were starting to go wrong in Ukraine. The nationalist drive was slowly being reversed by Stalin, and more and more Russians were coming in to take over control and squash any further trends to a separate identity.

The very next morning, they heard a loud banging on the door.

"Open up in there, quickly now."

They opened the door, and there were three of the local policemen with an official-looking paper, which they shoved under Ivan's nose. He quietly read it and his spirits sagged. It was an eviction notice, a demand stating that it had been decreed that their house was now required by the state, and the state was confiscating the house for the needs of the proletariat. There would be no discussions on the matter, and any resistance would be punished. There was nothing for it—they couldn't resist, and if they resisted, they would lose the house anyway and possibly their lives. Sadly they packed their belongings. They had little furniture at this stage as they hadn't even had time to buy or make furniture before their house was confiscated, but they left even that behind. They packed their personal belongings and moved out. Lydia was crying quietly to herself. It seemed to her that she was doomed to a life of sadness. Whenever she experienced a moment of happiness, it would be wrenched away from her. Ivan was silent as he looked back at his house, his home that he had so carefully built with his own hands. He turned and walked away with a bent head, bitter and angry at the new communist regime. He felt powerless and impotent: resistance would lead only to destruction.

They moved into Ivan's mother's home. This was already very crowded, being only a small flat with a living area and one bedroom. One of the sisters and her husband were living in the only bedroom, and the mother and the other sister were living in the main living room. The arrival of yet another couple was an extra stress that was difficult to tolerate. They stayed only a short time and tried to find accommodation in the city, which was just about impossible. Because of the deteriorating conditions in the countryside, urbanization was exploding and living space was now at a premium. And to complicate matters further, Ivan's income had badly deteriorated because the countryside's woes had stopped the kulags spending their money on paintings and all other non-essential items.

Ivan and Lydia considered the problems, and decided to see if things might be better in Dniepropetrovsk, another large industrial city, on the banks of the Dnieper River in the south. Conditions were supposed to be better with the increasing pace of industrialization.

The trouble was that all this happened in 1928, at the start of Stalin's first Five-Year Plan. Even flight to another city was not going to save Lydia and Ivan from the tragedy of the megalomaniac in Moscow.

****

Olga and Maria Goltz-1924.

Chapter Six

The Road to Russia's Ruin

Ivan's armory of skills was the main reason the family managed to survive the terrible years that followed. Dniepropetrovsk was a town in the heart of the area earmarked for rapid industrialization in Stalin's wildly ambitious Five-Year Plan, and the move into industry was a change Ivan easily adapted to, when circumstances required it.

He obtained a key job in the construction of new electricity infrastructure on the Donbas, a large mining and industrial complex in the eastern part of Ukraine. It would only maintain Lydia and the family in a one-room flat in Dniepropetrovsk, but at least they managed to eat in a period when thousands starved.

Stalin's aim was to transform Russia, Ukraine, and the other republics from a collection of largely peasant societies with individual ambitions for independence into a single modern, industrialized culture. The Plan's goals were formidable, including a three hundred percent expansion in heavy industry, together with all the building and infrastructure construction that would require, in just the five years of its title.

This would mean sacrifices by every household in the state, but particularly on the part of the peasants and the *kulags*, who, as a class, were to be eliminated altogether. The Five-Year Plan involved the collectivization of all the arable land in the country. Stalin expected to obtain cheap grain from these ventures, and at the same time, remove the bourgeois influence of private farm ownership.

The hoped-for cheap grain from the collectives was supposed to feed greatly expanded numbers of industrial workers, with the surplus sold overseas to provide the capital required for industrialization. The program would transform the countryside, and it was carried out with the zeal of war. Ultimately, the entire Five-Year Plan revolved around the sacrifices of Russia's peasant society.

The Soviets moved first to eliminate the kulags. They were the land owners and owned on average ten to twenty acres of land, and employed several peasants to help farm the land—something the Soviets regarded as exploitation. Committees were set up to identify kulags, headed by a secret police representative, with the regional head of the Soviet Counsel and the party secretary. These arbitrary decisions could not be appealed against. Often the process deteriorated into a way of settling old grudges and eliminating any political deviants or opponents. The more obstinate kulags who resisted were exterminated, and the rest were sent to Siberia to labor camps: altogether nearly one million people were either shot or deported. It amounted to virtually the same thing, because the Siberian conditions usually proved fatal to those who were weak, particularly the sick, the old, and the children. There was no escape for the kulags, as those who managed to avoid deportation or shooting could not get work in the factories. In an awful way, though, the quick death suffered by the kulags was preferable to the much worse fate that awaited the poorer peasants.

The peasants rebelled against the 1928 decision to force rapid collectivization of all farms. There were armed uprisings, brutally quelled by the army and police. Other peasants carried out individual protests by killing their farm animals and eating or selling the meat. The peasants' reaction was so severe that Stalin had to reduce some pressure in 1930, realizing that he would not have an agricultural base left if collectivization was pursued too rapidly.

He continued the pressure, but subtly and more slowly. Peasants who left the communal farms were given land that was not arable and were not provided with any equipment, so that they had no choice but to return to the collectives. The directors of the collective farms were Russians, or some dedicated communists, who had no idea how to run farms or how to plant or what to plant, so initially those collectives were less productive and less efficient than the individual farms run by the peasants. As a fairly natural consequence that anyone but the Moscow megalomaniac might have foreseen, the sums failed to add up.

And now the climate contributed to the devastation created by Stalin's grandiose plan. A drought struck in 1931. The harvest was catastrophic.

Stalin was not deterred. Grain was his only currency to pay for industrialization, so exports had to be maintained to keep overseas equipment purchases on schedule. He ordered troops and secret police to confiscate all the grain in the villages, including much seed grain required for the following crops. The 1932 harvest was lower by ten percent. Regardless, Stalin increased the following grain quota to be provided by Ukraine by a further forty percent. The demand was impossible and produced a man-made famine in 1932–33. Millions died of starvation.

With nothing to eat, the peasants tried to stay alive by eating anything edible, including pets, leaves, bark, rats, mice. There were even cases of cannibalism. Yet even as the village people died, the party members, mainly Russians, still went marauding through the villages, confiscating food virtually from the mouths of the dying. Usually the men tended to go first, because they were less endowed with body fat and had no energy reserves, followed by the children. The women would die last in the family after losing their loved ones.

Stalin knew that he was destroying the peasantry of Ukraine, but from his point of view, that had its advantage. The landed peasantry was the main source of nationalistic spirit, so he was breaking any future political resistance.

No one has fully calculated the total deaths caused by this man-made famine, but estimates range from six to ten million people, about twenty percent of the population. Those who survived were scarred for life.

Most of the world remained ignorant of what was happening. Stalin hid all evidence of the famine from outside observers. The frontiers were sealed, and journalists, particularly from America, were either unable or ideologically disinclined to discover the truth.

In 1933 thousands of officials, even at the top, were purged and exterminated on charges of nationalism. All the intelligentsia, writers, poets, actors, and teachers, were also exterminated, and the whole country started down the path of "russification," so that even the language spoken in the different republics was officially changed to Russian.

* * *

Back in Dniepropetrovsk, Lydia was not working, but caring for her two-year- old daughter, Ludmilla. Life was hard for her. The one-room flat had no running water or toilet, and facilities were shared on a communal basis. There was a hallway on every floor, with similar rooms opening to the hallway. The water was outside, served by a communal tap, and had to be carried into the rooms. There was only one gas ring in the flat, which was not always working, since the supply was unreliable. She was subject to food rationing, as she was not working. She was starting to worry that Ludmilla was getting thin and losing weight, even though she tried to supply her with all the food that she could get her hands on, at the risk of starving herself. They were barely surviving even with the money that Ivan was sending them.

Ivan himself was well fed, since he was working in a critical industry, electricity distribution being fundamental to the industrialization program. All the factories had their associated kitchens and cafeterias, and the critical workers were adequately fed at work.

One afternoon Lydia went outside to the common tap to take some water up to her room. Ludmilla did not go down, but remained in the narrow hallway. She was skipping along and singing, a happy little child unaware of the tragedy around her in the grown-up world.

Their neighbor, a thin, old Jewish woman, was also suffering. She was generally irritable, unfriendly, and impatient with the children on the floor, who were always making a noise in the corridor. She suddenly opened the door to see what the racket was in front of her door this time. She saw Ludmilla skipping and singing and called out shrilly, "Shut up, you little German brat. Get back where you came from and leave this place in peace."

Lydia was just coming up the staircase and heard the interchange. Suddenly she was enraged that this woman should talk to her child in such a manner. Ludmilla was doing nothing more than being a child. Lydia raced along the hallway, tipped the bucket of cold water over the old lady's head and started hitting her with the empty bucket around the head and shoulders. This was most unlike her usual pattern of behavior, but perhaps hunger and strain had pushed her to the edge.

"You Jewish witch, how dare you talk to my child like that? She has no choice to be where she is, and God knows, we would rather be anywhere else than this forsaken hole where everyone's dying of starvation."

The poor woman was taken completely by surprise. She ran inside and slammed the door shut. Lydia was left panting and puffing outside, still shaking with rage, and calling out further insults in her direction. By this time, the other residents had heard the noise. Doors were opening and curious heads looked out to see what had caused the commotion.

They were all pleased when they heard the story. None of them liked the old woman, who at some time or other had insulted all of them. Of course, there was also the strong animosity between the ethnic groups, particularly Ukrainians and the Jews, though the Russians were not very pleasant to the Jews either. However, there were State laws forbidding ethnic animosity, vilification, and fighting. Breaches were supposed to be severely punished, and normally people kept their dislikes and hatreds to themselves. But at this spat, the residents laughed and clapped. "Well done," "Bravo," were the calls.

The woman reported the incident, making a formal complaint to the nearby police office about the way that she was assaulted and vilified by the violent "German" woman who lived in her corridor.

Within days there was a knock on Lydia's door. She answered and saw a police officer with a clipboard and paper under his arm. He was rather arrogant, as most officials were in those days, basking in their unlimited power.

"A very serious charge has been reported to me, and I'm investigating this matter. I believe that you were involved in an assault on your neighbor. You used foul language, insulting her Jewish ethnicity."

"Come in, please, Officer," replied Lydia meekly. "I'll explain the circumstances to you." She escorted him in and sat him at the table. It would have been helpful if she had a glass of vodka to give him, but she had nothing, so she apologized for her lack of hospitality.

"It is like this, Officer," she continued. "My husband is away performing his patriotic duty, building the electricity lines to new industrial complexes in the Donbas, and I'm left here all by myself to look after my little child to bring her up as a patriotic citizen. The child was singing patriotic songs when she was abused by the old reactionary woman." She said it all so meekly and appealingly to the young officer that he had little hesitation in warming towards her. It also helped that Lydia demonstrated Ludmilla singing a few words of a patriotic song. She explained how she had lived in Ukraine since she was eight after being lost, and she was not really from Germany, but her parents were sent to Siberia during the tsarist regime. That made them heroes of the republic immediately.

The Jewish woman's story was not nearly as convincing, as all she could do was to lay blame for the whole affair on Lydia. She claimed that Lydia attacked her for no reason at all except for the fact that she was Jewish. Lydia shed a few tears explaining the whole matter to the official. Her whole effort was very effective: the policeman's report leaned quite heavily in Lydia's favor, influenced by the fact that he was anti-Jewish himself and he would have reacted the same way if his child was abused for singing the new patriotic songs of the communist regime. Why, this was nothing less than a defense of the Socialist Republic by a loyal citizen against reactionary elements.

Eventually the whole matter came to court. Lydia and the old lady presented themselves before the magistrate. After reading the police report and asking a few questions, the magistrate came to a decision. He took off his glasses and looked at Lydia sternly and said, "Your case is very serious, madam. You've been charged on two counts. The first count is attacking a defenseless woman and causing severe bruising around the head and shoulders. The second count is vilification of a member of an ethnic minority, namely a Jewish lady. Now how do you plead?" He looked at her quizzically.

"Well, of course, I hit her. Anyone can see that I've done it, and she's a Jew. What more can I say about it? If she talks to my child in that manner again I will hit her again," said Lydia.

"Well then, I must impose your sentence, which will be severe, as you have no remorse. I sentence you to community service for vilification of an ethnic minority. This will be a maximum of nine months to serve without pay in the kitchen of the local steel mill. I dismiss the charge of violence against you."

The Jewish woman got up in disgust and walked out of the courtroom. Community service in a factory cafeteria in the middle of a famine was equivalent to throwing a life buoy to a drowning man.

When the legal procedures were over, the judge relaxed and asked Lydia in an inquiring manner where she had lived in Siberia.

"We stayed mainly in the vicinity of Odinskoe until my father died."

"Ah," said the judge. "I know that area well. I was also deported to the Lake Baikal area by the tsarist regime for my revolutionary activities. Your father must have been a true patriot to die for the sake of the Party. I hope you bring your child up with the same high ideals."

He gave Lydia a wink, so maybe he didn't entirely believe all this, and walked out of the chambers. Lydia left in a daze. She had thought she would be severely punished, but all she received was one of the most desirable prizes going at the time.

She started working in the steel mill cafeteria, starting very early each morning. She needed to be there before the first day shift to prepare their breakfast. Then she helped with the midday meal, the biggest of the day. This was mainly basic high-energy foods, such as potato soup and *casha,* buckwheat cooked like rice. There was no meat, just an occasional sprinkling of *salo* or pork fat belly, cut up finely, fried with onion and spread over the buckwheat or potatoes.

Lydia's job was to peel potatoes, wash up the pots, pans, and dishes, and clean up as required. It was hard, but she was used to that kind of work. The big plus was that she could always sample the food, which meant that during the day she managed to be reasonably well fed. She was also entitled to a meal of her own, as a worker in the factory.

Peelings and scraps were taken to a local collective farm involved in pig production and used as part of the pig feed. Lydia regarded it as something of a waste that the food was being virtually thrown out and fed to pigs when humans could have eaten the scraps and survived instead of dying of starvation in the streets. But anyone caught removing food from the cafeteria was punished.

Lydia would come home well fed and quite comfortable to a home with no food, hungry child, and hungry neighbors. Some of her friends were looking after Ludmilla while Lydia was working out her sentence. In the end, she felt forced to take a risk. She put on a very large pair of underpants, modified by putting tie strings in the leggings, which came half-way to her knees and were fitted with a strong string at the waist to keep them up. During the working day, she would put some of the potato peelings aside, and in the evening, making sure that no one was looking, she would stuff the peelings into her underpants. When she put on her overcoat the increased girth around her hips could not be noticed. Once she got home, she could empty her underpants into a pot and help out the neighbors. When she was peeling potatoes now, she would make sure the peelings were fairly thick, containing a good portion of the potato.

With some salt added, the peelings made a rough meal for hungry people, since the potato skin actually contained the most nutritional parts of the vegetable, particularly high levels of vitamin C and other vitamins. Together with the potatoes' complex starch, it would certainly stave off starvation—as, of course, the Irish had discovered a century earlier.

The Jewish woman, who had started the whole process, could never work out why Lydia was so friendly to her now and always said hello and smiled whenever they met on the staircase or in the hallway. Lydia worked in the cafeteria for practically the whole of the year until the famine started to ease, so she and Ludmilla were sheltered from the ravages of the famine.

* * *

Ivan and Lydia gradually became wearily acquiescent to the demands of the government. In the aftermath of the famine, they realized that they were just lucky to be alive, and struggling against the regime in any way would be fruitless and even dangerous. Ivan tried to build two more homes after the first was confiscated in Kiev, but each time he completed a house, it was confiscated within six months by a communist bureaucrat as "necessary to the workings of the state." It was better to conform and try to survive within the system.

After the famine, most of the peasants left alive were either in Siberia as deportees, or working on the large farm collectives. A few gave up farming altogether and joined the population influx to the cities, working in the ever-expanding industrialization program.

Lydia went to work in industry as well. She trained as a small truck driver, and she got a job picking up farm produce from the collectives. This varied, and could include sacks of potatoes, radishes, onions, carrots, turnips, or any of the other vegetables and grains that were harvested off the farms. She would deliver her cargo to the local government stores, and help unload it. She enjoyed the independence and freedom of movement the work brought her. She felt free when she was driving, which at the time was restricted to lorry drivers involved in goods transport, and not enjoyed by the general population at large. She would meet the farmers and chat to them about conditions on the farms and their produce. It was never boring, and she could joke with the workers on the farm and the government store.

She finished her day late in the afternoon and went to the store's purchasing areas, where long lines were building. No matter what was being sold, there was always a demand, since there was always a shortage of every conceivable product. People just lined up on the off-chance that by the time they got to the head of the line there would be something left. The desirable goods were sugar, rice, flour, and sometimes tea, if they were lucky. Lydia could generally walk up to the front of the line, where Ludmilla would already be waiting. She went straight to the store after school and saved a place for Lydia.

People were inured to the system now. There was no evidence of impatience or irritation. The population had become weary and docile after the famine. They felt fortunate if they could get enough to eat, and having to wait for food in the government store was not a huge issue, except that it made the whole system very inefficient. People would even laugh at the situation. One of the jokes summed it up:

"An old, toothless lady comes up to a line and decides to join on the end. All the people ahead are young women who start laughing and whispering to each other. One of them calls out to her, 'Babushka, babushka, why are you joining this line?'

'Well, I hope to get whatever they are selling. I don't care if it's sugar or lollies. If I don't have any teeth, I can still eat whatever they sell me.'

'Babushka, they are not selling anything to eat. This is a line to see a doctor.'

'Well, I probably need a check-up and some medication as well,' says the old lady. 'You can't be too careful.'

The young woman laughs. 'Well, babushka, this doctor won't help you—he's an obstetrician.'"

In this time, Ivan, like most males, was conscripted into the reserves of the Red Army. Because of his electrical and electronics skills, he was made a communications operator, with the job of maintaining his unit's radio system and handling their messages. This was always a very sensitive position, since it gave him access to all the communications and orders transmitted. For that reason, the Army regarded it as absolutely essential that he and his entire family could be classed as utterly reliable.

But Lydia was still receiving mail from her mother, at least once every two months. These letters were a great joy to Lydia. They maintained her contact with Louiza, so she knew how things were going with her and felt that her mother still loved her. Lydia was able to feel she was still part of her family. Of course, she couldn't read them herself, but Ivan would read them aloud. Whenever she felt down, she would get Ivan to read them again, to bring her the glow of warmth from this tenuous contact with her mother and Ludwig.

Naturally there was no chance of a reunion while the communist regime was in power. The borders were sealed so no one could escape the country, and there was no possibility of being released on humanitarian grounds to rejoin her family. She was part of the "great proletariat of the Soviet Union," and her major function in life was to work for the welfare of the communist system. Everything else was a minor matter.

In addition overseas mail was very strictly monitored, and all letters were censored. They were not delivered normally by the postman: Lydia had to go to the post office, and fill in a form with the help of the postmaster, reporting the address where she lived, what relationship she had with the sender, and other personal details. She was then required to sign the form to acknowledge receipt. The regime regarded any contact outside the Soviet Union as suspicious: overseas mail judged inappropriate and a possible threat to the regime could easily bring death to the recipients.

One afternoon Lydia received notification of an overseas letter's arrival, summoning her to come and pick it up. She was ecstatic. She knew it would be from her mother, and she made her way joyfully to the post office. When she was asked to sign as recipient, it did not strike her as strange that this time the piece of paper was blank. Told to sign at the bottom of the page, she scribbled her name awkwardly. All she was interested in was getting the precious letter from her mother. She raced back to have Ivan read it to her when he came home from work, and to reread it repeatedly.

What she didn't realize was that when she left the post office, the paper she had signed was handed to an official of the NKVD. There were NKVD officers planted in every organization in the country to monitor all activity, everywhere, and that naturally included the postal service.

And as Lydia learned years later, the NKVD man simply wrote a letter to Louiza on the blank page Lydia had been made to sign. It read that she no longer wished to communicate with Louiza.

When Louiza received it, she was devastated. Now she had to face yet another loss, the severance of this tenuous connection with her daughter, whom she had not seen for eighteen years. She couldn't think of the reason for this break in communication but suspected that it was some government interference. The writing was different from Lydia's signature, but that was always the case because Lydia could not write anything more than her own name, and she always had to get someone else to write for her.

Louiza did not write again because she was afraid further letters might cause trouble for Lydia. Lydia tried to re-establish contact, but her letters were confiscated at the post office: the break was complete. When it was obvious the letters had stopped, Lydia became increasingly depressed and worried. She feared the worst, thinking that something dreadful must have happened to her mother and brother.

The regime did not take any chance of information leaking out of the country. The same clamp-down was imposed on Lydia's sisters, Olga and Maria, who had to tell her they also no longer received Louiza's letters.

They were all worried, and Louiza was heartbroken to think that she had been rejected by the children that she had lost years ago.

Olga and Maria had both moved from Kharkov to Stalingrad in Russia by now, because there was more stable work for their husbands there. They had suffered severely in the famine, and one of Maria's sons had died. Russia had been less affected by the 1932–33 disaster, and the sisters felt they would be safer there if living conditions deteriorated again.

Ivan and Lydia tried to have more children, but with no medical help and no one to assist during labor, Lydia had a series of six still-births. Sadly, Ivan was often forced to be away at these sad times.

The last miscarriage was twins. Ludmilla came home from school one afternoon and found her mother lying on the floor. There was blood everywhere on her dress and the sheets were stained. To Ludmilla's horror, just near Lydia's feet were two little bodies, twins. They were blue and still, their bodies still wrinkled, the umbilical cords still attached to the placenta. She was only nine years old, but she rushed around, cleaned her mother up, and made her a drink. She coaxed her back from semi-consciousness and helped her drink a large mug of tea. Ludmilla cleaned up the blood by repeatedly washing the floor, stripped all the blood-soaked sheets, and placed the two cold bodies of the dead twins into a basket, which was meant to be used as their cot. She did all this in a daze, her body responding to the needs of the moment, and her mind dissociated, somehow watching the whole tragedy from a distance. As she continued cleaning up, she cried. She had been looking forward to having a brother or sister to love and cuddle. Placing their bodies in a cot made her incredibly sad. For months after this tragedy, she experienced nightmares with dead babies around her, and would wake up screaming until she could cry herself to sleep with Lydia soothing her by gently stroking her back.

Ivan was not there at the time—he was away working on installing high voltage electricity connections throughout the country. When he finally came home and heard about the twins, he was devastated. He was determined that next time this was not going to happen. He made enquiries of friends and neighbors about the best midwife in the area. He went and talked to her. He asked her advice about the best conditions to ensure the greatest chance of a normal birth and how much rest Lydia should have. The midwife told Ivan that in the last one or two months of pregnancy Lydia must stop working, improve her diet, and rest as much as possible to ensure that the maximum blood supply would be directed to the placenta, and that premature labor would not be precipitated. Trying to make as strict an impact as possible, Ivan passed all this advice to Lydia.

Lydia became pregnant again in late 1939. This time Ivan was ready. He collected all his resources to ensure that Lydia enjoyed an adequate diet, plenty of fresh fruit and vegetables in season, and he even managed to obtain some vitamin tablets to ensure healthy development of the fetus. He went to see the midwife again and arranged for regular visits to monitor progress, and to give Lydia advice at various stages of what to do. He also made sure that the midwife would be there for the birth so that Lydia would not have to go through the trauma on her own again.

His preparations and care were rewarded. On August 4, 1940, with the help of the midwife and her expert care, Lydia delivered a healthy, screaming, kicking boy. When he was told, Ivan was ecstatic. He emitted a glad "hurray," promptly downed a large beaker of vodka, and offered one to the midwife. She accepted.

He rushed into the room to see his new arrival and to congratulate Lydia. They began to think about possible names, and finally decided on Valerie, after a recent hero of the USSR. Ivan raced down to the registration office to record the birth, but in his excitement and possibly the effects of the vodka celebrations, he forgot the name of the hero and entered his new son's name as Valentin. When he got back home, they realized his mistake, but Lydia just laughed and said that it was close enough—so long as the child was healthy, they did not care what he was called.

Ludmilla turned out to be the perfect big sister. After waiting so long for a sibling, she finally had a real living baby to play with instead of pretending with her dolls. She took every opportunity she could to cuddle him, play with him, and bathe him.

Ivan's friend, who worked in a metal fabricating factory, celebrated the birth by making a baby bath out of galvanized sheeting, as a foreign order. The final product was huge, and could fit three babies in it.

It turned out to be a very useful item, and not only for bathing the baby, and indeed the whole family, but one or two other valuable activities the family was to turn to in the future.

* * * *

Ivan during Electrical Technology Course in 1926. Left side in back row.

Chapter 7

Enter Barbarossa

It was a lovely late summer morning in the middle of August, the time of year when Ukraine weather gets really warm. Today, though, there was a sinister difference. The alien sound of a distant artillery bombardment rumbled ominously somewhere over the horizon.

Ivan hurried up the street to his home. He had just finished frantically loading his army unit's wireless truck to join the ordered retreat across the Dnieper River. It was August 14, and the Red Army was collapsing in the face of the *Wehrmacht's* lightning Barbarossa campaign. The Russian Army was fleeing east to try to create some obstacle to stop or delay the invaders on the far bank of the river.

Ivan was supposed to go straight back to join the rest of the already-moving unit, but he thought he just had time to sneak home and say a final good-bye to Lydia, Ludmilla, and Vala, now one year old. He hoped his short absence would not be noticed in the disorganized flurry of activity, because in principle he risked being shot for leaving his post.

Lydia was astonished when he appeared. "Ivan, what are you doing here?" she exclaimed. "I thought you were on the way across the river by now."

"We will be soon. They have started moving, but I will catch up with them in a few minutes," replied Ivan. He sat down at the rough table, picked up the young child, put him on his knee, and started bouncing him up and down, to squeals of delight from Vala. He was pretending he was riding on a horse like a Cossack, not understanding what was going on. Ludmilla cried softly. She was old enough to know something terrible was happening, and her parents' apprehension was transferring to her. She understood that the Germans were advancing: she had heard the rumors of the brutality and danger facing every person in the city.

Ivan just sat there and played with his son, time standing still. Lydia thought of making some tea, but gave up that attempt as it would take too long, and poured Ivan a small glass of vodka, which was all that remained in the bottle. She hoped it would fortify him for his departure.

They had talked about this moment many times: what if the Germans did come? There was no way that Ivan could escape, he was part of the military, and any hint of desertion or dereliction of duty would mean immediate death. There were no court martials or tribunals. Officers, particularly the political commissars, had the right to shoot on the spot anyone suspected of collaboration, desertion, cowardice, or even drunkenness on duty. Lydia, of course, because of her German parentage and background, decided that she would stay where she was with the children and take her chances. The Russians were more terrifying to her than the Germans. Indeed, many Ukrainians saw the Germans as their liberators from the scourge of communist oppression.

But Ivan could not bring himself to leave. He feared that when he left he would never see his family again. He wanted to prolong this final moment. He had initially planned to stay a few moments only, but half an hour had already passed when he stood up to leave. He kissed his daughter while holding the little boy in his arms, and he put his arm around Lydia to kiss her good-bye. She was facing the window, and as she looked out, she saw the flitting movements of men darting from cover to cover. She looked closely. The uniforms were a different color than the Russians', and she suddenly noticed their helmets: the famous flared rear to protect the neck.

"Ivan, have a look at this!"

"My God, *the Germans*." Ivan's face turned pale; he just could not comprehend how he had been so stupid. He was in a house surrounded by Germans. His unit had gone. Either way, he was a dead man. If he managed to get back to his unit now, accidental mistake would be no excuse, and he would be shot as a deserter and shot immediately: if he ventured outside or the Germans came into the house, his Russian uniform would get him shot by the other side. At best he might be captured, facing an uncertain future.

But Lydia was the practical one in the family. "There is only one thing to do—get completely undressed straightaway and put on your working clothes, the older the better." While he obeyed, Lydia took the uniform and everything else connecting him with the Soviet Army and burnt them. Her heart pounded while she was doing it, hoping and praying that no one would come in and discover her in the act. A Russian soldier in civilian clothes out of uniform would be regarded as a spy or a saboteur and shot.

Since theirs was a ground floor apartment, they had a cellar, which was used to store food for the long winters when it became scarce. Lydia took Ivan down and arranged some boxes and old rubbish to make a place for him to hide. She covered him with some old bags, and put boxes in front of him so that he would look like a lump of rubbish rather than a person. Then she smashed the light bulb to make sure that there would be obscuring shadows and darkness, even if somebody looked inside with a torch.

Then she ran upstairs to the apartment and made the children lie down behind the up-ended table, put all her goose-feather eiderdowns around them and just waited. There were still occasional shots ringing out, as some poor wretch was shot by the Germans or the Russians. The Germans gradually took over the whole west side of Dniepropetrovsk with little opposition. There was only sporadic fighting as the Russians withdrew to the east side of the river. This was one of the few times when Stalin did not issue his familiar "fight and don't surrender" command, which had caused carnage to the Red Army in the last few months. He was probably too drunk to issue any order. As a result, the city escaped the usual widespread destruction by bombing and artillery. The citizens could not escape and put up no resistance.

After some hours, the firing seemed to die down. The front moved on further east, leaving the citizens of Dniepropetrovsk to pick up their shattered lives. The tidal wave of the German blitzkrieg had passed: the survivors were left bewildered and unsure of the future, but they had to go on living. After a few days, hunger forced them out of their homes or cellars or wherever they might have been hiding to try to find food.

Once the combat units had gone, the German occupation forces took control of the community. Everyone had to register and be issued with passes. Records were made, not only of name and address, but such details as ethnic origins, place of birth, parents, and religion, particularly Jewish religion. Peasants who had been working on the land were directed to stay there, as food production was not to be interrupted. The Germans needed food production not only to continue to feed the population now in their hands, but in the hope of producing excess wheat for export to Germany and the German Army.

Stalin's scorched earth directive was only partially successful in Ukraine, because the Red Army was forced to retreat in such rapid disorder that there was no time for the commissars to force the peasants to obey it, and they certainly weren't going to do it of their own volition when the result would be death in a few short months by starvation. Instead of destroying everything in the Germans' path, the population simply plundered all government facilities to snatch anything useful to survive the winter.

The first target was the government bulk stores, which held all the food supplies in Dniepropetrovsk. A flood of desperate people rushed the buildings and cleaned it out. The snows would start all too soon in October.

Lydia made her way there with her little cart to try to bring something back. Ivan was left hidden in the cellar. There was not much left by the time she arrived. The place was empty except for a few boxes and a number of large metal drums. Some of the boxes were open, and a powdery material was spilt on the ground. It had a tobacco smell and was clearly not edible. The drums were also open and contained a whitish flaky substance, also not edible. That was the reason the hungry mob left the strange material behind. With the philosophy of "something is better than nothing," she decided to take them back to Ivan, who might know what to do with them.

With a heavy heart, Lydia, helped by Ludmilla, heaved the two drums onto the rickety cart and placed two boxes of the dusty material on top. She dragged the cart all the way home around the streets under the watchful gaze of the soldiers, who were guarding every street. She was always friendly and spoke to them in German and wished them a good day. The fact that she originally came from a German family helped her in getting around, as she could always talk to them in German. She was, in fact, starting to be rather pleased with their presence. For one thing, they were not Soviets. The soldiers were used to her now and let her pass unhindered.

On arrival back from the expedition, she invited Ivan. "Come and see what I've got. I'm afraid it's nothing to eat, but you might know what it is." He looked at the powder, smelled and tasted it, and his eyes lit up with joy. "This is just what I desired, this is tobacco dust. It is probably residue from exhaust equipment in the cigarette factories. Of course, it's a waste product and no use for cigarettes in normal times, but in our situation, it's a case of making do with the available resources. I'm dying for a smoke, and this is just what I need. This is better than food, Lydia—this is food for my soul." Ivan was a heavy smoker, hopelessly addicted to tobacco.

Then he looked into the drums of flaky chemical. He spread it onto his fingers, and rubbed and smelled them. They burned and he hastily washed them off. "I think this is caustic."

"Caustic—what's caustic used for?" asked Lydia.

"Soap, among other things. This could be very useful."

"Don't you need something else as well to make soap?"

"We'll need fat—mixing fat and caustic results in a chemical reaction, and soap is the product," explained Ivan.

Lydia looked at him blankly. He had a good scientific knowledge of chemical reactions, materials, and other scientific matters, but she wasn't a scientist and didn't understand much about reactions, fats, or molecules.

Ivan felt happy. Here was a twinkling of hope. At least one of his needs had been met, his craving for tobacco. He had been a victim to cigarettes in whatever form since young. Denied them, he became irritable, moody, withdrawn, and desperate for tobacco, more precious to him than food. And here, in one stroke of luck, he was able to gain access to two large boxes of tobacco dust. He was thankful to Lydia, who took the risk to go outside and bring this to him.

Patiently he tore a small piece of paper from an exercise book, carefully conserving every grain of the precious dust, and rolled a cigarette. He tried to light it. The tobacco grains were too loose, and as he inhaled, he was rewarded with a mouth full of grainy tobacco particles, catching in his throat and making him wheeze and cough for quite a few minutes before he could get his breath.

"My God, I'll have to think of a way of improving these."

One way and another, life was resuming an appearance of normality. The German occupation encouraged the population to become productive. Any facilities that were still standing and not taken away or destroyed by the retreating Russians were brought back into production. The Russians had sought to re-move all the major plants in the effort to transfer munitions man-ufacture east of the Urals, but these instructions were not carried out to the letter. If they had been, a large part of the population would have died that winter, as there would have been no food in the occupied area. The occupiers were hardly likely to import food from Germany to feed the fifty million Slavs under their control, particularly given their low regard for the Slavic race.

Activity gradually picked up as the remaining population gained confidence. They restarted normal activities, bakeries, communication lines, trams, trains, and so on, to try to bring life to the familiar pattern. Food and other products started to be manufactured locally for the population, as well as the German occupation forces. Eventually food was even exported to Ger-many, where shortages also reigned.

The Germans encouraged this process by systematic reward and punishment. Every working person was allowed a food ra-tion, which ensured the hungry urban people were keen to partici-pate. If the Soviets ever came back, this would, of course, have been regarded as aiding the enemy, and the "collaborators" could expect to be shot. The citizens tried not to think of that, consider-ing the alternative was dying of starvation, and chose cooperation as the saner option. The future could look after itself.

For the time being, the most fortunate section of the popu-lation was the peasants who stayed with the earth. They were encouraged to continue farming, and anything that had not been taken away by the Russians, such as the livestock, was still under their control. Food staples were a precious asset: chick-ens and vegetables that were still in the ground, like potatoes or wheat that had not yet been harvested. The harvest season would shortly begin. Unfortunately, this would have to be done by hand, since all the tractors and harvesting machinery had been either smashed or taken away by the retreating Reds. Vast areas of wheat were also torched, either by brush fires start-ed in the fighting, or by the Soviet troops' attempt to carry out the "scorched earth" policy. But many orchards, full of apples, plums, and other fruit, remained. If properly managed, preserved or dried in the sun, these could provide valuable sustenance and also would be a ready source of trading currency.

No one had any currency initially, and everything had to be exchanged. Food, of course, was the staple commodity, but such things as tobacco and vodka were even more highly prized. Good boots to protect the feet from the harsh winter cold were also coveted, and virtually unobtainable. Even the Germans were on the lookout for good footwear, particularly as the winter approached, and the bitter cold would drop as low as 20 degrees centigrade below zero, causing frostbite and the loss of toes.

The Germans set up an administration for food coupons. People such as Lydia, who were of German origin historically, were given some priority, but this still was below subsistence level, because so little food was available. The general population got an even lower ration. The lowest rank of all was the Jews. They were identified as part of the registration process and, as in the rest of Europe, forced to wear a yellow star on their clothing when in public. Their food ration was so meager they quickly lost weight, and within a couple of months, the entire Jewish population was at starvation level.

By this stage, Lydia was known by the regular German guards. She moved around freely and was friendly to them, chatting in German. Her German language skill was improving with practice, and she started to remember more of her native language. She had actually nearly forgotten it. She had not spoken German since being lost and separated from her mother at the age of eight.

She felt increasingly comfortable to be under the control of her own race. She had always sensed non-acceptance among Ukrainians and Russians: they tended to treat her with disdain once they discovered she was originally German. Now she was popular with the local soldiers. She chatted to them, asked about their families and how they lived, and she herself was interested to hear of the life in the "homeland" she had never seen or experienced.

The general feeling was that this occupation would be permanent, that the Germans had conquered the land. By now the *Wehrmacht* had just about completely taken over Ukraine. It was destined to become part of the German sphere of influence like France, Belgium, and Holland, all now under Third Reich control. The German occupation certainly wanted to have this concept accepted, and the people had no reason to believe otherwise. With identity cards, travel was possible anywhere behind the German lines, and the population had freedom of movement, providing they could show legitimate reasons for it. Occasionally Lydia began to wonder if she might one day try to find her mother.

Once his hair had grown, Ivan could finally venture out of his hidey hole in the cellar. The shorn head of the regulation Red Army haircut was instantly recognizable, and he would have been shot on sight if he had gone out on the street with that haircut and civilian clothing. The Germans would have interpreted the combination as either a Red Army man in disguise as a saboteur, or an escaped prisoner of war. But with long hair and in Lydia's company, he was accepted as part of the general population without suspicion.

Electrical skills were very much in demand, and Ivan got plenty of work preparing and restarting the various plants that had escaped destruction. He was duly registered and provided with identity cards, and as a working participant also received the most prized possession, a ration card.

But to supplement the family's meager food rations and feed the children, extra activity was required. Ivan perfected a way of making cigarettes out of the tobacco dust and granules that Lydia acquired. He picked some grass and dried it in the sun. He made a slightly runny paste with some of the tobacco material and mixed the grass and the paste together and spread the mixture as a thin layer on cardboard to dry. This way the tobacco dust was integrated with the grass strands, which acted as a base. When everything was thoroughly dry, he rolled portions in paper, making something quite like a cigarette—certainly the nearest thing to it that Dniepropetrovsk could produce at the time.

Once the manufacturing production was started in earnest, a few hundred cigarettes could be made in one day. Lydia would take them and her little homemade cart out and go into the countryside. This would take hours. She walked from one farm to the next and bartered cigarettes for their basic produce, particularly wheat and potatoes. She had to be careful not to take too much at once, for fear of becoming a target for some hungry residents if too much food was visible on the cart. Every trip was a risk.

She became adept at bartering. She knew the value of her cigarettes, as most men were quite heavy smokers, and they would invariably be tempted to offer an exchange.

"Come and try one, you probably haven't had a cigarette for a while. Have one and see how you like them."

The poor peasant would try the cigarette, coughing and spluttering as the acrid smoke hit his throat and then would smile and enjoy the nicotine.

"Ah, that was good. Do you have a lot of cigarettes?" he would ask.

"There is probably plenty more where these came from. I could come on a regular basis and supply your needs."

A few kilos of potatoes or a bag or wheat would be exchanged for the cigarettes, and Lydia would then be on her way again to the next farm. When she thought there was enough produce and not too much to make her a target, she would head home. This usually took the whole day of slow, heavy trudging through rutted country roads, which after rain became quagmires.

Things were looking a little grim after about six weeks because the tobacco powder was starting to look depleted, so that the little production line of cigarettes was eventually going to run out, with ominous implications for the family food supply.

"We'll have to slow down on the cigarettes," said Ivan. "We're running out of tobacco powder. I'd like to keep a bit for my own use, although that'll leave us with less to barter."

Lydia had foreseen this. "I've been thinking about that, Ivan. One of the farmers asked me the other day whether I had any vodka for sale, as well as cigarettes, because he wouldn't mind a few glasses. There might be an idea in that."

This set Ivan thinking. How could he produce vodka? At the best of times, it was a pretty scarce commodity, with the 1930s famine restricting the use of grain or potatoes to anything but survival. Turning food into alcohol had been unthinkable. Since the war, of course, everything had disappeared, and any vodka that was available was treasured and meted out only on special occasions. This was a pretty savage result because in Ukraine and Russia, vodka is seen as practically a necessity of life, particularly in winter. It is regarded as a vital antifreeze: if you go outdoors in minus twenty degree frost, a jolt of vodka is the only thing that provides warmth right inside the body. During the war, of course, with its scarcity, it became a prime bartering commodity.

"Now, let's think about this, Lydia! What do we really need to produce vodka?"

"I suppose you start with plenty of grain or potatoes as a basis for the fermentation. We've got some of that, and we can build a supply by bartering the remaining stock of tobacco."

"Right," said Ivan. "Then we'll need something to ferment this in. Some sort of a vat or container."

"I know," said Lydia. "How about the baby bath?" This large bath made for Vala was big enough to fit an adult, if he sat on his haunches, and twice as big as anything for a baby. It was now used as a liquid container as well as for Vala.

"That'll do it—it's big enough for one batch, and we'll have to fix up a still so that we can make the vodka from the fermented juice. I think I can rig something up. Now, have you got a large cooking pot?"

"Yes. And I think I could get an even bigger one from the neighbors."

"Well, that's fixed then," Ivan said. "I'll start planning the still and work out the requirements for fermentation."

Ivan set to work on the new project. He realized that he needed some copper pipe for the distillation plant. He went out to find some friends who worked in a factory, and through them eventually managed to obtain some lengths of copper piping in exchange for cigarettes. He bent this into a spiral roll, made a hole in the lid of the large cooking pot, and soldered the copper pipe on the top. He led the copper tube pipe into another container filled with water under a slow-running tap, to provide constant cooling for the distillation. The pot was then set on the wooden stove, and the distillation contraption attached to the lid was supported by wires in the cooling bath. The outlet of the copper spiral was set close to a small table, where a container collected the vodka in steady drops. The whole thing looked quite professional by the time he finished.

In the meantime, Lydia was also busy trying to build up a stock of grain and potatoes in barter with the peasants on the land.

Ivan spoke to as many people as he could who might know something about the fermentation process, getting first-hand coaching on brewing and distillation techniques.

After weeks of preparation, the time finally arrived to try it out. Lydia boiled the grain, pot after pot, and emptied them into the baby bath. Then the other ingredients, including yeast, were placed in the bath, and she covered the whole container with a sheet.

They were excited with anticipation, and kept peeking under the sheet to see what was happening. Nothing was, and they went to bed disappointed. But the stove was kept burning during the night and the mixture left close to try to keep it warm.

The next morning, as soon as Lydia got up, she raced over to inspect.

"Ivan, Ivan, quick—come over, look at this!"

The mixture was giving off bubbles of carbon dioxide: the process was working. They kept the container covered, and eventually, after some days, all activity ceased.

It was time to taste the mixture. Lydia took a mouthful. "Mmmm, tastes foul. But it's got a bit of a kick in it."

Ivan took a glassful, and his face lit up. "I've certainly tasted better, but you could get drunk on this. Now we'll try the next step of the process."

He filled up the large cooking pot with the murky liquid from the fermentation process, put it on the stove, and placed the lid firmly down. He tied it down tightly with wire to make it vapor-proof.

Before long it began to boil, and he turned on the water flow into the cooling tank. Everybody was quite excited now. This was the final test. Could they make vodka in the middle of the war? They waited expectantly, and before long a few drops of clear liquid started to come out of the end of the pipe. Ivan put a spoon underneath. He waited until it was half full, then very slowly put it to his lips and tasted the liquid, which was still warm. He smacked his lips and exclaimed, "Ah, beautiful!"

They started cheering and dancing around, looking delight-edly at their creation. They had just succeeded with what in the circumstances was the equivalent of the alchemist's dream. Vodka in wartime Russia was just about as precious as gold. It not only provided warmth in winter, it also soothed the pain of a wound, and many a medical procedure was performed using only vodka as an anesthetic. It raised the spirits and provided some relief from the intolerable brutality, pain, and suffering, both physical and mental, of the poor wretches on both sides of the war. It could even be used as an antiseptic for wounds when nothing else was available.

"Lydia, we'll have to build up a small stock before you can go out and start bartering for more potatoes."

"How many bottles do you think we'll get out of this batch?" asked Lydia.

"I don't know—we'll just have to see what comes out. Just keep on boiling the liquid until vodka stops coming out. I'll just sit here and be the taster. When it stops having a kick in it, we'll change the liquid in the pot and boil another batch," said Ivan, with a smile on his face. He liked the prospect of sitting there all night and tasting the vodka emerging from the equipment.

"What a job," he thought. "I should have designed this years ago."

And that is how he spent most of the night. When all the liq-uid was processed, he had three and a half bottles of vodka. He was well pleased with this result—and in addition a nice warm glow now flowed through his body. His thoughts were happier than they had been for a long time. When he finally went to bed, he slept through the morning and into the afternoon.

Lydia and Ivan were in high spirits the next day. They knew that they had a good working process in place and all they needed to do was to get the production cycle smoothly under way.

Lydia took the results of their first efforts, six bottles, and went on another bartering trip into the countryside. She had no trouble at all disposing of it for a good return, and over a short time managed to obtain enough grain and potatoes to replace many times what they had used to actually produce it. Crude and inefficient as their equipment was, they were able to produce six to eight bottles a week, enough to replenish the stock of wheat or potatoes they used for the process, and also provide enough food for the family. There was also some vodka left over for their own use, and to give to friends on special occasions. From time to time, they gave a bottle to the local German soldiers, who greatly welcomed the gift. Lydia became quite popular with the soldiers, and if she met one when she was out, there was always a recognition or friendly greeting from the patrolling guard.

Altogether, Ivan and Lydia were now in a better situation and enjoying a better life than they ever had before. With ingenuity and a little technical skill, they had managed to achieve what in wartime circumstances ranked as a comfortable position. Unlike others around them, they'd been able to assure a reasonable food supply for their immediate family. They were, admittedly, uncertain about Lydia's sisters—Olga and Maria were married and living in Stalingrad, on the path of the main German attack. Karlov had been immediately rearrested in Kiev when the war started and sent to Siberia. On the other hand, Lvov was firmly part of German-controlled territory and reopening contact with Lydia's mother should be possible.

But to crown everything else, they were free for the first time in their lives of all-pervasive, dictatorial, blustering Soviet domination. Underneath it all, though, was one stark fact that some points of view might one day find awkward. Eventually it would contribute to the rift that divided Ivan and Lydia for a long while.

Whichever way you looked at it, it was the *Wehrmacht* who had liberated them.

* * * *

Chapter 8

The Jews

At the beginning of the German occupation, most people in Ukraine were only dimly aware what was happening to the Jews among them. Part of the reason was that like most Jews, the Ukrainian Jews preferred to keep their lives separate from their neighbors. It's an historic characteristic—so ancient it was mentioned by writers in ancient Greece and Rome—and seems to have unwittingly contributed to widespread anti-Semitic prejudice down the ages. Largely because of this gap between them, Ukrainians did not immediately realize that Jewish rations were being cut down even further than their own, and in the end were reduced practically to starvation level. And when it first leaked out, many Ukrainians were not particularly sympathetic, such was the antipathy towards this separate race. There was a local political side to this as well: they were seen as participants in the forced formation of the communes when independent farmers had been made to give up their land to consolidate into large state-owned farms. Indeed, some Jews might well have been involved in that process, but it was as individuals who were already party members rather than from racial motivation; the driving force in the communes' foundation was the Russian Communist Party members and commissars prominent in the tribunals that ran the acquisitions.

A Jewish family living in the same street was friends with Ivan and Lydia. They also had two children—Jacob, aged ten, and Rachel, who was about eight. They played frequently with Ludmilla, being the only children around her age in the neighborhood. Since the arrival of the *Wehrmacht*, however, Jewish people were strictly segregated: even talking to a Jew was frowned on by the Germans, and certainly trying to help any of them was likely to get the helper shot. There were strict instructions to the general population not to assist the Jews in any way.

The synagogue in the area was just around the corner, but it had been confiscated by the Germans and used as a storehouse for equipment and produce. It was defaced and covered with swastikas and other graffiti. Every morning Mr. Goldstein, their elderly Jewish neighbor, would slowly walk to the synagogue in his black hat and coat bearing his yellow Star of David. He would pass their front door carrying a broom, go to the synagogue and sweep the sidewalk, tidy up any rubbish or paper that might be hanging around, then walk back home.

While standing at the entrance to her building, Lydia saw Mr. Goldstein slowly approaching. He had been a scion of the old Jewish establishment, but now he was haggard and walked with a stoop. Nonetheless, his deep brown eyes and white beard still gave him an air of authority.

As he walked past, Lydia said good morning, and commented that the weather was getting cold.

"Yes," he replied in a heavy voice. He was obviously weak from lack of food.

"Why do you still go and clean up around the synagogue? You don't worship there anymore, and it's only a German storehouse."

Mr. Goldstein looked at her and smiled. "It might be only a German storehouse to you, but to me it still remains the House of God, no matter what it is used for, and it will be to the day I die. I serve God in any way I can, and if that means cleaning the footpath around God's house of German trash, I'm happy to do so."

As he walked slowly away, Lydia looked after him and felt uneasy and somehow guilty. She was surviving well, and Goldstein and his family were slowly starving. Where would it end? Would this be a repeat of 1933, when people were dying in the streets? Fear gripped her heart at what could happen to her and her small family, and, in fact, to everyone in the city.

Ludmilla played with the Goldstein children every day. While she was Rachel's friend, she always had her eye on Jacob. He was a big brother she never had, and she was rather fond of him. Jacob led the games and was always best at everything they did together. He taught her how to spin the top. Children don't seem to play this often these days: the wooden top was about ten centimeters high, and had the string of a small whip wound around the top. When the string was pulled quickly, it started the top spinning on the ground, and the game was to keep whipping it to see how long you could keep it spinning before it collapsed. Jacob usually won. Of course, they played other common games, such as hide-and-seek, sliding down the hills, chase, and everything else that young children played in those days regardless of whether they lived in Russia, Ukraine, Germany, or England. The spirit of the young was the same everywhere. There was no hatred. They didn't need much to be happy, just companionship, somewhere to play, and something to eat. The school was, of course, permanently closed; so the children played every day to keep themselves occupied. The parents taught their children, if they could, had the time, or wanted to. Some older children formed gangs and survived by theft and also served the German masters by hounding and baiting Jews.

Ludmilla always had something to eat for the middle of the day, a piece of bread with some cottage cheese, some dried apple slices, or sometimes just dry bread with garlic rubbed on. She would sit down to eat it, and after a while she noticed that the other children had stopped bringing bread with them.

"Where's your lunch, Rachel?" she asked. Rachel looked down and mumbled, "Mum's got no food."

"No food?" Ludmilla was incredulous.

"No, we only have one small meal a day now."

"Have a bit of mine—I'll share with you." The other two grabbed at the chance. Ludmilla broke the bread in half and she gave half of that to each of them. They ate it quickly.

Over the following days, Ludmilla noticed they were both getting thinner, with skinny legs and arms and sunken eyes that actually looked bigger in their gaunt faces. Their play also changed. They stopped active games, the chase and hide and seek, and just sat around. They were gloomy and slow, and not really much fun to be with anymore.

One day when her mother was preparing the snack before she went out, Ludmilla asked, "Can I have more?"

Lydia looked at her. "This was always enough for you. You didn't want more before."

"I know, but Rachel and Jacob don't have any."

"You're not supposed to help the Jews—you will get me into trouble."

"But Rachel and Jacob are just my friends. How can you get into trouble helping children?"

Without a word, Lydia cut two more pieces of black rye bread, took a clove of garlic and rubbed it on the bread to give it some taste. She gave the three large pieces to Ludmilla and sent her on her way. "I suppose I can't help the Jews, but I can feed some children," she thought, and felt less guilty.

That became the pattern. At lunch break, the children, after playing, found some cozy spot out of the wind, which now was starting to get cold, and had their midday meal, just plain bread, smeared with a bit of garlic. There was no butter, meat, jam, or any condiment, but bread tasted like a delicacy when children were hungry.

With slightly more to eat, the children got back a little energy for active games, and Ludmilla looked forward to the playtimes again. A few weeks later, Lydia met Mr. Goldstein again as he was walking past the door, and as he passed her he mumbled under his breath, just loud enough for her to hear, "Thank you. Thank you for the children."

It was now near the end of October. The days and nights were much colder, and as some snow began to fall, frosts began to seep through the earth. The cold came earlier that year just to add further misery to the already wretched people. Puddles started to freeze over, and the children used them as small skating rings, running along and going for a slide on a piece of ice.

The population's suffering increased with the cold coming on top of inadequate food. Pretty well everyone was more miserable. If the sun is shining and you are warm, even if you are hungry most of the time, life can still be bearable. In the cold, dark, dank countryside, without any food, life is much harder. The sun was rising later and setting earlier, and its rays, on the days when it was not covered by thick clouds, were weak and watery. Fewer people ventured onto the streets. Everyone who could stayed indoors away from the biting wind, which now cut through the thickest clothing.

Then people noticed the arrival of a different type of German soldier. They heard the word "Gestapo." These men wore different uniforms and behaved differently—they were officious, cruel, and arrogant. Everyone soon learned to avoid them if possible. Lydia, at this stage, decided not to go on her bartering trips since they were officially considered black marketeering, and with the newcomers now running the occupation, she risked being challenged by soldiers who did not know her, with unpredictable and dangerous results.

One day the population was woken up by the jarring sound of a loud speaker mounted on a car. It was a loud, piercing "*Achtung, Achtung*," then something further in German, which most people did not understand. Then it was translated into Ukrainian, to the effect, "All Jews are to be ready in three days to be relocated. They are to pack all their personal belongings in one suitcase per person. They are to leave everything else, but their special personal belongings. They are to congregate at dawn in three days at the Central Station to board transports."

There was a lot of excitement about this new development. There were numerous theories about its meaning. The Jews took it as the fulfillment of their prayers. At last they were going to be resettled, given a place to live, and a chance to get back to normality. Some even predicted that they would be sent to Palestine, where they could make a permanent homeland. It was well known that Hitler hated the Jews and wanted them cleansed out of the countries that he controlled. Perhaps this rekindled hope: there was animated talk and planning about what they were going to do when they settled.

The next day Rachel and Jacob again played with Ludmilla, but at lunchtime when they were set to share the bread that Ludmilla always brought, they looked glum.

"We're sorry we have to go, Lucy," Jacob said. "But Daddy is pleased. He thinks it is the answer to his prayers. He will finally be given a homeland and be permanently settled somewhere that's a Jewish area." The Jews yearned for a place where they could be left alone by the Christians and practice their faith. That hope had grown since the coming of the Germans.

"I'll be sorry to see you go," said Ludmilla. "I don't know who I'll be playing with now. I'll probably just stay at home. It will be too cold to go outside soon anyway."

In her heart, she was inconsolably sad. She knew she would probably never see her friends again, no matter where they were going.

The next day, just before dawn, the Jews assembled at the designated spot. Each carried a bag that was obviously heavy and packed full of their precious belongings, all they could carry with them. Everything else would be left behind to be pilfered or destroyed by the Germans or the remaining Ukrainians once they were gone. By now they looked a sorry lot, thin and sallow, wrapped in the heaviest clothing they could find, with handkerchiefs and hats as meager protection from the wind. The young children were crying, and mothers tried to soothe them with little success. They didn't look as if they were going to the promised land of Palestine. They were hungry and cold, and the misery before them was still unknown, like a deep abyss whose bottom cannot be seen. Ludmilla was there, as were many of her people, to see them off, either out of old friendship or curiosity. They were slowly loaded into trucks by the barking orders of the Gestapo soldiers and the frequent use of the butt of a rifle. As Jacob passed Ludmilla, he waved good-bye to her gently. Rachel gave her a smile as she passed. She was hopeful of the future. Ludmilla just stood there with a few tears rolling down her eyes, and whispered, "Good-bye Jacob. Bye Rachel," and then slowly turned away and walked home feeling miserable.

Following the departure of the Jews, the Gestapo detachment left town to the regular *Wehrmacht*, but life became harder for everyone. There was less food about, and the Germans were testier since they too were suffering the cold with lack of food. Communication difficulties interfered with supplies. Trucks had difficulty getting through the snow-covered roads. Horses were often used for transport, but they were brutally ill-treated, whipped mercilessly to make them move their loads through difficult terrain, up hills, through slush or snow. Some six hundred thousand horses were used by the Germans, but they did not last long, particularly in the harsh, cold winter. Russian and Ukrainian horses were much more suited to the conditions. They were smaller, but tougher. Many broke down and collapsed from their labor, and when that occurred, they were shot. The meat was used, particularly to feed the Russian prisoners, who now numbered over two million, and also used by the hungry peasants.

Lydia and Ivan were keen to obtain a carcass. They had worked out a way of making soap, using the caustic soda salvaged by Lydia at the bulk stores months before. Every time she went on a bartering trip she would have a chat with the sentries that she knew.

"*Guten tag*" (Good day), she would say. "*Wie gehens sie heute?*" (How are you today?)

"*Nicht sehr gut. Das verfluchten kald*" (Not real good in this cursed cold) was the usual response, in the cold of minus thirty degrees. It was near the end of December, with long cold winter nights and only very short days with practically no sun. It must have been miserable to be a sentry on duty. Even though they had boots and greatcoats, it was insufficient for a winter campaign in Russia.

"Here, have a bottle of this. This will warm you up considerably. Don't drink it all at once or it will make you sick," said Lydia, as she handed over the bottle of homemade vodka to the guard. She was a popular figure with the regular sentries, as from time to time, she would slip them a bottle to keep them on her side and ensure they turned a blind eye to her frequent movements around.

"By the way, ah, do you know of any horses that have been recently destroyed?"

"They are very hard to come by," said Franz. "The commandants of the prison camps grab them as soon as possible, to feed the prisoners."

"Well, if one should become available close to home, I would be very interested in obtaining an animal. Of course, a few bottles of vodka will be a reward to warm up the boys."

That brought a smile to his face. A few bottles of vodka were always welcome, bringing a bit of warmth and lifting the spirit for a short time.

The soldiers in their inadequate clothing were suffering miserably. Hitler had not prepared for a winter war, believing a Blitzkrieg-type attack would bring victory within two or three months, as it had in the rest of Europe. It wasn't the Russian army that stopped him, but the sheer hostility of the vast terrain. Inadequate roads turned into quagmires with any rain, and the dust and dirt permeated the *Wehrmacht's* mechanized equipment, resulting in unexpected and frequent breakdowns. The soldiers were now so miserable that some of them were committing suicide while on sentry duties. But how do you punish a dead man?

Lydia gave Franz a wink and walked off, pulling the sled behind her on the thick snow, which now nearly came to her knees, even on the roads.

A few weeks later, there was a knock on the door late at night. Lydia and Ivan looked at each other in trepidation. They opened the door and there was one of the guards, Fritz.

"Come quick," he whispered. "There is an animal that has been recently destroyed. We haven't reported it yet, and even if we did, no one would bother to come out so late, in this miserable cold and wind. If you want it, it's yours to be taken away. So come, follow me."

Lydia got dressed quickly into her warmest clothes, put on her boots, grabbed her hand sledge, and went trudging after the soldier in the deep snow. They went about one kilometer before they came to a steep part of the road where a poor wretched horse lay dead on the side. He was broken by the effort of having to pull up a wagon as part of the supply column earlier in the day. There was no time to fix up sick animals, so they were just shot where they lay while the column continued on. The horses were usually local Russian stock commandeered for the Army's use; the German variety was incapable, as were the soldiers, of working effectively in this climate.

By the time Lydia got to the horse, it was already getting cold, and if left during the night it would probably be frozen by the morning. She quickly started, laboriously butchering the animal with a small knife Ivan had made from a wide hacksaw blade. It was effective, but the work was hard, and she was puffing and sweating with the labor, oblivious to the blood and fat splattering all over her clothing and face. She loaded as much as she could on the sledge and slowly pulled it back home. She and Ivan unloaded the sledge into the cellar, and Lydia trudged off again to repeat the process. She worked all night, and in the morning she was exhausted, but most of the animal was safely at home by first light.

Ivan was also busy. He had a huge job to do. First he cut the hide away from the thin fat layer, trying to be careful with the skin. This was a very valuable part of the horse; when tanned, it could be made into high quality boots, which were invaluable at that time. He then cut out as much of the fat tissue as possible and placed it into a drum. The rest of the meat he cut into slices and wrapped in paper, and the next day he did a few trips around the neighborhood and dropped it in to some friends to use as food. Any protein was in high demand at this time, since the only thing to eat as a rule were potatoes and some vegetables frozen in the fields. Consequently, horsemeat was a delicacy not to be wasted. Ivan kept part of it for themselves and managed to freeze it just by keeping it in the unheated cellar. They slowly consumed it through the winter.

Now Ivan tried to perform more alchemy. He finally had a use for the caustic soda, which had been just sitting there in the two drums. He dissolved the whitish flaky crystals in buckets of water, producing a strong solution of caustic, and poured it into the large metal baby bath over the fat, cut into small pieces. Drops of caustic splattered on his hands and burned small areas of skin. Then he brought the fatty mass to a boil and kept it at a very slow simmer for two days. When the solution was finally cooled, slowly, the top layer had separated. He skimmed it off and poured into a long wooden mould, which he had previously made. As the material solidified, it was cut into hand-sized pieces.

Lydia could not believe the result—to think that soap, a very sought-after commodity, could be produced by mixing together fat and the flaky crystal-like material. The Germans were wrong when they thought the Russians were a dirty, lice-infested race, who could not be bothered to wash. The fact was that they wanted to be clean, but soap was in such short supply that frequent washing was impossible. There was so little fat to eat that making soap out of it was an extravagance.

Lydia now had another commodity to barter. In addition to vodka, she also purveyed soap—the tobacco powder that had produced the cigarettes had long been used up.

With the horsemeat supply and with the grain, potatoes, and vegetables that had accumulated from the previous bartering forays, the family was reasonably well supplied, and by being careful, they managed to stretch the food resources through the winter. The main activity now was to forage in the woods to try to keep up a supply of wood to keep the house warm and not freeze.

At last the first harsh winter of the German occupation drew to a close. As the days grew longer and the sun started to melt the ice and snow, the whole place turned into a quagmire. It was difficult to get around because the majority of the roads were not sealed, and in the spring, the melting snow turned them into rivers of mud.

But slowly the country started to erupt into springtime life. Flowers were budding, new grass was growing, and birds, bees, and insects started their frenzied activity of life. This was the time of year to forage into the woods for mushroom-gathering, always popular in Ukraine but more attractive than ever in those lean times.

Ludmilla and a few friends she knew from school decided to join together to go mushrooming into the forest. Lydia was initially doubtful.

"No!" she protested when Ludmilla asked permission. "It is too dangerous. You don't know who's out there. There may be partisans in the forest, or you could even be shot by some of the German sentries."

But Ludmilla looked so crestfallen that Lydia relented.

"Well, not with school friends, anyway. But I'll go with you. We will go together. It is too far for you to go by yourself, and it's not safe."

"Oh, I wish I could go with my friends. I don't want to go with the family. We have been together all winter, nothing but you, Dad, and Vala, who is noisy and such a nuisance." Ludmilla was feeling lonely, and missed the Jewish friends she played with previously. Lydia, however, was firm. There was no way she would allow the young ten-year-old girl into the forest. Ludmilla went off sulking.

"We'll go in half an hour—be back by that time," Lydia cried out after her.

Lydia got some dried fruit together and a little bit of bread and a hard-boiled egg between them. She placed it in the container she was taking to hold the mushrooms they were hoping to pick.

They trudged off towards the south of Dniepropetrovsk to explore the forest areas on the west side of the Dnieper River. In the warm sun, the exercise of walking made them sweat. When they reached the forest, they started to explore underneath the trees and beside the rocks for a collection of rotten vegetation, the perfect site for the mushroom spores that survived the harsh winter to grow. They were successful from time to time and found groups of two or three, which went into their container and gradually filled it.

Ludmilla ventured more towards the river, but kept within calling distance of her mother. She kept smelling a fetid, bad smell, which was getting stronger as she came closer to the river. The area was flatter, and the trees were sparser. She saw a large, cleared rectangular area, which seemed to be a muddy field, and from time to time it was active with a few bubbles bursting on the surface. She didn't know what it was, but the smell was horrible, and it was obviously the source of the smell she noticed previously. She took a stick and poked into the muddy morass. There was a hard object, and when she dragged it up it was an arm, which was still attached to a body.

"Mummy, Mummy!" she screamed. "Quick, help, Mummy!"

She raced off to find Lydia, who wondered what the trouble was. Lydia too was starting to notice the fetid smell.

Ludmilla ran into her mother's arms, sobbing and crying and pointing behind her to where she had been. She could hardly get the words out. She was shaking with fear.

"There's a body there, Mum, there's a body, it's covered in mud, it's black and dirty."

"Ludmilla, what is the trouble, what body, what is it?" Ludmilla would not go back to where she came from. She only pointed and became agitated and cried more loudly, stamping her feet in frustration.

As she sank to the forest floor, sobbing hysterically, Lydia moved back in the direction she had pointed. She thought the grisly find might have been the body of a single partisan or Red Army soldier frozen over in the winter, but no: it was a large quagmire of mud, issuing occasional bubbles of fetid gas. Worse, close to the surface were bodies—not one, but a number.

Lydia took a stick for a closer inspection and gingerly felt through the mud. What she found and smelled very quickly made her sick. She lurched over to a tree close by and started to vomit with her arm against the tree supporting her forehead. The whole thing just disgusted her. How could her people—her liberators—just kill everyone irrespective of age, sex, or guilt? She made her way back to where Ludmilla was still sobbing and took her by the shoulders, and they walked unsteadily back together. The mushroom delicacy they had so looked forward to was left behind. They had no stomach now for any delicacies.

They walked as quickly as they could to the town, and there they spread the word of the horror they had found. Ivan, with a group of men, went back to the forest with some shovels. They poked around and found other sites of equal horror. They tried to find out who the victims were, and some of the townspeople could recognize a few bodies, mainly from the clothing. They were some of the Jews that were meant to be resettled or repatriated to Palestine.

They didn't know what to do. They didn't feel up to digging the bodies out, so in the end they piled more earth and rocks on top to try to bury the hellish mess.

When Ivan returned home, Ludmilla and Lydia were sitting pale and morose, shocked by their experience.

"Who were they?" asked Lydia.

"Well, I'm not sure exactly. Some of the boys recognized clothing their neighbors had worn previously, mainly on some of the women."

"But who were they really? I can't remember a lot of people missing. There must have been a lot of them."

"Yes, there were a lot of them. They were the Jews who were to be resettled, who left here early last winter. Obviously the ground was too hard to dig very deep, so the killers could only make a shallow grave after they were shot. Really, they were just covered over. When the weather warmed, the ground thawed and the bodies started to decompose. That's what those bubbles of gas and smell were all about."

"My God, not the Goldsteins. Were they among them?"

"I don't know," said Ivan, "but I imagine so. It wasn't the only site; there were a number of places through the forest, so the whole lot were probably shot and buried.

"Anyway, keep it quiet. We don't know anything about it, and don't tell Ludmilla. She is heartbroken and scared as it is."

After the revelation of the Jewish massacre, Lydia was inconsolable. She was racked with guilt, thinking that she could have been more active, perhaps even kept the children back if she had known what was to come. But no one did know. She thought she might have been kinder to Mr. Goldstein, and the children could have been provided with a bigger share of the food that she had been able to barter. She was also bitterly disappointed that the Germans, her own countrymen, in whom she had so much faith, who promised to bring justice and humanity to the long-suffering country, were no better than the communist Russians. Both were adept in killing innocent victims, for reasons that she could not fully understand. Her simple mind just could not fathom the reason for the death of those Jews, who were just living there like anyone else, or for the death of all the Ukrainians, who were merely living in the country, and whose fates had been remorselessly sacrificed for purely political purposes by Stalin. She could no longer understand this world. It made her angry and also scared.

Ludmilla could not fully recover from the horror either. She was morose, had frequent nightmares, and often woke up screaming with flashbacks of the horrible sight in the forest. She gathered from some of her friends and from hearing the grown-ups talking that the corpses were the Jews. She knew that Jacob and Rachel, her two friends, were probably among those in the forest, and she was very, very sad to lose them.

* * * *

Chapter 9

Return to Lvov

After the Jewish massacre was discovered, Lydia felt constantly miserable. Nothing pleased her: she could not just sink back and settle into life as it was before. Even the thought of going on her bartering trips, something she usually enjoyed, failed to cheer her shaken spirit.

Somehow she had to find a fresh dimension. Then it came to her—she could try to find her mother. It had always been in the back of her mind—Lydia had not seen Louiza since she was eight and they were separated in the move from Siberia—and if she managed it now, the achievement might bring a cleansing fresh start.

Because now, of course, the frontiers were *open*. The Germans controlled all the countries west of their front line, from

Ukraine, through Poland and Germany, and into Europe. They were all governed as a single German dominion, and in theory the residents could move around, providing they had some excuse and valid papers. In practice it was much more difficult to get the right documents. In the German zone, nothing could be done without a piece of paper and a stamp on it. Everything people had to carry—identity cards, ration cards, travelling cards, and any other activity cards—needed prior approval from the right authority. But Lydia had her identity card proving her German descent, and trying to find her mother gave her a very valid reason to travel.

The first task was to acquire the necessary funds. Lydia got to work selling and trading vodka and soap, building up food and money for the trip west. Next she obtained the necessary travelling papers.

There was quite a line at the occupation headquarters. The people had become used to the occupation by now, and with the coming of spring, they were starting to move around and becoming more adventurous in doing business, finding jobs, and visiting relatives.

Finally, Lydia and Ivan reached the head of the line to be confronted by an officious bureaucrat in uniform, thin, austere, and demonstrating obvious disdain for the local population.

"Show me your identity cards. Oh, you are *Volksdeutsch*, your parents were German," he said, becoming more friendly immediately. "And where do you want to go?"

"To Lvov."

"To Lvov?"

"Yes, I was born in Lvov, and I believe my mother is still there. The last time I heard from her, her letters came from Lvov."

"It is no longer called Lvov; it now has a German name, 'Lemberg.' And why is your mother living in Lemberg, while you are living in Ukraine?" he asked.

"We became separated when we were returning from Siberia. My mother caught the train to Lvov, I mean Lemberg, and I, with my sisters, had to catch the train from Siberia to Ukraine.

Once the communists took over, of course, they did not allow us to cross the border to rejoin my mother, and I have not seen her since 1918."

"Those filthy communist swine," he said. "They have no compunction in separating mother and child of honest German people."

Those words sounded hollow to Lydia in view of the recent atrocities she had discovered committed by the Germans on the Jews, the Russians, and the Ukrainians, and any other ethnic group or country they controlled. But she said nothing, naturally, and without much further ado he completed the documents and duly stamped them, assured there was no ulterior motive for their trip.

"Thank you, thank you," said Lydia, as the family quickly made their exit.

As they left the administration office, they both heaved a sigh of relief that the major hurdle was overcome and now it was only a matter of travelling and finding Louiza—if they could. They'd been given only two months, and they had no idea where she lived. Indeed she might well be already dead. But it was Lydia's first chance in twenty-three years of actually getting to see her again, and she was excited inside and somewhat scared.

A week later, they finally started on the journey. They had a good rucksack filled with bread, a bit of sausage, and also a few bottles of vodka for the trip. A separate bag contained their remaining stock of six vodka bottles, considered "hard currency" for the trip. It was a long way and food could prove a problem, even though their ration cards assured them of a little.

The train started very early and headed first about four hundred kilometers northwest to Kiev, the capital of Ukraine. The trip was an adventure for Ludmilla, and she was alive with excitement. Waiting on the platform, she jumped up and down on the spot and asked incessantly when the train was going to arrive. When the train did steam in, she rushed ahead and managed to get a seat near the window, but the carriage was quickly crowded. People filled the seats and spilled over onto the floor, and many were left standing. The carriage slowly turned stuffy with perspiration and wafts of garlic and onion. One of the men had already opened a bottle of vodka, although it was only early morning. As the passengers relaxed, the noise became louder with various groups having loud, spirited conversations. Then a group broke out into song and the whole carriage joined in. These were old Ukrainian ballads describing fractured or unrequited love and the lonely life of the old Cossacks on frontier duty. They were songs learned by children on their mother's knee, but forbidden under communist rule as nationalistic and not in accordance with proletarian philosophy. At least the Germans allowed this cultural outlet.

After a few glasses of vodka, Lydia joined in the singing with enthusiasm. Tears were running down her cheeks from emotion. She was happy. She was on her way to find her mother.

It took the whole day to get to Kiev, but the views were lovely. The trip went through the basin of the Dnieper River, with fields of new wheat just coming up, green and lush. They passed small villages with clusters of thatched roofed houses and whitewashed walls. Small farmhouses nestled in orchards, a mass of blossoms. The sun shone warmly and the war seemed to be far away. The scars of the previous summer's battlefield were healing, although there were still burnt-out buildings and farmhouses visible from time to time, and junkyards of derelict tanks, rusty with the turrets at odd angles, marking the sites of tank battles fought not so long before.

Ludmilla was interested only in the countryside and the animals she could see in the field. As a city girl, she saw few animals, but she had a child's interest, and she kept pointing at them and saying, "Look Mum, a cow!"—or a horse, or a goat, or chickens.

But Lydia was more struck by the burnt-out tanks. Her thoughts returned to the stupidity of war, the people who were killed, the maimed men and the mothers, sisters, and wives who now faced a lifetime of sorrow and loneliness because of the madness. And the massacres: it wasn't just her own people who had proved capable of atrocity, because Lydia knew full well that the Soviets had been just as monstrous. Disasters like the Katyn massacre were still unknown to most people at that time, but what Stalin had done in the thirties was no mystery to the ordinary Russian, and, of course, when the scores were finally clarified, they proved that Stalin wiped out far more innocent lives than Hitler.

When the train finally arrived at Kiev, some thirteen hours later, it was already dark and cool. The springtime nights were still cold. They were glad they had brought blankets with them.

They ate some bread and sausage. Everyone had a swig or two of the vodka bottle, and Lydia managed to find some tea at the station. They did not move out of the station, but stayed the night there, sleeping fitfully on the platform's hard wooden seats, with many passengers doing the same.

Regular patrols of German soldiers came by on the lookout for suspicious characters, particularly escaped prisoners, Jews, or possible troublemakers. They were supported by Ukrainian militia helping the Germans keep order. The Ukrainians, of course, believed they had been liberated, and would finally gain control over Ukraine when the war was over.

The next morning, they boarded the train to Lvov and managed to get a seat again since they were the first in line when it started to take on passengers. This time the train travelled directly west. The trip was slightly longer than the previous day's, hillier but still beautiful country, with peasants working the fields.

The peasants were very active that spring. This was the first time they actually thought they would enjoy the fruits of their labor themselves. The collective farms had collapsed, and the Germans hinted that the land and the stock would now belong to the peasants, so there was some hope of reward for their efforts. The Germans were keen to foster the idea and encourage activity on the land, although they used slave labor in the factories successfully enough. Everything was running smoothly, efficiently, producing maximum production at minimal cost to fuel the war machine.

By the end of the second day, the children were starting to get very tired and irritable in the cramped conditions, particularly Vala, who tended to cry more when he was not sleeping. He couldn't run to stretch his legs, because of the crush of noisy, smelly bodies filling the seats and standing areas, unwashed, unshaven, and reeking of garlic.

Lydia, of course, was very excited. This was something she had dreamed of and talked about for half of her childhood and most of her adult life. She was at last going to see her mother and the city where she was born, which she couldn't remember. After all, she'd been only four when she left. She kept quietly thinking about that part of her life, trying to recall.

They arrived late at night and again, without friends or contacts or anywhere to stay, they slept at the train station. In the morning, after a quick bite to eat of stale, hard rye bread, and some weak tea from the station, they ventured out.

Lydia was bewildered as she walked into the streets. She remembered nothing of her very early years, and Lvov, in any case, was a novelty, different from most cities in Ukraine. It is the most western of the urban centers, and it was ruled over the centuries by a variety of countries, depending on the outcome of the latest in the endless succession of Eastern European wars. Lvov became the main gateway of the trading route between west and east Europe and even the Far East, so it became a very cosmopolitan and cultural center, with a mixed racial make-up. About three hundred thousand to four hundred thousand people lived there at this time, made up roughly of a third Polish, a third Jewish, and a third Ukrainian ethnic groups, divided by the usual racial tensions. The Ukrainians believed that the Poles maintained a superior, upper-class attitude in the belief they were culturally above the Slavic Ukrainians. The Poles had indeed been the real governors for most of Lvov's six-hundred-year history. The Ukrainians hated the Poles; both the Poles and the Ukrainians hated the Jews, because of their self-imposed exclusivity. The Jews controlled the financial and commercial life of the city and always appeared richer, living in better homes and suburbs than the others. The others felt the Jews were somehow robbing them. In addition, wasn't it the Jews who killed Christ? The majority of the Ukrainians and Poles in Lvov were unreconstructed Roman Catholics, who had still not forgiven the Jews for that.

The town's major buildings, like the town hall and the university, had been built two hundred or three hundred years before and were more Italianate than Ukrainian and Russian architecture. Wide tree-lined streets carried tramlines on the major routes, the roads were still well maintained, and the whole place was in better condition than other Ukrainian cities. Stalin only got his hands on Lvov in 1939, and the debilitating effect of communist rule had not set in, although it had already exacerbated racial tensions. Both the Poles and the Ukrainians blamed the Jews for the Soviet yoke, for no reason other than that there were a number of Jews in the Communist ranks. Since the Russian takeover, Ukrainian patriots had been savagely put down. The NKVD made a determined effort to destroy any embryonic Ukrainian nationalism.

The final horror had been the massacre of all Ukrainian prisoners by the NKVD when the German attack started in June 1941. This event was still very fresh in people's minds—so many lost their dear ones, husbands, brothers, and friends.

"Well, Lydia," said Ivan, "this is your city, where do we go? Where do you think your mother could be?"

"I really have no idea—she could be anywhere. She is a widow, but she has one son and a daughter-in-law that could be living with her. I don't know what work or business she might be in. I don't even know if she is still alive—it's been six years since I heard from her."

"Well, I don't know, I thought it would have been a bit easier than this. This is like looking for a needle in a haystack we don't even know exists. The authorities won't be a help."

They went outside the central railway station and looked around. It was an imposing building with two towers on each side of the main doorways and large windows some two stories in height, with a dome over the major structures. There was an open square in front of the railway station and a large circular garden with a fountain. Its flowerbeds were filled with flowers in spring bloom, making a beautiful display, something they had not seen in Dniepropetrovsk for a long time.

"Let's catch a tram, Lydia, and just ride around. Who knows, we might see something to give you an idea where we should go."

They boarded a tram, lugging the small child. Their bags were now light and empty. Ludmilla and Vala jumped on the tram with excitement as they had not been on one before and were thrilled with the idea of the ride. They went up one street in the tram and then down another, and everything was just as strange as before, without anything Lydia recognized. There were beautiful buildings, however, with fine architecture quite novel to them. The city's living quarters were also well built, with flats two or three stories in height and clean, with the appearance of being well looked after—not the shoddy workmanship of the Stalin era in cities where the only owner was the State.

But everything was not perfect; there were areas of bombed-out buildings, with a space filled with rubble among the elegant buildings on each side. The gaps stood out like a missing tooth in perfect dentures. The few people walking the streets walked quickly with a nervous and scared air about them. There were also gangs of men with a white arm band and a yellow Star of David, working to remove rubble or repair roads guarded by the local militia, with an occasional German soldier. The Jews were being used for forced labor while they were still useful. This brought a sad feeling to Ludmilla as she thought of her friends Jacob and Rachel. She now knew they were no longer alive.

The family travelled around for about an hour in the tram, just looking and observing, when Lydia heard two women talking further away in the tram. She heard the name Goltz mentioned. Mrs. Goltz this and Mrs. Goltz that. She thought she was imagining it as a result of the emotional state she was in. She heard it again: "Mrs. Goltz." They were talking in Polish. Her

Polish was very rusty, but she could understand most of the conversation, as it was a Slavic language and close to Ukrainian. She went up to them and said, "Excuse me, I just heard you mention Mrs. Goltz. That wouldn't be Louiza Goltz?" They looked at her in surprise. One of them said in Polish, "Why do you ask?

"Louiza Goltz is my mother and I am looking for her. I haven't seen her for twenty-three years." She was starting to get excited, nearly fainting with the thought that this freak accident might finally bring her mother back.

"Yes, it is Louiza Goltz. She runs the haberdashery shop. We were just talking about some new material she had and how lovely it would be for the spring."

Lydia could not contain herself. "Please, please, tell me, where does she live? We have to go there straightaway."

"Well, it's not too far from here. Stay on this tram and go a further four or five blocks. If you get off then, turn right, and follow the street for a short time, you will come to her shop, and she lives just above it."

Lydia could hardly wait. She clutched her bag and was ready to jump off the minute the tram stopped at the point suggested by the two women. She ran ahead followed by Ivan, and Ludmilla holding Vala. She raced to the shop, which had not yet opened for the day, and beat on the door, calling out, "Mother, Mother!"

The top window opened and somebody called out in Polish, "What's all the commotion about, what's the trouble? I'll come down in a minute."

* * * *

Chapter 10

Reunion

A tall lady of medium build opened the door. She was dressed in a rather austere, simple, but tasteful dress, her hair pulled severely back and tied up in a bun. There was a dignified air about her, and she showed no emotion. She looked exactly how Lydia remembered her that fateful day in Siberia. By now Louiza was around sixty, and the added twenty-five years certainly showed, even though she was still well preserved. At that moment, she wore a look of quizzical confusion—she could not, of course, recognize Lydia, because her mental picture of her daughter was that of a little girl of eight, and in front of her was a mature woman of thirty-two.

She just stared at this short and rather plump woman, with a thin man beside her and two children. They were all

124

looking at her. And then the woman started shouting "Mummy, Mummy, I found you at last," rushing towards her and hugging her.

Louiza shook her head. "Who are you? I don't know you."

"I'm your Lydia, I'm your Lydia! I haven't seen you for twenty-three years."

Now the realization dawned. This *was* Lydia. Her little Lydie, the youngest child she lost so long ago. Suddenly she recognized the round brown eyes and the smile that she still remembered of her baby girl.

"My God, you are Lydia! Where did you come from? How did you find me? What is happening? What's happened to the others?" She fired questions without waiting for an answer and almost immediately burst out crying. Then she grabbed Lydia and just hugged her. Louiza could not believe what was happening. She felt like she was floating in a dream surrounded by characters she did not know, but who looked familiar and were apparently close to her. Could this be a continuation of the recurrent nightmare she'd had over the years? Louiza had never recovered from the traumatic loss of those three girls on the railway platform in Siberia. She had only briefly managed to make contact with them since then, had never, of course, seen them, and once contact was cut off, had not even heard from them. And now, as if back from the dead, the youngest daughter arrived unannounced and with other people who were total strangers. Louiza wanted to cry and shout and laugh, all at the same time.

After a while, the two women finally stopped hugging each other. Lydia gestured to the strangers and said, "I would like you to meet my family, Momma."

"This is Ivan, my husband; Ludmilla, my oldest daughter; and Vala, my son. He is only just one."

My goodness, Louiza thought, the daughter is just a little bit older than Lydia was when she was wrenched from me, and look how small she is. How did Lydia survive all those years without me in a strange country?

She gave Ivan a kiss and a hug, hugged Ludmilla and Vala together, kissing them both, and then she turned round and dragged them up the steps.

"You must be hungry and thirsty. Get something to eat and drink, and then we will talk and talk and talk."

At the top of the steep steps was a little apartment above Louiza's small shop. "Kate, Kate," she called out as they got through the door. "Look who's here, quick, come."

A young woman appeared, thin, blonde, with a rather angular but neat appearance, and pale blue eyes, fair skin, and straight hair set in a pageboy bob. She looked quizzically at the commotion coming up the steps, everyone shouting, crying, and talking all at once.

"What on earth is going on?" she said, "Who is everybody?"

"Kate, Kate, you won't believe it. This is Lydia, my youngest daughter. She just walked in off the street, without anything. I can't believe it. God has created a miracle. I've been praying and praying for this for years, and it has finally happened."

They all filed into the small lounge room and then she introduced Lydia and her family to Kate, her daughter-in-law and Ludwig's wife. Ludwig was the only child who hadn't been lost on that fateful day in Siberia, he was still with her on the train when it pulled out and left the rest of the family behind.

"Kate, make some tea and something to eat. They must be hungry and thirsty."

She sat down and gave Lydia another hug. Tears were still running down her face, but she smiled, and launched into her barrage of long-preserved questions.

"Now tell me, Lydia, how did you find me? I haven't heard from you—for what, six years? Seven years?—since your last letter, and you didn't know where I lived because this wasn't my address then."

"Well," said Lydia, "we hoped you still lived in Lvov because that was where you were the last time you wrote to us, and we thought the chance was that you still would be. So we came once the German control system settled down and we had right of movement in the whole area. When we got here, we just decided to get in a tram and ride around to see if something might trigger my memory to suggest some idea of where you lived. But guess what happened! We heard these two women talk about a Frau Louiza Goltz, and a clothing shop where they bought some cloth for summer dresses for their children. I asked them about this Louiza Goltz, and I realized it was you. They just happened to start talking about my lost mother while I was travelling in the tram!"

"It has to be a miracle," said Louiza. "How else could you have been brought to me after twenty-three years in such a way? I think we must owe it to God." And she started crying again, unable to control her emotions.

"But what stopped you writing?" asked Lydia.

Louiza burst out in an agonized voice, "You sent me a letter to say you wanted me to stop writing, you no longer wanted to know me. *You* cut off our correspondence."

Lydia looked at her incredulously. "Me, stop correspondence? I remember receiving a letter from you, signing for it, and never again receiving another one."

Louiza got up, went to a set of drawers, and searched among some papers. Finally, she drew out a small paper folded in four, old and creased. She opened it up gently and showed Lydia what she had taken as her last letter. The single sheet carried some hand printing that simply said, "Dear Momma, I no longer wish to write to you and this will be my last letter, nor do I want you to write to me again. I don't need this." And at the bottom of the page was Lydia's scrawled, childlike signature—the only lettering she did recognize as her own.

Lydia looked at it and could hardly believe it. "I didn't write this, Mother. Neither did Ivan. Who did, then?"

Ivan took the paper and had a look at the date. It was 1934, and then he started thinking. He said slowly, "I think I have an explanation. This was about the same time of my promotion to communications operator of my battalion. The army was probably very uneasy about my wife corresponding with somebody outside the Soviet Union. As you know, I often got information that was classified, and they were probably concerned that you might hear of it or I might discuss it with you and it might leak out through you writing to your mother. Can you remember the last time you received a letter, Lydia?"

"Yes, I do," she said. "You know we have to sign for every letter we receive from overseas, usually in a book. But the last time I got one, they told me to sign on a blank piece of paper. I wondered at the time why that was, but now it's obvious. This is that same piece of paper, this is my signature, and after I signed, they just wrote a letter to Louiza to say that I didn't want any more letters, and they sent it off in my name.

"You would have thought it was my letter, Mother, because my signature was real and I always got other people to do the writing for me. You wouldn't have seen any reason to be suspicious."

Louiza looked at her and whispered, "All those years wasted. I cried and cried for nights over this. I just didn't know why you rejected me. I thought maybe it was because I lost you when you were a child—I couldn't tell."

Gradually they all recovered their composure. Kate brought some tea and biscuits. Vala and Ludmilla tucked into them. They couldn't remember having biscuits like these before. They were properly made with lovely creams in-between, strikingly sweet with an almond flavor. The biscuits just melted in the mouth and disappeared. "Food that doesn't have to be chewed," thought Ludmilla, in wonder.

Kate was very familiar with the family's troubled history, since she was Louiza's only confidante and friend in recent years. She was also the only other adult in the household.

"What happened to Ludwig? Where is he?" asked Lydia. At this point, it was Kate's turn to burst into tears.

"Well," said Louiza, "we don't know where Ludwig is. He was conscripted when the Germans took over in June 1941. Since he was *Volksdeutsch*, he was expected to show loyalty and devotion to the Fatherland, so as soon as he was processed he was posted to an infantry battalion. We haven't heard from him for about nine months and we're not sure where he is. But he is fighting somewhere on the Eastern Front, and as yet we haven't heard that he has been killed or wounded, so we're praying he is still alive and well. There's a good chance he survived the winter because he is pretty resourceful, and unlike the boys from Berlin and the German cities, he was brought up in Siberia and knows how to cope with the cold."

Louiza showed Lydia around the little flat. It was tiny but comfortable, and tastefully furnished. There was one main bedroom, and there was another small room, no bigger than a cupboard, where Kate's two children had their bunks. Louiza slept in the lounge room and a bed was made up every night for her. The flat was just above the shop where Kate and Louiza worked. Louiza explained that when she came back from Siberia, there was still some money left over, and she had decided to buy into the small business that her friend Rosa owned, hoping to be able to support the children if she could get them back.

"And what happened to Olga and Maria?" asked Louiza, pushing on with the scary task of getting up to date.

"They left Kharkov after they each got married, and went to Stalingrad. Industry was growing there, and they hoped to get some work there since they were offered training in a factory.

"I haven't heard what happened to them since the war started. The Germans haven't reached Stalingrad yet, and there's no way of communicating while it's still under the Russians. We'll have to hope we hear from them when the Germans have taken the city, and maybe we can meet up again."

"My God, I hope so," said Louiza. "Maybe this war can be a catalyst for reunion, since it's already brought you back to me, even if it took Ludwig away. But tell me about your life. Tell me what happened to you. Tell me everything. I want to know. I have been imagining so many things that happened to you and the other children, how you were living, how you might be surviving, and not a day went by without me going to sleep crying, thinking, and praying about you all."

Lydia began to feel her mother's sense of loss had been perhaps even more grievous than her own, which she'd always assumed was the ultimate.

Just then there was commotion at the door, and three children made their way up the staircase: Kate and Ludwig's children. The eldest was a twelve-year-old girl, carrying a small boy aged just over one, chubby and fair-haired, and there was a girl with them of about six.

"Come in, come in," said Louiza. "Look who's here! Your cousins and your Aunt Lydia. You have never seen them before, but I've always talked about my other children, and now Lydia has arrived!"

She ushered the children in and introduced them in Polish.

"This young fellow is Alfred, and my oldest granddaughter is Wilhemina, and this little girl is Emma. Meet your cousins from Ukraine, Ludmilla and Vala."

All the children were shy and retreating, but eventually Wilhemina and Emma started asking Ludmilla questions in Polish. They had difficulty communicating because although the two languages sound similar, there are a lot of differences. But eventually the children managed to communicate. The two boys, who were both just toddlers, did it easily by chasing each other, wrestling, and touching.

The girls took Ludmilla away and showed her their dolls and other toys. She was astonished how many they had, because children's toys were a scarce commodity for Ukrainians.

The family's prized possession was their bike. This gave them enviable mobility for shopping, visiting, and certainly the children loved it. Ludmilla had never been on one before, and Emma and Wilhemina had to show her how to ride. After a few days and several falls and grazed knees, she was able to cope. The children were firm friends by now, and shared stories about their homes and friends, in between expeditions around the city on trams and sharing the bike.

Lydia and Louiza spent every minute they could together, talking and catching up with each other's experiences. Early on in the exchange, Louiza turned to Karlov—she knew that despite his capture, he had reached his sisters in Kharkov after the Soviets proved unexpectedly lenient on him, but she had no idea what had happened since.

"He was just under city arrest," said Lydia, "so that as long as he stayed within the city he could work there. He eventually married a Ukrainian girl called Anastasia, and they had a son, Markov. He had a reasonably happy life, and made the best of it in the circumstances. We visited him sometimes.

"But immediately when the war broke out, the Soviets re-arrested him because of his history and his *Volkdeutsch* parentage. They sent him back to Siberia straightaway. We haven't heard of him since."

Lydia only knew even this because Anastasia had contacted her in total distress when Karlov was sent away.

Louiza was distraught again. "That cursed wilderness Siberia, it's kept rising from the dark to swallow everything I hold dear, my home, my husband, my children. And now it is still there and takes my son."

They talked on, long into the night, with Louiza insisting Lydia repeat some stories and further details of others.

The time went quickly. The children played well together, the two cousins taking Ludmilla to the local park and shops, where she was amazed at the range of goods that were still available in Poland. The girls spent hours riding the bicycle around the footpaths and the local park. One day Ivan even borrowed it and went for a trip around the city and the local area, with Vala sitting precariously in front of him on the framework. Young Vala couldn't get enough, enjoying every minute.

Lydia and her mother spent as much time together as possible, although they had to work in the shop below. Lydia was practicing her rusty Polish and German, and after a month, her speech had improved.

Louiza's small flat was very congested now with the five children and four adults, but Lydia and her family were sleeping in the small lounge, and the rest managed in the bedroom and the small box room was used for the two older girls. Ivan managed to dispose of the "liquid" currency that he brought with him, as vodka was in the same short supply in Poland as in Ukraine. He managed to barter some bread and other food, so that they were contributing something to the family's food budget. Time, however, was quickly drawing to the end of their permitted two-month stay.

Ivan was ready to go. He felt constricted in the flat day after day, and he did not want to spend too much time on the streets for fear of being picked up by German guards who didn't know him as well as their equivalents did in Dniepropetrovsk. They were likely to be suspicious of any able-bodied Ukrainian from out of town, and questioning might well reveal he was ex-Red Army, in which case forced labor in Germany was the best he could expect. But Lydia, of course, dreaded the time when they would have to go, although she knew they must. If they overstayed their authorization, they could be picked up and thrown into camps or sent back to Germany. It was wise to give no reason for authorities to inquire.

Just before they were ready to leave, early in June, the postman called at the shop.

"Hello, Frau Goltz—letter for you. It looks like it's from the Army. You can't mistake those cheap Army envelopes. I know them only too well."

"My God," she thought to herself. "Ludwig!"

She grabbed the letter and saw that it was, indeed, from him. It was addressed to both her and Kate, and the envelope was in Ludwig's handwriting. Her fear subsided, and she ran excitedly up the steps calling out for Kate.

They tore open the envelope, and Louiza rapidly scanned what was inside. Once she was sure it wasn't disastrous news, she read it aloud to Kate and the children.

Ludwig said he was well and quite happy for the moment. Things in general were looking up. All supplies were being replenished, and his unit's morale had risen greatly since the winter months. They had just come out of a major battle in the Kharkov area. It had started on the twelfth of May, when the Red Army attacked in what the Germans first feared would be a major advance. Fighting was fierce at first, but the more experienced Germans quickly encircled the Reds, and a large part of the Russian army was captured or destroyed. Ludwig could not give any details, but a general success in the engagement had been widely reported in the German press, and Lydia and Louiza both knew that there was a lot of action on the Eastern Front.

Ludwig did not say where he was, but the news reports claimed the Army was moving relentlessly east and that there was nothing to stop them attacking Stalingrad. That seemed to be the general direction they were heading.

Kate was quite buoyant after the letter, and the children were happy their father had written to them at last and that he was well, not wounded, and seemed to be fairly cheerful.

At first Louiza was just happy to think that her son had survived another battle, and was still well, alive and uninjured. After a time, though, she started thinking about the possible implications of his news. If Stalingrad was the next battle to be fought, her other two daughters, Maria and Olga, would be at risk. How ironic, she thought, her son Ludwig had been with her since leaving Siberia and had been her life and support. He had given Louiza the pleasure of being the grandmother of his three children and helping to look after them. Now he had been taken away by another mad regime, likely to be sent to fight in Stalingrad where another crazy regime would probably force the other side of the family to defend it. Would Ludwig be instrumental in killing her other daughters, or their husbands?

"My God," Louiza groaned to herself. "When will it all end?"

Finally, the time arrived for Lydia and Ivan to return to Dniepropetrovsk. Louiza did a lot of baking the day before. She prepared sweet cakes, bought fresh white bread from the bakeries, and got a big Polish salami on the black market. They were going to eat well on the trip back. After the evening meal, Lydia and Ivan packed their few belongings and were ready to go.

Louiza and Kate came back to the flat after closing the shop, carrying a roll of material. It was large and a little too heavy for the old lady.

She put it on the table and said, "Lydia, I want you to have this." Lydia was quite surprised.

"Why?" She was a bit embarrassed, as that roll of material was clearly worth a lot, and even more in Ukraine, where everything was in short supply.

"Lydia, my darling, I have given you nothing in your life. I lost you when you were eight. You brought yourself up, and I couldn't give you any love, support, or comforts. I feel an absolute failure and I don't know what will happen in the future. I have been a poor mother, and this is just a small token to try to make up.

"Think of it as your inheritance, for who knows what might happen. A bomb might drop on my house here and kill me, and then everything would be lost anyway. The material will be enough to sew some warm clothing for everyone for the winter, and there will probably be some left over to do with as you please."

Lydia could hardly refuse. She gave her mother a long hug and a kiss. "I didn't stop loving you when you were lost to us, Mum. I probably loved you even more, and I dreamed of being with you every day. Those dreams have been fulfilled in the last eight weeks, and now I will always treasure them."

That evening was the worst of the whole stay. The knowledge that Lydia and Ivan had to leave the next day removed any chance of light-hearted smiles, as they all tried to keep emotions under control, and the children picked up the adults' mood. Lydia could not sleep that night, thinking of the next day's departure and the loss of her mother for the second time. She had to say good-bye, not really knowing if she would ever see Louiza again. But at least she had actually talked, touched, hugged, and kissed her after twenty-three years, and had the pleasure of seeing her children actually meet their grandmother. She wept as softly as she could, trying not to wake the family.

The next morning, they were up early, long before sunrise. By 4 a.m., the coffee pot was already on the stove, and the aroma permeated the little flat. The children were dressed and fed, and after a hurried breakfast of bread and sausage, Lydia and Ivan said good-bye to Kate. The other children were still in bed. She kissed them all, and Ludmilla also hugged and kissed her two cousins. She had a great time with them over the weeks. She thought how lovely it would be to live close by and play with them every day. She started to think about Jacob and Rachel, her friends whom she lost, but put those thoughts out of her mind. Louiza, of course, was going to accompany them and see them off at the station.

"Come on, everybody, we had better go because the train will fill up very quickly, and we want to be the first ones in line. We have a long, long way to go over the next few days," Lydia called.

Louiza finally got them out of the flat, and they made their way on the tram. Everyone was quiet and subdued. There was no talk—even the children were quiet. Lydia looked at her mother's face, set in a stoic and determined manner. She thought this was not because she was being hard, but because she was trying to control her emotions underneath and not burst out crying. There was just a glimmer of light in the eastern sky, where the sun was struggling to rise. All the trees and buildings that they passed had a magical, unreal quality. She had the impression that she was somehow in a dream, that everything that had happened to her in the last month was part of it, and she was about to wake up to the nightmare that was her real life.

Lydia came back to reality when they arrived at Central Station, busy and bustling even at that time of the morning. Many people, mostly Poles and Ukrainians, were leaving to go east for jobs. Central Station was also a dangerous place, because a person trying to escape the city could try to use it and the Gestapo was on the lookout. There were sentries at all entrances, and soldiers circulated the platforms watching for anyone looking or acting suspiciously. Their targets were Jews, saboteurs, escaped prisoners, and even German deserters. Ivan was at risk here, since they would see him as a young able-bodied man who should have been in the Army, or working in some essential industry instead of on a railway platform.

The family group found the right platform and stood waiting for the train to arrive. Gestapo guards were mingling with the waiting crowd and checking documents randomly. There was a flurry near the clock on the platform where a young man was standing in the shadows reading a newspaper. When the guards demanded his travelling papers, he dropped the paper and tried to run. They quickly caught him by the scruff of the neck and dragged him away.

"That is probably a young Jew trying to get away from the ghetto," whispered Louiza. "There is usually somebody trying to get away, but they generally get caught. The ghetto is a hive of activity, and the Jews produce a lot of clothing there. Sometimes I supply them with material when they can't get it any other way. Recently I heard that some of the older ones and the young children have been taken away. They are finally coming to realize their fate, so the numbers trying to escape have soared."

Just at that moment, one of the guards noticed their little group, and headed towards them. His gaze was on Ivan, and obviously he was going to investigate them all.

"You," he pointed to Ivan. "Papers."

Ivan was shaken and nervous, fully aware how vulnerable he was in this city. Lydia quickly smiled at the stern-faced sentry, who obviously enjoyed his power over people. That and a gun in his hand made him feel like a god. But Lydia was used to talking to soldiers and guards at Dniepropetrovsk on the way to her bartering trips.

She said, "*Guten tag*" in a friendly tone. "How are you today?" He was surprised by the welcome in place of the terror and dismay he generally provoked. Louiza immediately took up the cue and also greeted him warmly. "It's lovely to see such fine German soldiers here. God bless you. Since my son Ludwig went to the Eastern Front, I have been frightened by the hooligans and gangs who run around the city, but I always feel safe and protected when your kind soldiers are around. It gives me heart to carry on."

Louiza spoke perfect German and was obviously of German background. The guard's face softened and lost the stern aggressive look. His voice became softer.

"Why, do you have a son who is a soldier?"

"Yes, I have," she said, taking out a photo from her wallet showing Ludwig in his Wehrmacht uniform. He looked quite handsome and dashing, with a soft smile on his face. He was obviously a credit to the Fatherland.

"And who are these people then?" asked the guard more softly, without the venom in his voice.

"This is my daughter, and her little family. Her husband had a short break from his work, and they managed to come down and visit me and encourage this old woman. I haven't seen them for years and years, and since your soldiers liberated them from Stalin, they have been able to visit me."

He looked at the papers, and yes, they were in order. Their travelling documents, their time of departure from Dnieprop-etrovsk, the expected time of return all fitted in. They were the lucky ones. He gave them a nod, wished them good day, and walked on to investigate other poor wretches.

Ivan was relieved and so too was Lydia. The two of them smiled at each other with relief.

Louiza said quietly, "I just treat them like I would Ludwig, and they feel the warmth. They are human beings underneath their brutality."

"I know," replied Lydia. "I meet soldiers and guards often and a smile always helps. It puts them at ease, and if you show a bit of interest in their background, their home and their family, they are ready to respond. It's as if there are two sides to them. One side is human, warm, loving in their relationships with their mothers, sisters, and lovers, but the other side of them is horrible. They are like demons from hell, out to destroy, kill, rape, and burn."

"I hope Ludwig remains warm and human and doesn't turn into a monster because of the war."

At last the family boarded the train, and Lydia pushed her way to a window seat. She was desperate to see her mother as long as possible. The poor older woman was standing alone on the platform waving a white handkerchief, and as the train pulled out with the black fumes and steam swirling around her,

Lydia had half her body through the window, waving and calling out, "Good-bye, good-bye, Mother." She thought how ironic this was: the first time it had been her mother on the train, calling out to her through the window, and trying desperately to see her as long as possible, and now she was aboard the train, and her mother stood on the platform crying and waving to her.

* * * *

Maria's son died 11/16/1941 in Stalingrad.

*Lydia, and family during visit to Louiza in
1942.*

Ivan and Vala during visit to Louiza in 1942.

Ludwig's children-Wilhemina, Alfred and Emma in 1942.

Chapter 11

An Interrupted Reprieve

The trip back was just as slow as the outward journey. To pass the time, the packed passengers started singing again, but Lydia was not in the mood. She felt strangely withdrawn after the re-union with her mother. It was rather as if it had focused her attention on the exact state of her life. With fresh clarity, she saw the position: her first thirty years had been overwhelmed by wars and revolution. She felt like an autumn leaf falling into a flooded torrent and being dragged out of control by the powerful currents. Her situation had not improved lately. There was still no certainty in her life—this war was not yet over and only God knew if any of them would survive and where they would eventually end up.

She had indeed managed to survive the traumas of the forces unleashed, but she had missed so much of normal family life, the love and companionship of a mother and brothers. The reunion with her mother, marvelous event as it was, also brought her deep sadness for the experiences she had lost. She realized her priority in life was now her family and their survival. She could never, ever contemplate a separation from her children. If she was going to be killed, she would prefer that they all died. The hurts that she experienced and, what she now also realized, the loss and grief her mother had suffered had convinced her that separation would be too much to bear. She sat in her seat quietly and spoke very little on the way back, and from time to time cried softly to herself.

The family arrived back at their apartment, and found no problems. The neighbors had kept an eye on the flat and made sure there were no intruders. Summer was beginning and the days were lengthening. Food was more plentiful, with a lot of vegetables coming on the market, early tomatoes, cucumbers, onions, and carrots. Other necessities, such as shoes, clothing, implements, or even vodka, were available for use or barter.

Lydia was wondering what she should do with the material her mother had given her. It was certainly valuable. People were already thinking of warm clothing for the next winter, and cloth was scarce. During the previous winter, even the German soldiers had only a limited supply and had resorted to confiscating the clothing and particularly shoes from some unfortunate wretches, resulting in death from the cold for some. Lydia now had enough material to make coats and trousers for Ivan and Vala, and probably some skirts and coats for herself and Ludmilla. However, it would take a long time for her to sew and would interfere with her continual trips to the countryside for bartering. It would take her all summer to do it all by hand, and she did not have a machine, nor could she borrow one.

"Well, Ivan, what do you think? What sort of clothing would you like me to sew you? It would make very warm trousers for you and Vala, and I could make some skirts for us."

Ivan looked at it, and turned his head sideways in a quizzical manner, his characteristic gesture while he was thinking about something, and finally said, "Well, I already have two pairs of trousers. Do I really need more? And you are pretty well attired. Your mother also gave you some clothing for Vala, and a few dresses for Ludmilla that her cousins outgrew."

"That's true. It would be an awful lot of work trying to use it all up for the family, so perhaps we could exchange it for something."

"Exactly, but what? What do we really need? We seem to have enough food from bartering our vodka production. We have clothing. We don't need much furniture, we have enough. We don't know how long we will stay here."

"I know what I would like," said Lydia. "A milking cow." She smiled, and her face softened at the thought. Lydia always loved animals, and the idea of having a cow with big brown eyes and gentle face really appealed to her.

"What! A cow. And what would we do with a cow in a small, one-roomed flat? Are you going to share your bed with a cow?"

"Think of the advantages, Ivan. We could have fresh milk every day for the children. We could make cheese, cottage cheese, we could have cream and butter and whey, and how lovely that is, a cool glass on a hot summer's day. Any excess we could barter for other things. It would give us another source of a constant food supply."

"Well, put that way, I suppose so. But what happens if the Russians come back? It would be confiscated and given to a collective farm."

"If they came back, our fate is sealed anyway, as far as you and I are concerned. Just consider what our position would be in their eyes. A Red Army deserter and a *Volksdeutsch.* We'd last five minutes. Anyway I don't think they will ever come back. From the way things are going, the Germans could go as far as Siberia, and they'll take over this country as part of the greater Germany.

"Nothing has stopped them so far, even Stalin's great armies are being swept away. Once they take Stalingrad, the Soviets will collapse, and the whole resistance will evaporate."

"You could be right," replied Ivan. "Maybe all this could become permanent, which suggests we should be more long-term focused. So far we've been living from day to day from force of circumstances, but you could be right. But we couldn't keep a cow in an apartment."

"We would need a shed, fields, and grass," said Lydia. "I know this elderly couple that live near the outskirts of town— Mr. and Mrs. Kulchenko. They are too old now to do anything with the land. I've often stopped for a drink of water on my way home from bartering trips and talked with old Mrs. Kulchenko. She is keen to be with her daughter, who lives not far from us. The daughter's husband was moved out when the army retreated and is still missing, and she has three young children. She needs a lot of help. But the Kulchenkos have been unable to move because the vegetable garden supplies a little food."

Ivan saw the attractions of the idea. "Well, why don't we offer them our apartment, and we can move into their little house. They can still come and work on the vegetable garden when they want to, and we will have the field for the cow and also start our own garden. There is still plenty of time to grow some vegetables before winter."

The plan was settled between them, and when the Kulchenkos were approached, they readily agreed to the exchange. There had been no private ownership in principle since the communist takeover, but after the Soviet retreat, people just assumed they owned what they had and where they lived. They had no formal documentation or title: possession was the law. All that was necessary was to register the change of address with the German authorities.

The exchange was arranged for the following week. There was no transport available, and they had only the hand-pulled trolley that Ivan made a few years before. On the other hand, there wasn't much to transport—a few suitcases carrying their clothing, the bedding, thick eiderdowns and large pillows filled with feather down. And, of course, the small metal bath used to ferment the vodka output and the homemade still Ivan had put together. Their rough furniture in the flat consisted only of a table and four chairs, a homemade wooden bed, and the children's bunks. They took the children's bunks with them, but the rest of it was just exchanged for the farmhouse contents. The swap still took two days. The distance to travel was eight kilometers, and they could only make one trip a day. On the return trip, the old couple's belongings were hauled into the city. The Kulchenkos could do very little to help, and just walked slowly behind and tried to keep up. Sometimes on a hill they might lean on the trolley to give it some extra push, but Ivan did the heavy work. Lydia and the children remained at the farmhouse to guard their meager belongings. There was always a risk of thieves because clothing and bedding were scarce and highly prized. On the third day, Ivan loaded his fermentation and distilling equipment on the trolley, his tools, hammer, saw, chisel, screwdrivers, and a hand-operated drill. His boot-making equipment was compact—a small-headed hammer, anvil, and bits and pieces of leather still in the process of being worked. This load was not heavy, but by the time the whole move was complete, he was tired and weary from the protracted effort. It was now the end of June, and the weather was hot. But when he finally stretched out in the house, he smiled with happy relief.

It was a small place, with whitewashed walls, and a steep thatched roof with a chimney at the back. The four-paned windows were small and square, and there was a single door with flaky paint and squeaky hinges, in need of repair. The old couple had done very little maintenance over the years. Inside the main room, the large fireplace was fitted with an old cast-iron stove. Once cleaned up, though, it would still handle the cooking and baking—and in particular the new occupiers' specialty, the distilling.

There was an old wooden table and three chairs in the main room, which was bright and sunny with sunshine streaming through the south-facing windows, double-glazed for insulation against the cold winters. There was little other furniture, except for a few boxes. The wooden board floor was loose and squeaky, but Ivan planned to repair all the problems. The other major room was a bedroom with a big old wooden bed with a Hessian bottom, but no mattress. There was also a small box room off the main room, with shelves from floor to ceiling for food supplies. It was empty at this stage except for a few broken old boxes, and a small cellar. It was really no more than a large hole in the ground with two hinged doors forming part of the floor. But once you were a few steps down, it was beautifully cool even in summer, and valuable for storing vegetables and whatever grains were available for the humans and the animals over winter.

Ivan thought this was wonderful. He had always wanted his own home, his own house and a little land. He was distraught when the house he built in 1928 was confiscated by the Soviets for one of their officials. This was perfect. Ivan was eager to start working the land, raising a few small animals, chickens, pigs, and the occasional cow to supply the family and barter at the market—the traditional life of the Ukrainian peasant before the Soviets.

He got busy next day with the urgent repairs, making sure that the chimney was cleaned and functional. He also cleaned out the well, the only source of water for the building. They had no electricity, naturally, and candles were the only light at night, but now was the middle of summer and the days were long: the nights were just for sleeping. The family reveled in their new environment. Lydia continued her bartering trips, but they were down to only two or three days a week. She had fairly regular customers, and knew what they wanted. Ivan went on with the repairs, and before long the place looked well cared for and anything that moved worked smoothly. It was amazing what a touch of oil on the right hinge and the tightening up of a few screws would do for functional efficiency.

On the bartering trips, Lydia carefully noted the types of farm animals the peasants had and, in particular, if they had three or four cows. She would discreetly ask how many children they had, the size of the family, and also whether they had sufficient clothing. She picked out a few families who might be interested in bartering not just half a sack of potatoes or turnips, but a cow for the much-prized commodity of a very large roll of material. It was a major investment both for the farmer and for her, and the exchange had to be fair, with both parties happy.

"*Dobry den*" (Good day), she called out to one of her regular customers, a peasant lady who personified the concept of "daughter of the soil." She was short but broadly built, with strong muscles and thick hands. Her hands were bare of rings, and heavily callused from constant hard work on the soil. She wore a colorful handkerchief on her head, and her face was round and ruddy from long hours in the fields under the hot summer sun. Her clothing was a bit tattered because she had not been able to replenish anything for over a year, and her children, who were working in the garden with her, were also less than adequately dressed. Lydia, however, knew that this woman and her husband had four cows, one recently in calf, which was probably much more than they needed for their family, and they might be ready to do a trade.

"It's hard to get clothing these days with all the restrictions, and no production!"

"Yes," said the peasant woman despondently. "With the shops closed and nothing for sale, I don't know how I'm going to clothe my brood here. They either grow out of clothing or tear it to shreds with their wild games."

"You know, I might be able to help," whispered Lydia, lowering her voice, as if frightened someone might overhear what she was about to suggest.

"How?"

"Well, I have been able to obtain the most beautiful English woolen cloth. It is thin, but warm, and it would satisfy the choosiest people. It has a lovely design with a brown, green, and red motif, but you would have to do the sewing yourself, of course. I imagine you could, though."

The peasant woman was interested immediately, narrowing her eyes and asking suspiciously, "What would you want for that? What can I give you?" She was already on her guard, knowing that if she could get her hands on this prize, it would come at a high cost.

"Let's not even talk about it until you see what I have to offer, and then we will probably come to some agreement, I'm sure. You would be able to exchange something and clothe your children, yourself, and your husband."

The peasant woman was hooked. Lydia waited a little bit and then went away, continuing her trip, to let the idea develop in the woman's mind. She knew that the woman was desperate to clothe herself and her children for the coming winter, and she would be prepared to negotiate.

A few days later, Lydia took a small square of the cloth to the woman. She laid it down on her table, pressed it out gently, and said, "Now look at this, isn't it beautiful? You can imagine beautiful coats, trousers, and skirts made from this. It is so warm, and yet so fine."

The woman took it into her hands and stretched it out and looked at it at different angles, with different light reflections, and had to gruffly agree. "It is good material, but I've seen better," she said.

"Not in this lifetime you haven't, because this is English wool, highly prized, and even English lords and ladies wear this very stuff."

"Well, what do you want for it, and how much is there?"

"Well, what do you have? What can you offer?" Lydia did not want to come straight out with her real aim. She was playing the familiar bartering game.

The woman, of course, knew those rules and played along. They talked around the topic and balanced items and their values, and what would be a fair exchange, and so on, and it became obvious that the only things of any value that would come up to the worth of what Lydia was offering were the cows. She did not want to say this was what she really wanted, but pretended instead that she had no need for them—but possibly she might be able to barter one for something else if that was the only thing they had to offer.

"Well, let's have a look at them," she said. She looked at the cows and into their mouths, trying to gauge their ages to see whether they had any disease or unhealthy features. She paid particular attention to the size of the udder, to make sure they were producing milk. Then she brought out the whole piece of material roll that was covered up in the cart and put it on the table, and the peasant woman and her husband dropped their guard, as they and their children all swarmed around exclaiming wonder and appreciation. It seemed a huge roll—it would supply their entire clothing needs and still leave plenty over for barter.

"Well, then, are you happy to exchange the cow for this material?" asked Lydia. The man was still slightly hesitant, not being as interested in the family's clothing as his wife. Lydia spotted this and said, "I would, of course, put in five bottles of vodka just to sweeten the deal for you."

That did it. With the material and the vodka, everybody in the family had their price. The man agreed to the exchange immediately. They put a rope around the cow, and Lydia took it and started walking slowly home with the cow in tow, leaving her cart to be picked up later. She was ecstatic. Here at last was a steady and constant supply of food for the family. When she arrived home, everybody gathered around, admiring her acquisition.

She was a beautiful cow—big brown eyes and dark brown hide with occasional patches of white. There was a white star on her forehead, and a big solid pink tongue would come out and give somebody an occasional lick. She was friendly and seemed to enjoy the attention of the family. She won their hearts straight away. She was called Rayka, and she became Ludmilla's responsibility. Ludmilla would take her down the road where the grass was lusher and rub her neck or her forehead. Rayka changed the family's survival struggle. All they needed to do was provide her with water and allow her to graze in the allotment attached to the house and the roadsides, to be rewarded with liters and liters of milk.

Lydia milked her at dawn and again in the evening. Each time she gave a pail of milk. In addition to the children's milk every day, some would be allowed to ferment, covered by a muslin cloth, and the resultant yoghurt formed overnight. It could be eaten as it was, as a highly nutritious protein dessert or snack, or it could be made into cottage cheese by placing it into a cloth bag and putting a large stone on top overnight to squeeze out the water. This was also a pure protein food used to make the favorite Ukrainian *varenicky* dish, cottage cheese dumplings cooked in water and then covered with fresh cream and a garnish of green shallots. In addition, the family at last had some butter if they scooped off the cream after the milk settled, and then churned it. So beautiful Rayka, in addition to being the family's favorite pet, also supplied a large part of the family's basic food. Providing the cow could be protected from being "requisitioned" by the occupying forces, she would serve as a vital food source for the family.

Lydia loved getting up early in the summer mornings while the sun was still rising, and there was mist and coolness in the air before the warmth of the day. Rayka would be standing there munching her hay while Lydia milked. She held the bucket between her legs, and pulled on the teats of the udder, with a long rhythmic movement, rewarded by a squirt of milk hitting the pail at every movement. Occasionally, when Vala was awake, he would come running out with a mug to taste the milk directly from the pail while it was still warm and frothy. Sometimes as he ran up, Lydia would turn the teat in his direction and give him a squirt, aimed right in his face. He would laugh and giggle, as he wiped the milk from his cheek.

Lydia was really happy at this time. At last there was some security in their lives: they had established their house, she was able to feed the family, and Ivan was content. Things finally seemed to have come right. She was blissfully unaware of two major problems looming unseen in the future.

In the meantime, there was a major trauma one morning. When Ludmilla got dressed and went outside to get Rayka ready for the early milking, she wasn't in her normal place, the small shed at the back of the house. Ludmilla looked around and could not immediately see her. She ran around the house, and there was Rayka on the ground, prostrate, looking very sorry for herself, her eyes red and her tongue rolling out at the side with froth around her mouth. Occasionally she gave a low, long, sad "mooooo." She was obviously sick. Ludmilla quickly ran inside, calling out, "Mummy, Mummy, come quickly. There is something wrong with Rayka. She's ill. She's dying."

Lydia was busy with the breakfast and didn't quite believe her. "Oh, don't be silly. There's nothing wrong with Rayka. She was a healthy cow when I saw her last night."

"Quick Mum, quick, she'll die if you don't come," pleaded Ludmilla pulling on Lydia's arm.

Lydia said, with some impatience, "Oh, alright. We'll go and have a look," and followed her outside. Rayka lay there on her side looking very sorry and sick. The sight sent a cold shiver of fear down Lydia's spine and her stomach knotted.

Lydia raced indoors immediately to call Ivan. "Go quickly to find Grigor in the village," she implored. "He knows about animals and he might be able to suggest a cure."

Ivan went off as he was told to fetch Grigor, while Ludmilla and Lydia put wet towels around Rayka's head and gently stroked her. Rayka, of course, did not greatly improve, and she kept up the low mooing. She seemed in a lot of discomfort.

Grigor eventually arrived and was immediately taken to Rayka's side. He looked at her closely, examined her tongue and her eyes, and smelt her breath. It was foul.

Then he walked around the paddock, went down on his haunches and poked at something with his finger and brought it up to his lips, smacking them.

"Ah," he said. "Now I know," and he broke into a smile. He came back to the family standing anxiously around. "You know what's wrong with that darn cow?" he said. "She's drunk."

"Don't be silly," said Lydia angrily, thinking that he was trying to joke.

"No, truly, she is drunk. Come, I'll show you." He led them away from Rayka to an area in the paddock where there were a number of mounds—the leftover waste from the vodka fermentation process. Ivan was in the habit of emptying the solids left from the distillation at the bottom of the yard, later to be dug into the earth and used as fertilizer.

"Of course, I understand it all," said Ivan with a laugh, and turned to Lydia. "Rayka's been eating the fermentation mash where I've been emptying it, and obviously she had more than was good for her this time."

"There must still be a lot of alcohol left in the mash to make her so sick," Grigor offered, "because it would take quite a few bottles of vodka to have any effect on an animal her size."

The family heaved a sigh of relief in unison. They saw the funny side of getting their cow drunk, and now they made her as comfortable as possible, bringing her a few pails of water she seemed to need rather badly, just like any human with a hangover.

As summer drew to a close and days turned short with colder evenings, Lydia and Ivan were busier than ever, trying to build up sufficient supplies for the coming winter. Once the blizzards started to blow across the steppe and temperatures dropped to minus ten or twenty degrees, movement, if not impossible, would be impractical, with meters of snow covering the roads. Ivan got to work, cutting grass to produce hay and buying as much as possible from the local peasant community wheat harvest. Gradually the cellar piled up with stored vegetables.

One autumn day, Lydia was on a fairly long bartering trip to acquire potatoes from a farmer who was harvesting a large crop. Darkness was not far away, the wind was blowing, and she did not relish the four-hour walk back.

The peasant said, "Look, why don't you wait a while. I have to deliver a load to the main storage depot in town, and I'll be passing your house. If you like, I'll give you a lift home."

Lydia didn't need to be asked a second time. The peasant's wife made her a cup of tea made from local herbs—the real thing was unobtainable—and she sipped it comfortably while waiting.

Finally he was ready. "Well, hop on. We have to get going—we don't want to be caught in the dark." Lydia climbed up on top of the cart next to the peasant, and they set off along the dusty, rutted road. For a while, they plodded along uneventfully, chatting about the harvest and the weather, and the coming winter. There was some talk that there was very heavy fighting around Stalingrad.

Lydia was very uneasy about that. "I have two sisters in Stalingrad. I only hope they survive. I suppose the best thing would be for the city to fall quickly before it's destroyed."

"Well," said the peasant doubtfully, "I wouldn't expect Stalin to give up his namesake. He's more likely to defend that of all cities to the last blood of his last soldier."

Just at that moment, they heard a screech of a car come around a bend of the road. As the car came near to the cart, the driver, who had no thought of slowing down for the cart, hooted the horn and shouted to get out of the way. The poor peasant was caught by surprise. He tried to get off the road, but the horse reared and bolted, frightened by the roaring steel beast that seemed to be after him. The horse, unused to motor vehicles, was spooked by the speed, the blast of the horn, and the roar of the engine. The cart ran for fifty meters on the side of the road, half on and half off, and then the outside wheels hit a rut, and it tipped over to the left, throwing both Lydia and the peasant onto the road. The Germans, having a clear run, accelerated off into the distance, laughing at the sight.

The peasant landed awkwardly in some low bushes at the side of the road, but apart from scratches and scrapes, and a few cuts, he was not seriously hurt. He looked around and saw Lydia. She was unconscious, lying in an awkward position, with one leg bent at the knee and folded underneath her and both arms out. At the side of her head, just above the left temple, was a large bruise and swelling, and the skin was lacerated by the jagged surface of the rock she must have struck. Blood was oozing out of the wound. She lay absolutely still.

"My God," the peasant said crossing himself a number of times. "I think she's dead." He felt her pulse and found a slow, weak heartbeat. He didn't know what to do—no ambulance or medical or hospital service existed here. Every doctor was at the front, and all the medical equipment was with them.

The peasant managed to capture the horse, and with the help of some nearby workers, he righted the cart. Once he had loaded the potato cargo back, he laid the unconscious Lydia on top, like one of the potato sacks. One of the older women workers sat beside her to support her head, and they made their painful way back into town. Lydia did not wake up. When they got to the house, Ivan rushed out, and with the three of them, carried her inside and into bed.

The peasant told him the whole sad story, and went off to make his delivery and take the woman worker home.

Ivan was beside himself with worry as he boiled up some water and washed the wounds with boiled water and drops of Condy's crystals, the standard antiseptic they kept for emergencies over the years. He wasn't so worried about the wound or the bleeding as the fact that Lydia was still unconscious. He could not rouse her in any way. She just laid there and moaned from time to time. Ivan tore up a clean towel, bandaged her head, and made her as comfortable as he could. There was really nothing more he could do but only hope she would eventually recover.

Panicked thoughts rushed through his head now about the future. They had a good partnership, and their complementary skills served them well through uncertain times, but should she die, he would have sole responsibility for looking after two children as well as providing for everybody himself. It was likely to be too much for one man—particularly one constantly at risk of being identified as an ex-Red Army member. He despaired of losing Lydia, his life's companion and partner. And without her as their front, he was certain to be noticed and picked up by one side or the other.

Ludmilla took over some of Lydia's chores, such as milking the cow night and morning, and she tried to do some of the cooking, managing some very basic meals. In addition she had to look after Vala, still only a toddler who was constantly falling over, scratching himself, and demanding attention.

Ivan fed Lydia with light vegetable soup, carefully strained. She managed to swallow a little, with a lot of effort and paroxysms of coughing when it went the wrong way. In a few hours, she developed a fever and the infected wound filled with pus. Ivan bathed it twice a day with the Condy's crystals and washed away the infected matter. He knew some first aid procedures from his training in the army and massaged her body daily.

After three days of uncertainty and constant nursing, Lydia appeared to improve a little. Her color was better, her breathing more even and not as labored, and her temperature settled. The next morning, she opened her eyes and woke up, moaning and groaning.

"What's wrong? Where am I? What am I doing here?" She raised her left hand and felt her head, which was still bandaged.

"Thank God, we're glad to see you alive," said Ivan. "We thought you would never wake up. You've been unconscious for four days, and we could only keep you alive with vegetable soup."

Lydia groaned and moaned a bit, and Ivan told her the whole story.

"I can't remember a thing, you know," said Lydia weakly. "I can't remember getting on top of the cart, or falling off. I can't even remember anything that day or leaving the house. I don't even know what day it is now."

"Well, I can tell you, it is the fifteenth of October, and not that far to go to winter."

Lydia was galvanized into trying to get up, but her head turned dizzy and she fell back on the bed. "Oh, my head," she groaned. "I feel like I'm going off the planet, I'm so dizzy."

"Never mind, you just lie there, have something to eat. You rest and get your strength back, and before you know it, you will be as good as new."

During the next two or three days, she did improve somewhat, but she was not quite the same. She regained her strength after she managed to start eating, the pain was not quite as bad in her head, and when she got out of bed, she was not as dizzy. But she was not back to normal. Lydia was no longer the happy, spontaneous woman who just went about doing what she had to as best she could, with gusto and enthusiasm.

She had become withdrawn, less confident, and worst of all, she began to show periods of sudden irritability and flare-ups of angry frustration. Poor Ludmilla and Vala got quite a few beltings as a result of this, and several times Ivan had to intervene and rescue Ludmilla from punishment.

The children were very careful now not to annoy her, speaking quietly in whispered tones. Ivan, too, worried that this change in character might be permanent.

Over the next few weeks, Lydia recovered her full strength and resumed her own chores. With the help of Ludmilla and Ivan, she completed the harvesting of all their vegetables, and packed them away for the winter, and did any pickling, putting cucumbers in jars with vinegar, brine, and herbs. She also made sauerkraut, another way of preserving food for winter. This was a process of cutting up cabbage into thin slices, pickling it with vinegar, salt, and herbs and then packing it into large containers, a small keg for choice.

By the end of all the effort, they were better prepared for winter than any year in recent memory. But the second major problem of 1942 was surfacing. The German Army was bogged down at Stalingrad. By November there was no longer any "good" news coming from the German side, with the whole army held up on the western side of the Volga River and slowly cut off from support. The temperature dropped and snow fell heavily, with cold winds cutting across the steppe.

On Lydia's forays into the town, she occasionally talked to some of the German soldiers. What they let slip filled her with misgivings. It seemed the Germans might even be beaten in Stalingrad: by the beginning of the New Year, Lydia even began to fear that German rule was not going to continue in Ukraine and western Russia. The unthinkable was again a possibility. The communists might come back.

By the end of February the Soviet return was virtually certain. For Lydia and Ivan, there was no choice.

They had to go.

* * * *

Chapter 12

Good-bye to Ukraine

This time, though, there was an easier way out. Because of the
Wehrmacht's constant demand for healthy conscripts, if German
industry was to keep running, it needed a steady influx of workers
from the occupied countries. The foreigners took the young Germans' place in factories involved in the war effort, on the railways
and particularly on the farms. Normally the Wehrmacht brought
in the slave workers through routine detention raids in occupied
cities, going through the homes and taking all the young people
they could find over fourteen, male or female, west to Germany.

But now the system was suddenly extended in the wake of
the Stalingrad disaster. The Dnieperpropeterovsk town commandant issued a proclamation blazoned on posters round the
town and on circulating trucks that an evacuation order had been

given: people in general were to be evacuated west, as long as they were fit and able-bodied, to work for the Reich. The evacuees would be allowed only one large suitcase each, and they should bring warm clothing and bedding.

Ivan and Lydia decided immediately to leave in the evacuation. They had mixed feelings about it even so, because leaving the home, their garden, animals, and stores of supplies they gathered for the winter for so long would hurt, but they had no choice in the face of the looming Soviet return. Once the communists got back, they would be labeled traitors, saboteurs, and collaborators with the Germans, even if all they had really done was try to survive in a very difficult environment. Ivan's Red Army background would inevitably bring a charge of desertion and immediate execution, even without a trial. Lydia's *Volksdeutsch* origin would mean either death or transport back to Siberia, a revisited fate that she could only contemplate with horror. The children would be unlikely to survive once the family was separated. Ivan and Lydia were both healthy and strong, and the Germans would happily take them for the factories.

"We have to think carefully what to take with us," Lydia said. "I think the baby bath is essential. Apart from anything else, it's pretty well provided us with a living."

Ivan agreed with that and worked out a way to make a canvas covering to contain it and their bedding. Lydia made up two eiderdowns with duck feathers she had traded from farmers, for extra winter warmth. This was enclosed in a canvas cover with handles, so that it could be carried as a suitcase. Another suitcase held a change of clothing for each person, a few kitchen utensils, and a battered pot, which had been with the family for years. As much as possible of the remaining space was filled with food: a large piece of smoked pork belly fat, and some buckwheat, a staple diet similar to rice when cooked in water.

"What are we going to do with the cow?" asked Lydia. "If we leave her here, she'll either starve or be killed."

"Send her back to the people we got her from, if they are staying here. They'll look after her again."

They left everything else apart from a few tools, which Ivan packed away. All their other possessions were given to friends and neighbors. And they were ready to leave.

The next morning, they rose before sunrise, dressed and checked the luggage, and then had breakfast. Nobody was very hungry and Ludmilla was quiet and glum. They were leaving their secure home for a trip into the unknown. It was strangely quiet—the normal noises of the home were absent. The cow was no longer there mooing for attention. Their few chickens had been disposed of weeks before. They loaded the luggage onto the little handcart that had served them well over the last few years. They took a last look at the thatched cottage, locked the doors, and made their way slowly into town to the assembly point nominated by the Germans.

Other people collected slowly and stood in line quietly. No one was happy. Although most of them were volunteering to go and work in Germany, they went only out of fear of the Russians' return. Not all of them were *Volksdeutsch*.

As the line moved slowly forward to the processing desk, Lydia held the two children close to her. She was thinking of a previous "repatriation," when the Jews were doing this very thing, collecting at the assembly point with their precious possessions and then disappearing, never to be seen alive again. She half-wondered if the same fate could possibly await them.

They reached the processing desk, and the uniformed bureaucrat asked for their papers.

Ivan handed them over. He opened them and had a quick look. "Ah, *Volksdeutsch*," he said, "right." He filled out a form, stamped it, and gave it to the family. Turning to Lydia, he said, "As *Volksdeutsch*, of course, your whole family is entitled to go to Germany."

The German nodded as he handed them their travelling documents and returned their I.D. "It is a great thing you're doing for the Reich, for the Fatherland, going back to support the war effort against the Bolsheviks."

"*Danke*," said Lydia, taking the papers, thinking silently that they didn't want to go anywhere, just run from the Russians and certain destruction.

They were told to wait while the rest of the people were processed, and then a German soldier led them to the railway line. A long train waited there. It had one passenger carriage in the front and nothing but freight cars behind. Its passengers were only human cargo, factory input like the coal and minerals stripped out of Ukraine and sent back to Germany.

The family groups were allocated their wagon, and ordered to climb in with their luggage. There was no platform, and there was a problem getting the women and the luggage up. Six families were allocated to their wagon, about eighteen people, men, women, and children, in an area no bigger than a large room. The wagon was cold and dark, with sliding doors on each side in the middle, but no windows. Horizontal vents in the top of the sides let in slivers of light and air. A bundle of fresh straw had been dumped in a corner for bedding. This was no luxury trip, Lydia thought, but they could put up with a bit of discomfort for the sake of safety. It shouldn't take long to get to Germany.

"Come on Ivan, let's take this corner spot," she told her husband, and they shoved the luggage into one of the corners of the wagon. It began to get crowded as the other people came aboard. Lydia knew some of the other families already, and started to chat with them, while Ivan introduced himself to the men. There were six children in the wagon, and the rest were adults. Apart from Vala, still only two, the children were all between nine and twelve, Ludmilla's age group.

Lydia noticed there were no facilities whatsoever, not even a toilet—nothing but the mound of fresh straw and a four-gallon drum with the top cut off.

"They're shipping us just like animals," said one of the women. "I'm not sure if I'll be able to cope with this."

"Don't worry," Lydia said. "It's only about four or five days to Germany. We'll be there in no time, and we can put up with a bit of discomfort."

When everybody had settled, they began to organize themselves, and set out operating rules to avoid conflict and run the wagonload smoothly.

Natalie, the woman in the next family, was quite adamant. "First thing to work out is the toilet routine." She was much younger than the rest, only twenty-five, without children. She was still shy, and the toilet problem obviously worried her greatly. The other women agreed, and while the men were less concerned, they left the arrangements to their wives. Natalie rigged up a makeshift cubicle near the door with blankets hung from rope between the ventilating shafts.

The other women divided the straw between the families and heaped up makeshift mattresses covered with blankets. Even in such grim surroundings, a family space, ownership, and belonging were important.

It took hours to load the train. The men stood talking near the door, watching the activity outside and smoking if they had any tobacco. Ivan opened one of his bottles of homemade vodka and poured a portion for each of the six men, and as the train finally started to jerk out of the station, belching steam and smoke and blowing the whistle, they drank a toast. "*Nasdorovia*," said Ivan, "a safe journey for us all."

The women showed less bravado. Some cried softly, as they waved white handkerchiefs to friends or parents who had not been allowed to go with them. Some prayed for safety for themselves and their children, crossing themselves. One or two were carrying little parcels of the dark black soil of Ukraine, to keep some part of a land they loved dearly.

Lydia did not feel that way, because as far as she was concerned, her birthplace in Lvov was part of Poland, not Ukraine, nor was she leaving any parents behind there either. She had always felt that she was an outsider: when she first arrived there after losing her mother she couldn't even speak the language.

She longed to establish her roots in the country where she belonged, and she now believed that was Germany. At least it was
a destination of safety and security, compared to the Russian
communists.

It was, alas, nothing like the efficient five-day trip Lydia had
so confidently predicted. By this time, the German railway system was badly disorganized after years of Allied bombing, and
the delays and day-long standstills were continual. They were
a low-priority cargo, so that the train was continually shunted
off the main line to wait at sidings for hours—sometimes for
days. Even getting to and from Siberia had been quicker than
this.

Life in the train wagon took on its own rhythm as it all
dragged on. After a time, the train almost felt like normal life to
the people aboard, rather as passengers on a long liner voyage
come to think of the ship as home and its routines as the pattern
of their native environment.

The families began with plenty of food they had prepared
especially for the journey, sausages or *salo,* a pork belly product
with high energy content highly prized in Russia and Ukraine,
loaves of dark rye bread, and, if people were lucky enough, a
bottle of vodka. The women made friends and chatted about
their family, children, and friends, and where they came from.
They sometimes nibbled on sunflower seeds, which, at this time
of the year, late August, were plentiful and a rich supply of nutri-
ents. They bit the seed with the front teeth, split the husk, and ate
the kernel, which tasted like a nut. It was such a popular custom
that many old women had indentations worn into the front teeth
from biting the sunflower seeds, and even Lydia showed a little
wear on her otherwise perfect front teeth, at the young age of
thirty-three.

The men talked about the political situation, forever con-
jecturing on the outcome of the war and the strength and
weaknesses of the German and the Red Army. Ivan was quiet
during these sessions. He kept his counsel to himself, in case
he revealed his background in the Red Army. He just said that

he was in electricity distribution engineering, which was the truth, and had escaped call-up for the army because it was an essential industry.

The days were still very warm, in the high twenties, and the wagon warmed once the sun was up and slowly grew suffocating with all the people in such close proximity. They left the side doors open to allow a breeze to come through. The mothers continually worried that the children would fall out and kept nagging them to keep away from the doors. By this time, the children were irritable as well from being cooped up in the confined space.

Progress was intolerably slow. In addition to the bombing, partisans targeted the railways to sabotage, and blew up a line whenever they could. Delays were constant as crews went in to clear the line of the tangled trains, bodies, and cargoes.

The families' food supplies ran out after about ten days, even with frugal rationing, and hunger started to become an issue. All the Germans provided was a kind of gruel with a piece of stale, hard bread, just enough to keep the "cargo" alive until the end of the journey.

And by now the sideline delays were lasting for days or even weeks. The occupants took to making a camp outside during the waits, building fires and foraging for food. The few guards allotted to the train did not bother to keep them aboard, since the travelers were reluctant volunteers for the trip. In any case, there was nowhere safe to run or escape in the isolated areas where they stopped, and anyone foolish enough to run away would get killed either by the partisans or the Germans as an escaped prisoner, if they did not die of starvation. The men went to the forest and foraged for anything edible, coming back with berries and mushrooms and even the occasional rabbit. It made a welcome addition to the bread ration and the bran gruel. But everybody was losing weight rapidly.

If the train was marooned in a farming region, the foraging had better results. The fields had now been harvested, and there were leftover potatoes under the ground, some sheaves of wheat left behind, or the occasional turnip or cabbage the harvesters had missed.

Vala started to lose weight. He needed protein, fat, and vitamins for growth. Lydia began to worry that he might not survive if the journey went on for too long. But Ivan found a temporary lifesaver on one foraging expedition. He came back, excitedly calling out to Lydia. "Look what I've got, Lydia. Come quick."

When Lydia peered out the wagon door, Ivan was dragging a nanny goat behind him. Her face lit up: this could be a boon for Vala.

"Where did you find her, Ivan?"

"Oh, grazing happily in one of the forest clearings. She wasn't very afraid, and no trouble to catch, but I had a devil of a job dragging her here. She just did not want to come."

"No wonder, she probably has a kid, and she was fighting furiously not to be separated. We could perhaps find the kid as well if you go back later." The goat had a partially-filled udder, which indicated offspring and meant milk for Lydia's children in the meantime. They tied a long piece of rope to her and tethered her to a small tree near the railway line. She ate anything—weeds, low-lying leaves of the beech trees growing at the start of the forest, or any grass at all. It was lovely to have an animal close by again, making noises and braying playfully from time to time. Ludmilla, of course, was given the job of guarding the goat and making sure it wasn't hijacked by some other members of the train. Lydia talked to the guard who was always on hand. He was a nice young man, fairly friendly, and always said hello. He understood that some of those people were of German origin, part of his own race, and he was there only to keep order and act perhaps as a protector, rather than a jail keeper. However, like every soldier in Ukraine, he had the power to shoot and kill anyone who appeared a threat to himself or to the German occupation.

"Good morning," said Lydia pleasantly, smiling. "We have some good news. My husband found a goat and I think we can milk it. Can we have your permission for this to be used as a milk supply for the very young children on the train?"

The guard knew that there were a number of young children on the train, and that they were starting to show signs of malnutrition. This new development was positive, if it kept the mothers happy and they had some milk for their children. He gave permission straightaway.

Lydia realized that trying to keep the milk to herself would create tensions, and probably would mean the goat being stolen or killed, or cause fighting between the groups. She called a mothers' meeting to coordinate a joint approach to give everyone a share.

As it worked out, each child got just over half a cup of milk, morning and night, which was just sufficient to reduce their physical deterioration. The goat became a symbol of hope for the whole train. But it was certainly not a real solution, and it did not last for long.

Vala got sick. One morning he woke in an irritable mood. He cried without any reason, and whimpered and at times screamed as if in pain. Lydia didn't know what was happening: this was unusual for her son, normally a quiet and well-behaved child.

As she tried to soothe him, he suddenly vomited. A short time later, he had a watery bowel movement. This was no mild tummy upset, but serious. Gastroenteritis can be lethal in a young child already suffering malnutrition, particularly without any hospital facilities. She suddenly realized that her only son, the miracle who had arrived after six stillbirths and late miscarriages without a doctor, the child she struggled for years to conceive and for whose survival she fought for continually, was on the verge of slipping away.

All her frustrations and impotence exploded into rage. Her child was dying and the train was stuck in that desolate ungodly place—if she could only get it moving to its destination, things might be right.

Lydia jumped down from the wagon without using the steps, stumbled, and fell forward on her knees and hands. She didn't feel the pain and or even notice her bleeding hands and knees. She rushed to the guard patrolling slowly around the train and screamed at him, half in German and half Ukrainian.

"Stop, get the train going! What are we doing here? We are all starving and dying." She grabbed hold of the guard's arm and started pushing him. He was taken completely by surprise. He really knew Lydia well, often talked with her, and knew she considered herself German. Out of the blue, here she was completely out of control—and the racket was attracting other transportees to the scene. The guard wasn't intimidated by this woman, but the others could be a problem. He was on his own, and his single pistol would be no match if they rushed him.

"Stop this at once, you idiot. Stop or I'll shoot!" But that would have made things even worse. He hesitated. In the nick of time, Ivan saw what was happening and ran up.

"Don't shoot," he pleaded. "Don't shoot, she is *Volksdeutsch*—something must have gone seriously wrong. Please don't shoot." Then he grabbed Lydia by the arm and pulled her away. "Don't be a fool, Lydia. Think of the children. What will become of them if you get shot?" "Children" was the magic word. For herself Lydia didn't care anymore; life was one long, hard, continuous struggle to survive and constant anxiety about an unpredictable future. Oblivion was not unattractive in those circumstances. But she could not leave her children facing the same dreary landscape, as orphans.

She collapsed like a pricked balloon and started sobbing uncontrollably. Two of the women led her away, talking to her soothingly. The guard was relieved. He thought this might have been a narrow escape for the woman and for himself. He replaced the pistol in the holster and tried to look in control of the situation.

"Danke, danke shön." Ivan took him by the hand and shook it thankfully, and followed Lydia into the wagon.

Ludmilla cleaned up Vala in the baby bath, and Lydia gave him some cooled boiled water to sip. He managed to keep that down and his pain seemed to ease.

By the time they settled him back in bed, other women were coming round to report their own children had started vomiting. Clearly there had been something wrong with the afternoon's milk. It was either infected or the goat had eaten some noxious weed.

"We can't take the chance of this happening again," said Lydia. "If the children are sick only for a few days, the way they are it would be the death of them."

"Well, what shall we do?" asked the mothers.

Lydia just sat quietly with her head bowed, drained and exhausted.

"I don't care. I don't know what to do—you can do what you like." She was usually the forceful leader of the group, but tonight a decision was beyond her.

Ivan suggested, "Well, if we can't use the goat's milk, we can use the meat." They agreed the goat would be slaughtered, and the meat distributed.

Ivan went to see the guard again and apologized for the earlier trouble. "And would you mind if we slaughtered the goat and distributed the meat?"

"No, do whatever you want to. I'm sick of the whole episode," exclaimed the guard. The affair had left a rather unpleasant feeling, and all he wanted was for everybody to get back to normal.

So that was the end of the nanny goat.

Ivan called to some of the other men from the wagon. "Come on lads, let's do it straightaway before they change their minds." The animal was duly slaughtered and the meat divided between the families. Ivan even gave a kilo of rump to the guards, who were very grateful. Their own rations were not much better than the transportees' by this stage.

That night there was a welcome addition to the normal supper. Most people made soup from their meat portion with a few vegetables and a little bran. It made a delicacy that they had not tasted or smelled for a considerable time.

By the end of November, it was obvious the train was not going much further before the onset of winter. Authorities decided to halt for the rest of the cold weather, and issued instructions to stop in a small town in the Carpathian Mountains of western Ukraine, where the passengers would be billeted with the townspeople. They were to be employed as much as possible in productive local activities.

The area here looked much more prosperous and cared for than eastern Ukraine. The Russian occupation only began there in 1939, and it had so far escaped the devastating collective farms and the pell-mell industrialization that had ravaged the east. The scenery was strikingly different to the vast steppes in the southeast, which were covered with monotonous fields of wheat or grasslands as far as the eye can see, occasionally interrupted by the rivers draining the area. Here there were dozens of small white-painted villages scattered over the countryside, with neat farms on the lower ground and oak, elm, and birch trees covering the hillsides above. Higher up in the mountains were pines, junipers, and occasional isolated green clearances.

The town was tiny, with only one main street with some shops and tradesmen. It was on the side of a wide shallow river where the water cascaded over worn river stones.

Ivan and Lydia were billeted with an elderly couple whose son had been missing since the start of German occupation in June 1941. It was a luxury to be in a house again. The fire in the kitchen burned quietly, with an occasional crackle, throwing out warmth through the whole room. Thick mud walls provided excellent insulation, and in comparison with the train, it was a cozy heaven. There were two other small bedrooms, and the elderly couple occupied one of these. Ivan's family billeting was a forceful intrusion in this family's home, but the Germans had made it quite clear that no objections would be tolerated. Lydia spoke to the woman.

"We are sorry to intrude on you like this, but we are so thankful that you can provide us with accommodation. We have been travelling for over three months in that cursed train, and now the snow is starting. Any longer and we would have been frozen."

"We understand your trouble," the woman said. "These days you really have no say in what is happening in your life. First we had the Poles lording it over us for years, then in 1939 the Russians came and told us what to do and not to do, and now the Germans have been running us since 1941. All we want is to be left alone and lead our own lives. Your presence will not inconvenience us too much, but you'll need to find your own food. We have none to spare."

Lydia went to her suitcase and rummaged around. She brought out a large colorful headscarf with bright red flowers intermingled with blue and green motifs. She gave this to the lady, saying, "Please accept this gift from me as a token of our thanks."

The lady was pleased, and she smiled and her eyes sparkled. It was a long time since she had received anything new, and the headscarf would keep the wintry wind out of her ears.

"Thank you, but you shouldn't have. You must have very little of your own, having to travel with such limited luggage."

And after that exchange, everyone got along quite well.

The town had two principal industries. It was the repair and maintenance center for this part of the railway line, and also the site of the local sugar-beet processing factory, which normally exported its finished sugar product to the rest of Ukraine, Poland, or Russia. At this point, however, it was supplying only the German Army. The Germans consequently wanted the factory operating at maximum capacity, but the town population had dwindled in the war, and labor was too short to run the plant at full bore. This was why the transportees' train had been diverted there for the winter months. Any workers the sugar-beet factory didn't need were to carry out necessary repairs to the railway lines, fell trees in the forest, and bring lumber to the town for distribution. The German Army used vast quantities of wood for building camps, bridges, repairing railway lines, and so on, so both the lumber and the sugar the town produced were rated important to the war effort.

Ivan's skilled electrical experience automatically assigned him to the sugar mill, where the machinery was ancient and poorly maintained, and constantly needed repairs. He was continually busy. Lydia also went to the sugar mill as a process worker loading the sugar beets into a crushing plant. The work was very heavy, but she was strong and used to that.

Ivan, strange as it might seem, started enjoying himself. He was always happy working on repairs and maintenance, regardless of whether the problem was electrical or mechanical. He liked making things run. He got this plant to function properly, and even started a preventive maintenance and wiring replacement program to minimize future breakdowns.

And one other point immediately caught his attention there. Sugar beets were very high in plant sugar. In the production process, liquid was filtered from the crushed beets, and the water in this sugar-laden solution was then slowly evaporated to concentrate it to supersaturated level, so that as it cooled, crystals of sugar were precipitated. Now, if Ivan could manage to get access to the concentrated fluid, it would be a prime starting point to add his precious yeasts…and, presto, vodka.

By this stage, brewing illicit alcohol had virtually become Ivan's second career, and so essential to the family's survival in the process that he wasn't going to let this opportunity slip away.

One evening after the meal, he asked his host, the old man Taras, innocently, "There doesn't seem to be much alcohol, vodka, umm, in the town…Has anyone ever tried to make vodka from sugar beet?"

"No, it has always been brought in from outside," said the old man. "We don't have a great tradition of making vodka in the villages. Brewing was always the landlords' monopoly, and they were Poles. It was illegal for the peasants to make their own. The Jews owned the taverns, so between them and the landlords, the Ukrainian peasants were kept out. Not that it stopped us drinking, but drinking was an expensive pastime."

"I'll see what I can do about changing that," said Ivan.

Over the next few weeks, he gathered the essentials—copper pipes, pots, and vessels—to replicate his former home distillery. With the help of a few fellow workers, he worked out a way to siphon off some of the factory liquor for his own work at home. He was going to have to be careful to conceal the theft from the Germans. They'd call it sabotage, with the inevitable result if he was discovered.

In the evenings, he started to put together the new still in the house, with the enthusiastic help of the old owner, who was excited about the whole prospect of a domestic vodka plant.

"I can't wait to sample it," he kept saying, with a toothless grin. "Just what we need for this winter cold."

Ivan took the maintenance fitter into his confidence, and with his help installed a small, carefully obscured valve in the pipeline carrying the liquor to the evaporating units. This was in a corner of the factory, out of sight from other activities. He also got Lydia transferred to the cleaners. Her job was to go around and ensure that the factory area was clean and hygienic, constantly sweeping and washing the floors, meaning the guards and the other workers continually saw her walking around with buckets in her hands. It was simple to take a bucket to the corner of the factory where the valve was installed, with her brooms and mops over her shoulder, make sure no one was around, and partly fill it from the sampling valve.

It was easy to carry a bucket of the sugar-laden liquor past supervisors, German guards, and other workers, because it looked a completely normal thing for her to do. No one noticed anything missing; spillage and waste in the factory was far more than a bucket. Back at the old man's house, the baby bath was called back to its familiar second purpose in life. When Ivan had four or five buckets collected, he emptied them into the bath, added yeast, and covered the whole thing with a cloth. Soon the bubbles of carbon dioxide arrived to show the yeast was acting.

When the bubbles stopped, the brew went into the large steam-proof pot to boil, and the vapour condensed in copper pipe wound inside a cooling box packed with snow.

As the pot slowly boiled on the old stove, the old man and his wife waited with smiles on their faces. They were already enjoying all this. When the first drops started to fall, Ivan took the first taste. He smacked his lips with appreciation and just said, "Mmm...beautiful." He handed over the spoon to the old man and said, "*Poproboy*" (taste it). The old man filled up the spoon.

"Ah," he said, "just heavenly." He closed his eyes, and his face wrinkled in appreciation. Vala, watching all this activity, realized the adults were trying some tasty food. "*Poproboyu, poproboyu*" (I taste it), he piped up. Ivan grinned and gave him the spoon with a few drops of vodka. As the warm liquid hit Vala's taste buds, his face screwed up immediately with a grimace of disgust and distaste from the liquid burning his mouth. The grown-ups burst into laughter. This episode became a favorite family anecdote.

"Well, this expert taster doesn't seem to approve of the product, but never mind—I'm sure the drinkers will fully appreciate this brew," said Ivan. His product was as good as ever, and while it might not have been quite up to professional standards, it certainly was a good wartime substitute. Ivan was able to produce about ten bottles each cycle, and one or two cycles every week.

Lydia regularly dropped one or two bottles to the German guards, for goodwill. Ivan's colleagues also received a regular bottle, as they helped with the process, and the old man and woman tasted the product whenever they felt inclined. The rest of it was used for bartering food: there was still a reasonable amount in the village, since the farmers here were not collectivized and the Germans could not confiscate all they produced, with the hills and forests providing good hiding areas. Deep searches were not made for fear of partisan attacks. The extra food built up the family's condition over the winter months.

Then, some weeks after the process started, the old man had a visitor very late at night. Lydia and Ivan were woken up by soft voices talking just outside the door. After a little while, the other man disappeared as quietly as he had arrived. In the morning, Ivan noticed new tracks in the snow leading up the hill to the forest edge, and they disappeared into the forest.

"Taras, who was here last night?" he asked the old man. Taras looked a bit worried and concerned.

"Yes, there was someone here," he answered, but he would not elaborate.

After the meal that evening, Taras lit his pipe and sat thoughtfully by the fire. The atmosphere was congenial and warm, with the fire burning strongly and the comforting aroma of fermenting yeast from the distillation plant dripping vodka into a bottle.

In the end, Taras nodded to Ivan and said, "I really have to talk to you about something important."

Ivan sat down beside him and said, "There's a problem, isn't there, Taras?"

"Yes. Last night I did have a visitor. I know I can trust you now: it was my son. He is part of the partisan group in the mountains, and he came to warn me that they planned to attack the village. This area is so lightly guarded, and they think they can blow up part of the railway line and any rolling stock that's there, and also destroy the sugar plant. He just wanted to make sure that I would not be around when this occurred, and would not be hurt."

"But he can't do that!" Ivan exclaimed. "That plant is running twenty-four hours a day, and the workers there would be hurt and killed, including me and Lydia, and many of our friends and your friends."

"I know that," said Taras, "but in his opinion, they are all collaborators anyway, working for the Germans."

"They are just working. They are not getting paid. All they're getting is a lousy food allocation. If they don't work they will be shot. That is hardly being a collaborator."

"Who knows what a collaborator is in these crazy times. A collaborator is a collaborator if he is defined to be one by the man who holds the gun."

"Well, it's all hopeless then. We will probably get killed by our own countrymen in the near future. I might as well get drunk on what's left of the vodka, and forget our worries," he said sadly, as he reached out for a bottle.

"Not so fast," said the old man. "We've still got some hope of averting this tragedy. I don't want my son near the Germans, involved in this stupidity, just as much as you don't want partisans blowing up the plant. Maria and I are sick with worry.

"I explained to him what we were doing here, producing vodka, and he was very interested. He says it's highly prized by the partisans—about the only thing that keeps them warm in the dreadful conditions up there in the hills. They can't light fires if

Germans are in the area, and they are continually being hounded by the Gestapo. When he discovered that we are actually producing vodka here, he decided that this would be so useful to the partisans that they might be prepared to change their target in exchange for a steady supply."

"You mean all the vodka we produce will go to the partisans?"

"Not all," retorted Taras. "I'm sure they won't mind if we have a nip or two to keep us warm, but the majority of the production will be required for them. They would consider this as a contribution to their war effort, second in importance only to guns and ammunition."

"Well, that settles it. We really have no choice. But we'll increase the production as much as we can, and we'll still have a few bottles to trade."

Ivan's new distillation system handled that problem easily, and all he had to do was boil the pot longer, but he did have to increase the brewing capacity—that came next. He cut a wooden keg normally used to catch water from the gutters of the house in half to make two vats. Lydia had to collect extra buckets of liquor from the sugar plant. During the evenings and nights, Ivan supervised the fermentation process, and the old man and his wife continued the distillation process. Ludmilla looked after Vala, keeping him occupied while their parents were busy.

They were making a full contribution to both war efforts, sugar for the Germans and vodka for the partisans. They weren't quite sure who they were collaborating with, Germans or partisans, but each side would find a good excuse to shoot them if their activities came to light. In reality, all they were trying to do was stay alive.

When the snow started to thaw, they resumed the trek to the west. Ivan and Lydia packed up the precious baby tub and their other belongings, and trooped to the station.

Ivan left his replicated distillation equipment with the old man, except for the baby bath. Taras had great plans for continued vodka production. He still had a ready market in the town, even though there was no profit in sales to the partisans. He came along with the family to the embarkation point, carrying some bags stuffed with pork belly fat and sausages.

This time the train was more congested. All the previous travelers were rounded up, apart from a few who had died over winter and crammed into a train only half the previous size. They had room only to lie down, and even that was crowded.

The winter's rest and improved food had invigorated Ivan and Lydia. Now they were keen to complete the journey without more delays. Finally the train got under way with a long whistle and puffs of smoke from the locomotive. Slowly it gained momentum and started again on the long journey west. A few people stood by the track waving good-bye, and the old man waved with a smile on his face, no doubt thinking of his inherited distillation plant and the benefits that would flow from it.

Ivan waved good-bye to the tiny town that never ever knew how he and his baby bath had saved it from the partisans' fury.

* * * *

Chapter 13

Germany

My earliest memory is having soot blowing into my eyes. I was about three years old, and my mother was holding me by my thighs in a crouched position, with her arms supporting me under my armpits. I was slightly over the edge of a train wagon as we were slowly making our way up a mild incline. My pants were down, and she was encouraging me to go to the toilet. Some potty training! On the other hand, it is quite a suitable way to enter this particular story.

"Hurry up, hurry up, please," she implored. "There might be a tunnel coming up."

I just sat there looking at the scenery. Most of it was a thick forest of pine trees with an occasional small clearing or stream, but it was a diversion for me, as this was the only time when I could look outside the wagon doors. It was still too cold to keep them open more than a crack.

We were on our way to Erfurt, the capital of Thuringia, which later became East Germany. My world consisted of a small corner of the goods wagon where Ludmilla, now about eleven years, and my parents rested on some hay covered with a tarpaulin. There were no other children in this wagon, and most of the adults were young single people who, like us, were being sent back to Germany to help the war effort. Some were just children wrenched from their parents at the age of fourteen or fifteen, going to Germany to work on farms or in factories.

The days dragged on, with nothing to do but sit there listening to the adults talk. From time to time, someone started a sad song and the others joined in. They all knew the words. That was pleasant and soothing, and I could drift away to sleep during these sessions.

There were a few men who made music with a thin paper and comb, resulting in a pleasant melody, and they accompanied the singing. The voices were better than the reedy music. The men had very deep voices, and the women high and bright. Sometimes there were even happy songs, even though they were leaving their homes—but afterwards many would need to wipe a tear from their eyes. They'd been singing about home, loves, and the bravery of the Cossacks in the old days. At the time, I could never see why anyone would cry over these things, because the stories seemed exciting to me.

I soon learned that if I closed my eyes during "potty training," the soot would not enter them, only build up in the corners. Mum cleaned it out with a handkerchief, together with any smudges on my face, licking the handkerchief and rubbing my face vigorously. I really hated that.

Early on in the trip, my mother had noticed a young girl who did not seem to be attached to anyone, looking lost and forlorn by herself. She seemed so sad that Mum could not help approaching her.

"Hello, little one, and what's your name?" she asked.

The girl looked up and smiled sadly at Lydia. "Natalka," she answered. She was a small and very thin girl who looked too young to be by herself, with curly dark hair cut short, and big brown eyes, emphasized by the thin face. She reminded Lydia of a sparrow in winter.

"Tell me about yourself. I didn't notice you on our train when we arrived at the village, but there seem to be a few new faces here this time."

"We were on a different train, but it was blown up not far from the village. Most of us survived relatively unharmed, because it was going slowly at the time, and once they repaired the line, they went on as far as the village and some of us remained, as there wasn't room for everybody, as some carriages were damaged beyond repair."

"Where do you come from, Natalka?" asked Mother.

"Poltava region. We lived in a small village not far from the town. My father was a teacher." Mother noticed that she was more sophisticated than the other peasant girls. Her clothing was better made, and she spoke without slang or dialect, seeming more self-assured and poised.

"So how come you are here by yourself? Is your family also going to Germany, or did they remain in Ukraine?"

It turned out Natalka had volunteered to go, when the Germans had given every family in the area a few hours to decide which member would be sent away for war work. The rest of the family was deeply committed to stay for children or other reasons. "If they had taken Father it would have left the whole family destitute—he's the only breadwinner."

She began to cry softly. My mother warmed to her and held her in her arms for a moment. It was the beginning of a long and friendly relationship.

I don't know how long the trip lasted—one day seemed the same as any other. But one evening the train slowed down and snaked slowly into a large compound. There was barbed wire in strong, straight lines, high fences, and gun-carrying soldiers everywhere. Towers stood along the fence lines, showing strong

lights illuminating the dark surrounds. Behind us another passenger said something about concentration camps, but I didn't
know the meaning of that.

We stopped next to some buildings and a soldier began banging on the wagon door, calling out, "*Raus, raus, schnell*" (Out,
out, quickly).

Everybody climbed reluctantly out of the wagons, Ludmilla
murmuring under her breath, "I hope we're not staying here.
This is a camp." She tried to pack her belongings, but the soldier
banged the side of the wagon and pointed with a stick, and said
to come straight out and not to worry about baggage.

They separated the men from the women. I went with Mother
and Ludmilla. We were led into a large room, and all the women
were told to strip. They did this rather reluctantly and with em-
barrassment, at first placing their hands in front of their bodies,
but soon they even stopped trying to be modest, as everybody
was completely stripped.

Everybody was quiet and somber, not knowing quite what
was happening.

Then we were led out of the dressing room into a room containing metal spray nozzles in the ceilings. The ground was made
of hard gray cobblestones, cold to the feet. They were given soap
that smelled like fly spray, I now realize, and then the nozzles went
on, spraying all the women with water that also had an unpleasant
smell. The women took the opportunity of washing all over, impossible in the train, and the lukewarm water was not unpleasant. Mum
seized the opportunity to thoroughly wash me, lathering my hair
and my face liberally with the soap. Things smelled awful, and I
really would have preferred her previous licks and rubs. Ludmilla
and Mother washed themselves thoroughly, and I could see that all
the women were enjoying this showering. Back in the other room
they were given towels to dry themselves. All our clothing must
also have been through some washing plant as well. It was still hot
and some leather items had been damaged by the heat.

Everyone went back to the train relaxed. It had been the first
proper wash that we'd had in many weeks. One of the young

men said, "They wanted to make sure that we didn't bring any dirty Russian lice into good clean Germany."

Once the train reloaded, we were on our way west again. The next evening, we were at Erfurt, pulling up slowly in a huge railway yard with many, many lines, wires, and posts stretching beyond vision.

I saw lots of steam trains, some stationary and some belching forth smoke and moving slowly, pushing or pulling other wagons. We pulled up in a quiet part of the yard and remained there for hours. We thought we would be staying the night, but without warning the guards started bashing on the doors, and again the familiar "*Raus, raus, schnell, schnell.*" We were already packed, because we knew we were close to the end of our journey. Dad jumped out and Mother passed me down to him on the ground, and passed the baggage. All the young people were lined up and marched off in a long line out of the train yard and down a road. It was late, still cold, and we were all tired, and I was tired. I was woken up out of my sleep and felt angry.

We were separated from the rest of the wagon and instructed to join another group of people. Most of them seemed older, with a few young people around Ludmilla's age. An old truck pulled up covered with tarpaulin, and we were ordered in with our bags. Apparently we were the *Volksdeutsch* passengers of the train, not slated to be treated quite as roughly as the labor conscripts from the Slav countries.

The truck drove away to an old building away from the station, two or three stories high, with dust and boards and rubbish everywhere. We were told to make ourselves comfortable: this was to be our home from now on. There were no guards or soldiers around, but the German who seemed to be in charge said that in the morning, he would return and everybody would be allocated to their workplace. Nobody unpacked their luggage. They just got their sleeping gear out and collapsed for the night, exhausted.

The next morning, the German who'd met us returned early. He was not a soldier, but he seemed to have a lot of authority, and was ordering the people around. He had something to do with "the labor allocation." Once he had everybody lined up, he questioned them one by one.

"You, what skills do you have? What can you do? Have you had any training?" He noted the answers on a clipboard in his hand. But when he came to the older women, he mumbled in disappointment, "Well, you're not much good for anything. You better stay here and look after the children."

Finally he addressed us all. "You have now been allocated to the various factories and work sites around the city of Erfurt. Now there are strict rules to be obeyed. Because you are *Volksdeutsch*, you will require no guards or supervision, and you will be going to and from your place of work by yourselves. You must never be late, or there will be strict punishment.

"But although you are *Volksdeutsch*, you are still Ukrainian, and you will be wearing these blue and yellow labels on your clothing. Sew these to all your clothing and you must not be seen without them—they are indications that you belong to the 'foreign workforce.'

"You can only leave this building to go to work. You are classified as part of the labor camp personnel, and all administrative arrangements will be done through them, including your food. You will be fed at work during the day, and go to the work camp for your main meal. The children can fetch their midday meal from the camp and bring it here.

"You will work six days a week, and Sunday will be a day of rest. You can't go to the market or shops, and you'll have no money anyway since you'll be fed and kept here free of charge, but you won't be paid for work.

"You are not to associate with the other ethnic groups, the Poles, Lithuanians, Jews, and so on. We have found in the past that you hate each other more than you hate us, and we had fighting break out when the groups mixed.

"In the meantime, get yourselves comfortable, as this will be your home. Don't go upstairs, as the building has been damaged by bomb blasts, and upstairs is unsafe. Remain in this area. It used to be an old hotel."

And finally the officious German turned on his heels and left.

"Where were you allocated?" Lydia asked Ivan.

"I'll be working in the railway repair shop," he replied. "And you?"

"The tank factory, making tank components."

"Looks like we changed our freedom for slavery. They will work us to death here for little food and no money," said Dad.

"Well, at least we are not going to get shot, and the Red Army won't catch you so Stalin can't have your blood."

Father hated this situation. He felt trapped, constrained, and he knew that he had nowhere to go. He either stayed there or risked the Russians shooting him out of hand as a deserter. Mum, on the other hand, showed a certain satisfaction at being in Germany at last. She was beginning to savor her *Volksdeutsch* status, and now she was keen to improve her command of the language and culture, and be a German in Germany instead of a hated German in Ukraine. She believed that there would be some corner here where she could, at last, be accepted. I realize now there were strains ahead I still don't like to think about.

The adults cleaned up the room, and swept and threw out some of the debris and boards. They made themselves comfortable in the particular corner where they chose to stay and unloaded their meager belongings. Some blankets were hung up to divide the large decrepit hotel foyer into private areas. Most had only a few blankets and a pillow, perhaps a change of clothing and a few utensils, such as spoons and pots.

Ivan still had his small tool kit, a hammer, chisel, small hacksaw, and a very sharp knife made from a hacksaw blade that he continually sharpened. He also had a long sharp tool consisting of a thick wire set in a wooden handle—a dowel, used for repairing shoes.

While the adults were unpacking and cleaning up, the children decided to explore outside. I couldn't believe that we were at last living in a house and not in that crowded, dark, cold railway wagon where we seemed to have spent forever. I could now run around and play and explore. On the other side of the street was a huge area filled with big dark buildings. Many of them were destroyed, however, and there was only rubble left, with partly demolished walls standing around like grotesque onlookers to the misery of the place. There was not a lot of activity in this area. Somebody was talking about this having been bombed out before. I wasn't sure what that meant.

Our house was on a large block of land with a garden at the front, overgrown and uncared for. Fencing and brickwork was destroyed and the windows were broken. The place was probably considered uninhabitable for most people, but to us it was like a palace after the months of crowded railway wagon travel. At the back was an area of overgrown grass and some trees, and there was also a small river flowing at the end of the block, overhung by some of the rooms. It was an old, interesting place. I thought I hadn't actually seen one more interesting. We had great fun playing and exploring, running around, shouting, throwing rocks into the river and playing chase. We had found a playground at last.

It was still cold, but the wind wasn't blowing and the watery sun was starting to warm the earth. There was no snow, and there were new, green shoots sprouting everywhere. The buds in the willow tree were starting to sprout, and there were some flowers starting to come out from what used to be an old garden. Things could be good here.

In the middle of the day, a man dressed in gray with a yellow and blue emblem on his chest arrived. He greeted everybody in a friendly manner and said that he had been sent to take them to the main work camp. He asked a few people where they came from to see if any came from his home region, and he asked eagerly what was happening in Ukraine. Any news that the people could give him was eagerly lapped up. He was a nice young man, tall, with blue eyes and fair hair, but very thin. We all followed him to the main work camp. I was carried by my mother on her shoulders as everybody was walking quickly, and Father also had to take a turn carrying me on his shoulders with my legs on each side of his neck—great fun. It was good to be walking on the firm earth instead of swaying and jarring in an old train wagon. The main camp consisted of a series of warehouses. We walked into the dining room, fitted with wooden tables. Everything was dark and black with tall ceilings that you could hardly see at the end. There were no windows, and the light bulbs were on long twisted wires with only one yellow bulb, which threw a meager light just underneath, leaving the rest of the room in shadows. The room was dark and unpleasant, and I did not like it. It was nearly empty. The guard explained that the people were working and were on day shift, and the people from night shift were sleeping and would have their meal later before leaving for work.

The group sat down at the tables, and the men went and fetched the food. This was one large steaming pot, and an old, battered tin tray with some pieces of bread. The pot contained soup, a green/gray mixture with small hard pieces of vegetables, which appeared to be turnips. Its only taste was salty. Even the bread had little taste. But everybody was hungry, so all the bread was eaten, but there was still some soup left when we finished. This was a work camp and this was the food.

Dad and Mum were very disappointed as they walked back to our quarters situated in the dilapidated hotel.

"Well, so this is the great *Deutsches Reich* for which we risked our life to come."

"I know it looks bad," said Mum. "But give it a chance. It might improve still. And we probably saved our lives coming here."

The rest of the day was spent getting settled in the large old hotel foyer. Dad explored the rest of the hotel and managed to find an old gas heater. With a little bit of fiddling, he got the old stoves working in the kitchen, and that was a bonus. The water was still running, we had heating facilities, and even the toilet was still working. This was certainly a luxury after the wagons. Mum got some pots organized, boiled some water, and before I knew what was happening, I was in a bath, getting scrubbed in our baby bath. Ludmilla was next, and the blanket, which was hung up in front, gave some privacy as she was starting to be shy. Before long there was a steady procession of boiling water being brought from the kitchen, and all the children and some of the adults had their first bath using our baby bath. This lifted the general mood considerably.

In the afternoon, the official came back with various papers, and gave these to every man and woman in the group assigned for work. He gave them instructions on how to get there and also special identity passes, allowing them to move between the place of work and the hotel.

That night we went to sleep early partly because everybody was exhausted and faced a very early start in the morning, but mainly because without electricity or other lights, there was nothing to do but go to sleep.

The next morning, the men and women got up about 5 a.m. and drifted off to work. I slept on. I woke up with the sun shining into the room through dirty windows, most cracked or broken with jagged holes. Three old women, an old man, and the children were still present. The old women were supposed to look after the children, but there was little hope of that. The older children—Ludmilla, two girls, and a boy about her age—were running around the yard exploring, and even ventured out into the other streets to explore the area. I was confined to the yard, and I wandered around poking at the corners to see what I could find, sitting and looking at the river flowing by in the backyard, under the general care of the old women sitting wearing their colorful headscarves and with bent backs. After a while, they saw that I was not getting into any trouble, and they left me alone to do my own thing. During the day, the older children were told to take some pots and go to the work camp kitchen to pick up some food. It took them about an hour, and by the time they brought the food back, the soup was already cold and tasted even worse cold than the night before. We were hungry, though, and we wolfed down the bread even though it was dry with no butter or other spreads.

At first everybody complained about the quality of the food, but as there was no change, they just ate it. The workers were not getting any money for their twelve hours of labor per day; the food was inadequate, and people were losing weight even more quickly because of the heavy working conditions. Everyone became more and more despondent.

The children also complained about having to carry the pots through the streets for their midday meal: they were heavy and the soup would splash out. Dad fixed that. He built a little trolley from some of the timber lying around, and he found an old pram, which provided the wheels. That pleased the children. They were playing with the cart when not using it to get the food, and often I would sit in the back and be pulled along by the other children. It was certainly something to do and occupied many hours around the streets, running up and down with the cart and getting rides down the hill.

I used to wander across this street whenever the old "babushkas" were not watching me, and poke around the demolished factory sites. There were all sorts of things one could find. Shiny pieces of aluminum, nuts, and bolts, and some of the items were even useful, such as the occasional spoon or fork. Pieces of shiny mirrors could be used as reflectors. I could sit on the steps of the hotel in a certain position and reflect the sun onto a wall or a garden. It was a game I played for hours.

Time passed, and one day melted into another. Sometimes all the parents slept after night shift together, and we were shooed out to try to allow them to rest. I didn't mind. There was plenty to do around the garden and the streets, and sitting on the steps watching the activities in the street was always interesting. I was much too young to play with the other children a lot, and whenever we were out in a group, Ludmilla always had to look after me, a responsibility she sometimes resented, worried I might hurt myself.

All the children became familiar with the town. They had no restrictions placed on them. They soon discovered the street markets. They had no money to buy anything, but now and again, they could pick up a piece of fruit or a piece of carrot or potato and bring it home to be cooked in the old kitchen. Now we were coming to the end of spring, there was some mouthwatering produce on the market, but all we could do was drool at the fresh red radishes, succulent green shallots, onions, potatoes, and carrots brought in by the farmers to sell.

Only a week after we settled in, the first air raid hit. Both Mum and Dad were working that night, and Ludmilla was playing with her friends. I was sleeping in a corner of the foyer when I woke to a deep rumbling hum gradually getting louder. It was overwhelming, as if a swarm of bees were inside my head. The air-raid sirens were screeching urgently. There was no one to stop me, so I rushed outside to see what was going on. To me it was a magical sight, even though I did not understand what it was. The sky was jet black, and from all points of the horizon, there were long shafts of light playing and moving around as if dancing to a tune. There were arcs of brightly lit tracers everywhere. The sky was lit up with eruptions of light, as intermittently huge explosions showered flames up into the air. Parts of the city were burning, and there was the continuous drone of airplane engines. The whole thing lasted for an hour, with waves of aeroplanes coming in, dropping the bombs, and then disappearing. I just sat there mesmerized on the steps—it was awesome. I felt as if the whole thing were a gigantic fireworks display, and I was the only spectator, with no one else around and the streets deserted.

As soon as the engine drone disappeared, sirens started to wail again for a short period. After that the whole place started to bustle. Cars were on the road again, and people were moving around hurriedly. There were shouts and orders, and the screeching of fire engine sirens in the far distance. I wasn't frightened at all. I just sat there watching the whole scene in wonderment, not really realizing the significance or the danger and the tragedies that were unfolding at that very moment. I went down to bed reluctantly sorry that the "show" was over, and as I did so, the people who were in the building who were not working were just drifting up from the cellar, where they had taken refuge. That was now our air-raid shelter. Ludmilla gave me a belting for "disappearing," as she had been worried sick, thinking I might have been killed in the air raid.

The next morning, when Mother and Father arrived, she told them about my disappearance, and I got another scolding and a smack for being so naughty. I couldn't really understand what I had done. I was just watching some fireworks. They didn't do me any harm, and I thought it wasn't fair to be belted and scolded for doing something that was not naughty or wrong.

The raids became a regular feature of our life. Erfurt was a major railway, commercial and industrial center, and a significant target. Mum became increasingly anxious. When she was home, she would be the first one to run into the cellar, dragging both of us down by the arms. We had to stay there well after the sirens sounded the all clear. If she was on night shift, she would always try to run back when a raid started: she worked about half an hour's walk away, but she ran it in much less time. At every corner, she would be stopped by the air-raid warden, instructing her to get into the nearest shelter. She would point to a few houses, and say, "It's okay, okay, I just live over there, and I will get into my own shelter with my family." Then she ran on until stopped again, to give another excuse and keep running. By the time she arrived home, she was in a lather of sweat, panting and blowing. When she hugged us close in the shelter, I could hear her heart beating like the piston of a steam train, her breathing fast and deep. But she was determined that if we were going to get killed, we would be killed together. Her anxiety soon transferred to me, and I began to be overcome with fear when the raid sirens wailed, scurrying down into the cellar, so my days of enjoying the fireworks at leisure were well and truly gone.

Otherwise the summer passed pleasantly enough for me. I had nothing to do and played either in the garden or dragging along with Ludmilla when she was with her friends. We could not mingle with any of the local children, as we were still regarded by them as *Ausländer* (foreigners), and they would have nothing to do with us, accusing us of having lice and being dirty. We had privacy in our own yard, and it was pleasant to lie on the grass by the river, looking up and seeing the white clouds scurrying across the blue sky. When you lay in the shade of the large oak, the light filtering through the leaves changed pattern continuously as the wind blew the leaves around.

Mother and Father set up a small garden on the grounds, and the old women and men tended it with loving care. They were rewarded for their labor with fresh vegetables, a welcome addition to the pea soup and bread from the camp kitchen.

Sunday was a day of rest, even in the work camps. The inmates were allowed to do as they liked so long as they stayed inside the camp. On those days, we would actually visit the Ukrainian section, where the young men and woman were entertaining themselves with song and dance. They were young, and even in those surroundings, I could see that many friendships were developing, with some of the people holding hands or clowning with an arm around the waist or around the shoulders. They sang Ukrainian songs, and there always seemed to be someone who could play the accordion. This raised the spirits and it was probably a good strategy used by the Germans. At this stage, Mother hadn't quite made the mental switch to German identity that tempted her, and she was always foremost in the singing, standing in a group with hands intertwined. Father looked on smiling, always with a cigarette in his hand or hanging from his lips if tobacco was available.

One day he took us to his workplace to show us what he did. I was fascinated. There was so much noise, clanging and banging, movement of trains and locomotives puffing and hissing steam. I was confused. I didn't know how anyone could make any sense of all this activity. We walked where there were large turning tables, which turned the locomotives around. The area was enclosed by a wire mesh fence. I could see an outline of a figure on that fence.

"What's that, Dad?"

Sadly he said, "Look away from that, Vala. A bomb went off nearby and a worker was blown through the fence, and those are his remains. He was only a Slav, and the Germans think it unnecessary to remove the particles from the fence, and everyone is too busy to do anything about it." I was frightened and tried not to look at it, but somehow my eyes were drawn to that site. For the next few weeks, I had dreams of this man blown through the wire meshing by the explosions. It made me more fearful of the air raids, now that I realized what they could really do.

One afternoon a large car pulled up in front of our hotel. This was a most wonderful contraption, driven by a uniformed soldier. It pulled up, and the driver jumped out and opened the door, and out came four apparently very important men, wearing high peaked caps and braid and medals all over their uniforms. I kept out of the way.

"And these were my quarters where I misspent my youth while going to the university," one of the men was saying.

"Ah, your student prince days," joked another man.

"There is a special back entrance here where we could always smuggle in wine and *frauleins*. But what a sorry state it is in since my last visit here," he said. "That was thirty years ago. These days I look nearly as dilapidated as my dear hotel." There was a round of laughter from his colleagues.

They walked into the foyer where we had made our home and saw the old people with bright scarves around their heads, and bent backs, thin as scarecrows. The others were all at work.

"And who are you? A group of layabout gypsies who have made a camp here?"

One of the women saw her opportunity, and in reasonably good German said, "Herr General, we are not gypsies. We are honest, loyal, patriotic Germans. We came willingly from the middle of Russia to help with the war effort, yet we are being treated like slaves. All the others are at work in the factories making tanks, bombs, and shells. We are here looking after the children, and for this we are not even paid one pfennig. We exist on pea soup and crumbs of stale bread. We are dying of starvation for our efforts."

This hit a chord with the general.

"We'll see about that," he said. "Who's in charge here?"

"You had better talk to the camp commandant. I think he is

in charge of everything."

"Right," he said, "that's the next stop." After looking around the garden and being sadly disappointed at the state of disrepair of the whole building, where he obviously had so many happy experiences in his youth, they went to the car. The chauffeur closed the door, gave a salute, and drove away, apparently to the commandant's office.

The next day, Mother and a few of the other workers were summoned to the commandant's office. He was furious.

"How dare you report me to the general! How dare you complain about your situation. You are only dirty rotten Slavs."

That was the last straw for Mum. In Ukraine she was called a dirty rotten German, and now in Germany, she was being called a dirty rotten Slav. She really felt these days that Germany was her only real heritage, and she increasingly wanted to be part of it. And now, after all the hardships of coming here, working in miserable conditions, no food, and dilapidated living quarters, to be called a dirty Slav triggered the "black rage" that had plagued her since the head injury in Ukraine. Her face went red, her eyes bulged, and she banged both fists on the table, picked up the large glass inkwell, and threw it at the commandant's head. It hit him on the head and the ink poured all over him.

He was a thin, frail man. His bureaucratic position gave him power, but underneath he was a weakling, and he was fearful that this stout woman was going to kill him. He was also frightened of the general.

"And if there is any more trouble from you," she shouted, waving her fist at him, "I will report you to the general, who has given me strict instructions."

Here Mum struck a piece of unexpected luck. Unknown to her at the time, the commandant was ripping off the State in an outright fraud: the *Volksdeutsch* coming back to Germany were supposed to be given full citizenship, including a work card so that they got standard rates of pay for working the various jobs. But the commandant was still charging this amount to the factories and other work centers, allegedly to cover food and accommodation costs, but in fact most of it went into his own pocket. Once an investigation revealed this, he would end up in jail or even in front of the firing squad. The Gestapo did not like fraud against the State.

He knew he was beaten. There was nothing for it but a dignified retreat.

"Alright, in this case you will be removed from my support. I will give you your own work cards, and you will be paid directly by your employer.

"The other rules still apply: you must stick to your direct route between the workplace and where you live, so you will not even be able to spend the money, and you will probably starve. The matter is closed, and I don't ever want to see you again." He slammed the door as they left.

Lydia and the others could not believe their luck. When she recovered from her rage, she had thought that they would be arrested and shot for what she had just done. She couldn't imagine how she had accidentally struck on the commandant's unsuspected vulnerability, or how she got away with it. This came to light much later.

The incident changed the life of our little community. All the *Volksdeutsch* now got the standard rate of pay. The children did the shopping. It was now full autumn, and a lot of vegetables were available and some meat, butter, or sugar on ration coupons.

Now we were not continually starving. There was nothing luxurious, but there was plenty of fruit, and even some nuts in the markets. There were good cooking facilities in the old kitchen with the gas working, even without the electricity. Everyone felt that the *Volksdeutsch* status and their diligence and hard work had finally earned them some respite from their misery. Unfortunately, the equal status did not apply to Ivan because of his Slavonic origin, and he was still working for no pay.

* * * *

Chapter 14

Bombed Out

We were deep into autumn now, and it was cold. I was so glad we had the warm eiderdowns, because even without Mum or Dad in the bed, it was still warm inside when I cuddled in with Ludmilla.

One night there was a major air raid. As usual it began with the urgent wail of sirens, followed by the distant hum of the airplanes becoming louder, then loud explosions and the rattle of the anti-aircraft fire. All of our workers were out on the night shift, and there were only the children and the three old women in the cellar. The explosions were nearer and louder, and at times the whole building shook, when a bomb went off nearby. Then, without any warning, I heard a huge noise. It was more than a noise—it was a force that enveloped my whole being. The cellar was filled with smoke and debris. The old women started screaming and praying and crossing themselves fervently. I could not hear anything—I was absolutely deaf and felt as if my whole head were split open. Breathing was difficult with the suffocating dust. In the darkness, we did not know what had happened. We made our way to the cellar door, but we could not get out—we were completely buried in our little cell. Mother did not make it home this night. I still don't know why. Perhaps they stopped her from leaving at work or made her go into an air-raid shelter, but no one came. We were there all night, buried, suffocating, not knowing what happened, but obviously a bomb must have hit either our house or very close. My ears were still ringing loudly, and if I stood up, I was dizzy and would fall down. We waited for many hours. Time was immeasurable in the complete darkness, and to me it seemed forever.

Finally we heard a movement above us, some shouts and bangs and scraping, and after what seemed a long time to me, there were some shouts: "Here we are, we're near the door now, a little bit longer." After a while, the door was opened, and we saw light and the fresh air came in. We were safe. The feeling of relief was overwhelming. Mother grabbed me and hugged me to her, with Ludmilla clinging to her side. We stood there blackened with soot and grime, our clothing torn, sobbing uncontrollably with relief.

When the workers came back in the morning, they found the whole house had been destroyed. The bomb had fallen close to our home, and the whole three-story building, instead of collapsing, which would have buried us forever, had actually been blown into the river, leaving only a little debris covering the entrance to the cellar. The workers were able to dig us out quickly. If they had been with us in the cellar when the bomb exploded, we would probably all have perished. There was no one else who was concerned about our fate and no one to dig us out, as we were a low priority.

When I emerged, I was placed on the front steps that had survived the blast. One of the old women was also there. She was distressed and crying. I could not hear anything, and my head still felt like the inside of a large bell. Everybody was busy digging, trying to retrieve some of their possessions.

When Mum saw the devastation, she went into a state. She wanted to get out of this situation, the bombings, the crisis, the work, everything—she just felt trapped. There was no visible way out, and bad things were happening to us beyond her control.

The whole area was devastated. All the houses in that street were destroyed, and piles of rubble were still burning. It must have been a whole line of bombs dropped from the same airplane. Some ruins were half in the river, but our house had not been hit directly, just blasted into the water. That was probably the only thing that saved us from being buried alive. If the whole house had collapsed on top of us, three stories of bricks, stone, and rubble could not have been moved without heavy equipment in time. No equipment of any kind was available.

Most of our people's meager goods and chattels were retrieved, and we even managed to get back our precious baby bath, along with our eiderdowns and the few pieces of clothing and equipment that we possessed.

But now we had nowhere to live. We could not stay in the open, and there was no viable housing in our street or even in the city, as the whole place was gradually being destroyed. As we were now regarded as German citizens with a work card, we no longer belonged to the work camp. This was certainly fortunate, because if we got into the hands of the camp commandant, life would have been difficult for my mother and father, after what she did to him. We were able to go anywhere where there was work available, but we had to be reassigned fresh billets and fresh work places.

My poor mother was in shock. She left me in the care of Ludmilla, and trudged with Ivan to the labor control office. They had to report the new circumstances and try to get either different housing or other allocated work in an area where housing was still available. After some hours, she came back beaming and relieved. There was a smile on her face again.

"Guess what, children, we are leaving Erfurt at last," she announced. "We are going into the country to a village called

Fermstad. We will be working in a small factory making travel luggage, and we've been billeted on a farm. I don't think we will be bothered with any bombs from now on."

She was hugely relieved to get out of Erfurt and get back to the countryside, where it was clean and safe, without the constant dread of being killed. Father somehow managed to arrange an old truck from the railway maintenance department to take us to the new billet. It was a long trip that ran on into the dark. There was a drizzle of rain, developing into sleet. The road was rough and the ride was bumpy and uncomfortable.

Brown and yellow exhaust fumes were sucked into the back of the truck, and I nearly wanted to throw up over the side. I couldn't, as there had been no food that day and my stomach was empty. It was hard to see where we were going. When we finally arrived, cold and hungry but still inquisitive, it looked like a small farm with outbuildings, some barn animals and a farmhouse.

The woman who met us saw our condition, our cold, hunger, and misery. She bustled around and prepared some food: a nice piece of fresh rye bread with cheese and real butter. We made short work of the food, and she prepared a warm glass of milk for us. She then took us up to the attic room where we were to stay. It was a large room, private and, to us, sheer luxury. We had not had a room of our own since we had left the little farm in Ukraine, and that seemed a lifetime away. After sharing a railway wagon with six families, a farmhouse with another family, and the dilapidated hotel for the last ten months with no electricity or basic facilities or even a bed, to be in a room with a huge bed, thick feather eiderdowns and big pillows, with fresh, crisp white sheets, was something I had never experienced. Everything was crisp and white, clean and comfortable. The windows, however, were left completely open, and the wind brought in the cold air, turning the room into a freezing chamber. The woman, however, heated some large stones in the oven, wrapped them in thick toweling, and brought them to us to warm the bed and our feet. I have never felt so comfortable and drifted off to sleep with my head still ringing from the bomb explosion.

Our lives changed completely. Father was assigned to work in the local factory manufacturing travel luggage, and Mother worked on the farm where we were billeted. My father had at last been given appropriate work cards and was being paid the basic wage, so we were able to pay the farmer's wife for the food and our lodgings.

The farmer's wife was pleasant and genuinely pitied us when Mum told her the story of our travels. She bustled around and managed to find some old clothing belonging to her own children, which she gave to Ludmilla and to me.

Ludmilla made friends with the local girls, and I played around the farm, making snowballs, sliding down little hills, and exploring. We still heard planes flying overhead, though, and I found that unnerving: after the Erfurt bombing, the fear of airplane noise remained with me well into my teens. I would feel a vague anxiety, and my heart would begin to race. Over the winter, more and more bombing missions came over. I heard people say that the end of the war was coming.

Chapter 15

The Yanks Are Coming

Spring came at last, and the ice began to melt into rivulets of water running into the streams. The warming sun brought life back to the frozen earth, and the first green growth started to sprout. One day I was standing by the road not far from the farm, enjoying the weather, when suddenly I heard a low whining rumbling noise, which was slowly getting louder. It was different than airplane noise, deeper and constant. The sound progressively got louder and louder, and then around the bend burst a column of tanks, followed by trucks filled with soldiers. People came running from their homes nearby and watched.

"Americans, Americans," they shouted, with a sense of excitement and anticipation. They all knew that finally the war was over—the Americans had come. The area was lucky, and they avoided the arrival of the dreaded Russians. Their ruthless treatment of the German population was well known and feared.

For me it was such a simple end, and I did not realize the full significance or how fortunate I was to be still alive. All I saw were different men in different uniforms and different voices and language, which I did not understand. They started throwing things at the children who were lining the road, and as they got nearer, I found lollies wrapped in paper thrown at the children. I picked some of these up and had my first taste of chewing gum.

There was exhilaration and excitement everywhere. Just then most Germans didn't care at all that they had lost the war—they were just glad that they had survived it. There was no immediate change in our lives, but there was more army activity around and a constant traffic of the olive green–colored trucks painted with a white star. The Americans were kind, smiling at the young children and giving them chewing gum or sweets.

But soon after they arrived, it was announced that they were pulling out again to let the Russians occupy this part of Germany. Now that caused great consternation. All the people like us who were displaced and who had been brought to Germany to work were going to be rounded up and taken further west into the American zone. My father was frantic again, fearful that somehow he might miss out on that and left to face the returning Russians, with a firing squad as the result. Mother, on the other hand, was absolutely weary.

"I'm sick of running, Ivan," she told him. "I'm sick of trying to beat the Russians and continually facing this threat. What can they do to us? I'm of German background and we are in Germany. This is my country. They will just come here and probably go back to Russia after the whole thing is settled."

"*But what about me?*" Father shouted. "I'll be shot! For God's sake, think about that."

Mother would hear nothing of it. She was sick of running. She would just face fate where she was, in a place she had been feeling safe for the last few months, and had come to love.

"You are as stubborn as a goat, and just as stupid," Father exploded in exasperation. "Can't you listen to any sense at all?

We are in danger. You are in danger, even if you are a German in Germany, you will be treated as a collaborator and also shot."

In desperation Dad went to the American Army Center, and explained his predicament to someone in authority. He told them that he was an ex-Red Army wireless operator, separated from his unit and that he had ended up in Germany, and Mother would not budge one centimeter to get out of the way of the Russians. They were immediately interested in my father when they heard his story and were keen to interview him further.

Just a little time later, an army truck arrived at the farm. Two burly soldiers got out of the truck with my father. They were huge and black and towered over my mother and father by feet. Without much ceremony or discussion, they picked up my mother and lifted her up as if she were a bag of feathers and just plunked her on the back of a truck. She was surprised and annoyed. Then they shoved two bags of luggage after her, followed by Ludmilla and me. Father was already in the truck. Mother was too surprised to say or do anything. She just sat there dumbfounded. One minute she was on the ground, adamant that she wasn't going to move, and the next minute she was on the back of a truck being driven to the train line for evacuation.

But by the time we got to the train line, she saw the sense of leaving to get away from the Russians. Her black mood disappeared all of a sudden, and she was just as keen as Dad to get on the way as quickly as possible. Now that was a quick change in attitude, but her survival instinct was reignited, the decision was taken out of her hands, and she had to make no effort.

When we got to the railway, a train was already there and a long line of boxcars were being loaded. Most of them were now full, and there were still some desperate people trying to hop on and make the final getaway. We made our way quickly to a boxcar that was not quite full. The occupants were very thin, sickly-looking men. Their heads were completely shaven and they still wore rough gray clothing, ill-fitting, tattered, and with a "P," indicating that they were Polish, from the forced-labor camps.

A number of them blocked the way to stop us from getting in. "You lot look too clean and well fed to be displaced persons. You German scum should stay behind and face the music when the Russians come, and explain to them why you are so sleek and clean."

This triggered Mum's "black anger" again, and in a frenzy, she hopped up into the boxcar with her arms flying and pushing people aside, at the same time swearing profusely at them all in fluent Polish.

"Hey lads," one called out, "she must be one of us. Only a real Pole would know this vocabulary." They all started laughing at this and welcomed her in. They gave us a hand with our two bags and helped us get into the boxcar.

Mum soon quieted down and started talking to the occupants in Polish. It appeared that they were from a nearby concentration camp. Some were prisoners of war, and some had just been grabbed by the Germans for the work camps. They'd been mistreated, starved, beaten, and forced to work in atrocious conditions—and they vehemently hated Germans after what had been done to them and their country.

After a few hours' wait, loading was completed, and all the people who were eligible to leave had managed to get on the train. The local Germans were refused permission, but many of them were trying to make their own way.

Now it was the same old story, like coming home, living in a boxcar again. And we went on slowly west again, with lengthy interruptions. Eventually we got to Mannheim. We disembarked from the train and said our absolute good-bye to a boxcar. Mind you, the trip had been better than most of them. The Poles became quite friendly when they heard our story and realized that we were just fellow refugees from Ukraine looking for sanctuary and also forced to work. And it helped that my mother had been born under Polish rule and had some Polish background.

Altogether there had been a curious mix of jubilation and expectancy about the ending of the war, mingled with a certain fear about our ultimate fates: no one had a real idea what would become of us. But at least the war was over. There had been singing and skylarking in the wagon, and the Americans' food was tasty and welcome compared to the German sawdust bread and pea soup.

Once at Mannheim, we were loaded into canvas-covered trucks, and driven to a very large camp with our belongings. The camp held all the ethnic groups of the countries that had been controlled by Germany: Lithuanians, Estonians, Poles, Russians, and Ukrainians. The members of each group clustered together like sheep for the comfort of language and background. We were assembled into a large hall and clustered together, with only sleeping room. There must have been hundreds of people there.

Everyone was given mattresses, which were quite comfortable when the lumps were straightened out, and they were certainly an improvement on what we had before, the hard floor of the boxcars or the cement floor of the foyer of the hotel where we had stayed before. Now at that stage, it felt good to be in the Ukrainian group. They were happy and chatty, asking questions about everybody's origins, where they came from and their stories, and Mother and particularly Father were at "home."

There were a lot of rumors going around, though, and we still did not feel the future was secure. We were safe only for the present.

There was even an Orthodox priest among the Ukrainian group, who still remembered what he was doing before the Soviets cracked down on any religious activity. He was a tall man with a full beard, and looked like he hadn't shaved in his life. He had a sense of dignity about him in his black robes, and everybody showed him respect. He was probably the first priest a lot of the people had seen, since he would hardly have shown himself under Stalin. That immediately gave Mum an idea.

"Ivan, I think Vala should be christened. He is four years old and he hasn't been, and who knows what the future holds," said Mum.

"Well, if you want to," replied Dad. He had some respect for the clergy, though he hadn't been in touch with a priest himself for over fifteen years.

"Anyway," he went on, thinking it through, "I think my mother would have very much wanted Vala christened, as she was a very devout Christian. Both my parents were Ukrainian Orthodox and wouldn't miss a Sunday without going to worship. This, of course, was before Father was killed," he said wistfully. "I suppose we should thank God for our safe deliverance from all the danger we have gone through, and christening Vala would be a good start."

So it was arranged. I was to be christened in the middle of this huge hall with hundreds of people around. I suppose I was going to be the center of attention. I don't think I liked the idea much, but I had no choice in the matter.

Mum and Dad consulted the priest, and he nodded his head solemnly from time to time. "It is an absolute disgrace that the word of God cannot be preached in Ukraine where it has been strong for a thousand years, and little children like this have been denied God's blessing for twenty-five years. Of course, I'll gladly do this christening. It may even soften the hearts of some of the people and make them think back to their own christening. This will be the first in the camp and will rekindle the Christian spirit in the people," declared the priest. He became quite enthusiastic about the idea. So it was decided that three days later a christening ceremony would be held.

On the morning of my christening day, Mum got me up early, took me to the communal showers, and scrubbed me vigorously until my skin burned.

"Stop it, not so hard Mum. Don't be so hard. I've got soap in my eyes," I protested.

"Be quiet!" she retorted angrily. "You're not going to be dirty in front of all those people and the priest on your christening day. Anyway, God will not be impressed if you are dirty."

"This God must sure be important," I thought to myself. Everyone was running around madly to please him.

A table was pushed over near our belongings, and my baby bath was placed on top of the table. Mother then filled up the bath with tepid water, using a bucket she had borrowed. All the people congregated around the bath. There were hundreds; some were watching from curiosity, and some were simply devout and praying and crossing themselves. I was stripped naked in front of everybody, and then plunked into the bath. The priest was there, dressed up in his robes and his golden cap, which looked like an onion, and he held a book in his hands. He started the proceedings, blessing everybody around with the sign of the cross in different directions to cover the entire crowd. He then started reciting the christening service. A large part of this consisted of singing the service and paragraphs interspersed with singing the words, "God bless us," always repeated by the congregation. He then waved a metal container filled with burning material. Smoke was emitted, producing a sweet-smelling odor. Someone mentioned incense. He kept waving this little pot, which was suspended on three thin chains, and he held the top of the chains while waving the pot around the crowd. I wondered why he was doing this. Perhaps he was trying to frighten off the devil with the smoke and the smell. He then put a brush into the water and sprayed everybody around, again while performing the singsong ritual of praying in song.

Everybody took part in the service, and at some stage, they would bend down on their knees and pray and then get up and pray and cross themselves, all in unison as if by some signal given by the priest. In between they sang various hymns. Many were crying, no doubt remembering their childhood and homes and the loved ones they left behind in Ukraine. I was very impressed with all this. Then for a finale, he filled a cup with water and poured it over my head, and declared that I was now a Christian. In the service, I was also assigned a godmother and a godfather—Mr. Pracuic, a friend we met in the village just before the war ended. He was always faithful to his promise and was a friend of the family until he died.

I thought at the time that Christians must be particularly clean people, because the whole thing seemed to revolve around being thoroughly washed before the process, soaked in water, and then poured with water and cleansed again. At this point, I was starting to get cold and hoped the whole process would end soon.

Thank God it did. I was wrapped in a towel, and Mum took me off and dressed me, glad and happy that I had been turned into a Christian in front of this huge crowd of Ukrainians. From that time onwards, I was known as the "boy who was christened."

The gathering of thousands of people of different ethnic groups in the same camp was an absolute disaster, if you expected to see some glimmer of hope from the end of the war. It seemed strikingly tragic that after going through all the ill-treatment by the Germans and the Russians, the people could still not get on: fighting broke out continually between the groups. The age-old animosities still smoldered. Poles hated the Ukrainians. Ukrainians hated the Poles. Poles hated the Lithuanians and the Lithuanians hated the Russians—an awful picture of the problem with Europe.

In despair, the Americans decided that all the ethnic groups should be segregated into separate camps and kept in Germany until somebody, somewhere, decided what to do with this mass of humanity. There had been something like seven million people working in Germany from the different countries that Germany conquered, and they would all have to be sorted out and the refugee problems somehow managed.

The Ukrainians were told that they were to go to Ellwangen, an old town not far from Mannheim. They were not keen to move again, being rather apprehensive of moving anywhere. They had heard rumors that Ukrainians, Russians, and Poles in the English zone were being sent back to Russia—with the familiar result that the Russians were dealing with them harshly, including executions and deportations to Siberia. While this had not happened here in the American zone, a fear was starting to build up that nobody really wanted us because we were a nuisance, and to give us back to the Russians would be an easy solution to the problem. The Ukrainian Committee therefore decided to send out a delegation to Ellwangen and to scout out the area to see if it was a real camp or if it was only a transportation point back to Ukraine into the hands of the Russians. This was done. However, the advance party came back enthusiastic. They reported that the proposed facility appeared to have been a large army camp, with good facilities for communal living. There were a lot of small rooms suitable for some families, but they had communal bathrooms and toilets. There were also large dining and kitchen areas where people would be fed. Approval was given for the transfer, and with the help of American army trucks, the whole Ukrainian ethnic group from Mannheim descended on Ellwangen.

This suited the new arrivals just fine, because most of them were young, single people, who had been taken by the Germans as young as fourteen, so most of them were now in their late teens or early twenties. They were billeted two or more to a room, and used the dining facilities so they didn't have to cook. There were a few families like us, with children of various ages. But in comparison to the total population of the camp, we were a minority.

We were allocated family quarters outside the camp, in a nearby street of two-story houses. Each story had living accommodations, three bedrooms, a bathroom and kitchen. Each family was allocated one of the bedrooms, and share of the bathroom and kitchen. This was wonderful. We actually had a whole room to ourselves. Dad made a bed for himself and Mum, and I shared a bed with Ludmilla.

Father immediately got involved in building. He discussed a project to build a church with the Ukrainian Orthodox bishop, who was also at the camp, and who took over the religious leadership in the community. His daughter, Mrs. Hayevska, a teacher, took over the cultural activities and educational responsibilities for the children at the camp.

Dad was allocated an empty building. It was only a square concrete box with a door, surrounded by protective mounds as high as the roof. Someone said that it was used for storage of munitions at the camp. It was completely cleaned out and painted. Dad scrounged around for various timber and other materials, which were very difficult to get in Germany just after the war. He built a beautiful church inside the concrete box. There were the traditional gates, altars, and benches for the congregation. He painted and decorated the whole thing in the normal traditional designs of the Orthodox Church, ornate and very colorful. This was the jewel of the camp. Church services were started. This was a major activity. Ukrainian religious activity was a major cultural identifier, which was probably the reason Stalin was so keen to destroy it.

I attended church every Sunday, and for my age of five, I was very devout. I would sit in the services from beginning to end. The services lasted for hours. And most children my age would quickly get bored and sneak outside and play around the area, but I thought that was a sin, and I stayed until the very end. My recent experience of being christened was foremost in my mind, and I thought that after being accepted by God, the least I could do was stay there for the full service. That did take a lot of perseverance and concentration on my part, as kneeling for long periods on hard concrete was painful.

After church was completed, the bishop's daughter was keen to start a theater, which was going to become the center point of the cultural activities in the camp. Dad was also deeply involved in that project. And you can see now what was starting to happen. My family was almost automatically slipping back into the Ukrainian lifestyle.

* * * *

Chapter 16

Louiza Returns

Once the war was ended and our position became secure, a lot of Mum's thoughts turned again to the fate and whereabouts of her own mother and the little family we left behind in Lvov after our visit during the German occupation. She worried continually, and often talked with Ivan about what might have happened. She wanted to find her mother again and renew contact as quickly as possible.

And despite the general post-war shambles in Germany, the Red Cross organization was up and running and busily helping people register and rediscover loved ones also in the country. They helped the reunion of many families.

At the first opportunity, Mum consulted the Red Cross to try to find her mother's whereabouts. She knew the Russians must have overtaken Lvov long ago, and the chances of surviving in the battles would be poor. In addition, once the Russians discovered that Louiza and her family were of German origin, and the fact that her son was fighting on the Eastern Front, and participating in the battle of Stalingrad, it would make life very difficult for them.

After constantly badgering the Red Cross officers at Mannheim, she finally, to her relief and joy, received a positive result. Her mother was alive, and they could actually provide an address where she was presently living.

Mum was ecstatic. She came rushing home, smiling and laughing.

"Guess what, guess what I just found out," she called out to Dad. "Louiza is alive. She's well, and what's more, she is out of the Russians' clutches, and is actually in the American zone. I have an address here, and I've been informed that it's just inside the zone, so she is safe." Mum was absolutely thrilled to know Louiza had escaped the battles that raged as the Russians swept in from the east, and she had a chance of seeing her mother again.

"I must go and see her as soon as possible," called Mum, and she rushed over and repeated the news to Ludmilla and to me.

Dad was also pleased, but mainly for Mum. He did not really know Louiza that well. He had only met her once for a short time, and had no emotional attachment to her or their family. So while he was glad for Mum, he was not personally over-excited.

"What are we to do, though?" he asked. "We've got this baggage here, and we can't go trailing all over the countryside in the state the country's in just now. Most of the trains are not running. There is very little food around. I'm nervous of going outside this camp where we have some security and stability—can we be sure we can come back in?"

It was obvious Dad didn't want to particularly go on an expedition to find Grandma. But Mum would not be put off. She was adamant that she would go and see her as soon as she possibly could.

"Well, I suppose the sooner you go and see her, the better," said Dad. "I'll go and see the people at the camp administration office and see what's required. I don't think it will be an easy matter to make your way in the present state of the country."

So it was decided that Dad would stay at the camp and look after our belongings, while Mum, Ludmilla, and I would try to find Grandma and visit her.

Mum was impatient and expectant. She had to be provided with some travel documents and make sure our identification papers were in order. She also obtained very detailed directions of how to get there, what trains to catch, where to change, and how to find the exact address after leaving the train station.

Grandma was staying in a very small village about six kilometers from the nearest railway station. The problem was that she was staying right on the border between the Russian and American zones, in a village that actually straddled both. We were warned by the camp officials not to stray into the Russian zone, as they had no jurisdiction there whatsoever, and we would not be able to get released.

I could see that this had a sobering effect on Mum. Her boisterous spirits sagged, and she looked worried and concerned.

"Do you think I should go, Ivan?" she asked Dad. "I'd hate to get caught by the Russians."

"Well, I don't think they could really do much with you, because you have the papers of a German citizen in effect, so they would probably just question you and let you go. It would be a different matter if they caught me, as I'm still classified as Ukrainian, and they would love to get their hands on me. That is why I'm not going, because being caught by the Russians would be the finish of me and the risk is too great. But you go anyway, so long as you're very careful. You will have the children with you. Louiza will love to see them again, and they do have a right to see their grandmother again, even if only the once."

This was actually just as fair as he could be.

We set off on our journey. The weather was getting into mid-spring, but the nights were still cold, so we took our heavy coats.

We expected the trip to take a few days, so we would probably have to sleep at some station along the way. We had a bag filled with bread, cheese, and a sausage, enough to see us through for at least three or four days. We also wrote to Grandma, so with any luck she might be expecting us.

Dad saw us off to the train. We boarded and managed to get our seats near a window. I poked my head out and waved my hanky frantically, feeling a little uneasy as the train pulled slowly away from the station with a loud whistle and belching of smoke. Dad was getting smaller and gradually disappearing from view, waving gently at us.

Mum was now getting more and more excited to think that she was actually on her way again to see her mother, for only the second time in the twenty-seven years since they were separated in Siberia. She just couldn't wait for us to get there, and kept on talking about her childhood that she could remember in Lvov and in Siberia, and wondering if the war had made any difference to Louiza since she last saw her. This time there wouldn't be the same shock for her as before, since we knew her address and Mum had sent her a letter to say we were coming and when.

The train journey was slow. The line was still damaged from the war, and there were several detours. Finally we pulled up at the large town where we were to catch another connection north the next day. We ate some of the food we'd brought with us, made ourselves comfortable on a long bench until the early hours of the morning. Then we boarded a two-carriage branch line train out into the countryside. Small villages passed, and country people got aboard, friendly and smiling at us. We would say *"Guten tag"* and smile back. They couldn't really tell that we were Ukrainian. This part of Germany had escaped a lot of the war as the small country villages were not worthwhile bombing targets. All the houses were still neat and looked after, even painted. The fields were different colors, some green, some had been ploughed, and the earth still brown, and some with cattle or sheep in the fields. The air had a clean and fresh smell about it. I was enjoying the trip. It was like a holiday, a few days in the country away from the camp.

Finally the train reached the end of the line at a small country station. We didn't know quite where to go now. We had the address, but no maps. Mum approached the stationmaster and asked, "Excuse me, please, could you tell me how to get to this address?" She showed the address written on a rough piece of paper to the station attendant. He took the piece of paper and looked at it scratching his chin. Then, as if he suddenly were struck with inspiration, he opened his eyes and shook his finger in the air and said, "I know where that is, it is no more than a few houses. It is not even a village, just a small hamlet." He led us outside and pointed down a road winding up into the hills.

"Now be careful, it is very, very close to the Russian zone. As a matter of fact, it is just beside the Russian zone, and there is some dispute as to whether the Russians should be in charge of it, so be careful where you wander."

"*Danke schön, danke schön,*" called Mum, as she hurried off excitedly in that direction, pulling Ludmilla and me behind her.

After a few kilometers of trudging the dusty, rutted road, we started to get tired and lagged behind her. She was impatient as she strode off. "Come on, children, hurry it up, don't lag behind so." But I was hot, tired, and thirsty, and the last thing I wanted was to be hurried along this dusty road on a hot day.

Soon after an old man driving a small cart pulled along by a skinny, tired-looking horse overtook us. I'm sure the only reason that the horse wasn't slaughtered and used as food by the starving Germans was that there was no meat left on his bare bones and it wouldn't be worth the trouble.

The man pulled up beside us. "*Wo gehen sie?*" (Where are you going?) "Can I give you a lift? The children look tired."

I was thankful to stop trudging. Ludmilla and I got into the back, and Mum sat on the seat beside him.

"Where are you going?" he asked. "This is a quiet place, and I know most people living in the area, but I haven't seen you people before."

"No, we don't live in this area," replied Mum. "We are actually from Ukraine originally, but we have been in Germany since 1943 as workers. I'm looking for my mother, who lives in this area, and we are trying to locate her."

Mum then pulled out the piece of paper and showed him the address of her lodgings.

"Oh, yes, I know where that is. It is at the end of the small hamlet we will be passing very soon. I can drop you nearly outside the door."

We kept going and I was comfortable in the back of the cart warmed by the sun, deliciously drifting off to sleep.

A shake from Mum woke me. "Come on Vala, wake up, we are here now," and I was picked up by Mum and lifted out of the cart. "Come on, Lucy, get a move on."

We were outside a small cottage, which looked shabby and in need of paint and repairs, but I imagined it would be very comfortable inside. Mum bustled around, brushing down my hair, and doing Ludmilla's hair. She was nervous and wanted us to look our best when we were presented to Grandma. She wet her handkerchief with her tongue and rubbed at my face, rubbing at a lot of smudges, which she knew Grandma would not approve of. Mum knocked on the front door, and a lady who looked old to me answered.

"What is it?" she inquired, when she saw us standing there, three forlorn creatures covered with dust from the road.

"Could you tell us where Mrs. Louiza Goltz lives?" asked Mum.

"*Ja, Ja*, I know this lady, this is the address, but she does not live in the house. She lives in the small outhouse at the back at the end of the garden. You can go along the pathway to the back, and you will see her."

Mum grabbed us again, and we went along the path at the side of the house to the small wooden hut at the back, no more than a shed. She knocked on the door and she waited expectantly. The door opened, and an elderly lady stepped out. She was tall and thin. She looked out inquiringly, and suddenly she recognized us. She rushed towards Mum, and they hugged and started crying and kissing each other. She then included us in their embrace, and said, "Come in, come in, please."

Inside was only one single room, but it was comfortably arranged with some bedding on the floor. There was no table or chair, and apart from a small box in the corner with a few utensils, little else was in the room. Another lady was sitting on the bedding, and there were three children, one boy about my age, of about five years, and two girls, one slightly bigger than Ludmilla and one slightly smaller.

Ludmilla recognized the girls and rushed over and gave them all a hug. They were all talking together and didn't make much sense. They were talking in German, and our broken German was adding to the confusion.

"You remember Kate, Lydia?"

"Of course, I do," Mum replied. "I still remember the lovely time we spent together in Lvov when we visited you during the war."

Grandma looked at me and said, "You have grown. You are twice as big as I remember you. I thought you were only a little boy, but now look at you." She picked me up and gave me a big squeeze and a kiss. They were all thin and drawn and looked even more badly nourished than we were.

"You must be tired and hungry after your long trip. I'll prepare some food. Sorry there is not much, but I expected you to come any day, and we've got some lovely cakes."

Grandma busied herself. She had an old black kettle that she put on the primus stove and started boiling some water. She cut up some pieces of cake that had pieces of fruit inside. I was famished and was really looking forward to getting my teeth into some of it. She made some tea for Mum and Kate and, with the children munching on the cakes, we were all happy, and for a short period, there was relative quietness in the room.

After tea Mum started asking questions about Ludwig and how they had survived the war. Grandma started crying quietly, and Kate also turned away.

"We haven't heard from Ludwig. He was in the Stalingrad battle before the 4th Army was surrounded by the Russians, and since that time we have not heard one word whether he's alive, dead, or where he is buried," she said, sobbing more.

"I have some letters from him up to that time, which I've kept, and I keep reading them and reading them, but that won't bring him back," mumbled Grandma, with tears still running down her cheeks.

"How did you get away?" asked Mum.

"Well, it was a very uneasy situation. When the 4th Army was surrounded, we knew it was the beginning of the end for the Germans in Russia. Once the Russians started reentering the conquered lands, I knew that we had no hope and had to leave. I couldn't face being captured by the Russians again. There are three children here and Kate, and if Ludwig is dead, his children still have to be looked after, and there is only me and Kate to do that. I was very frightened," Grandma went on, "but also frightened to leave our home and shop and everything that we owned until the very last minute. But when the Russians started to advance, we decided to just run for it."

"We didn't know where to go—we just walked west away from the Russians as quickly as we could. The roads were blocked with people moving west to get away and trucks and supplies going east—we were nearly killed the first day by Russian planes flying up and down the roads and just shooting anything that moved. People were not even burying their dead, just leaving them by the side of the road.

"We decided it would be better to travel at night when the roads were a lot lighter and sleep during the day. We just walked as far as we could for one or two hours at nightfall, then rested with the children for a few hours, and continued walking later. During the day, we got off the road into some wooded area and made camp. We lost all sense of time. We just went on walking and walking, racing the Russians."

"And how did you end up here?" asked Mum.

"Well, eventually we couldn't go on any further. All the food was gone, we were absolutely exhausted, and we just could not take another step. We asked this lady if she could put us up, and she said she really did not want us in the house, but we could use the shed at the back as shelter but we had to pay her. We just stayed here. The Russians came right up to us and stopped only one or two kilometers away. We were absolutely astounded that we had actually got in front of the Russians, and they came so close to overtaking us. We can still hear their maneuverings and tanks, but this has been declared an American part of Germany, and we are in the American zone, and the Russians can't come any further. We are still frightened in case something happens and they make another push west, but at this stage, we just can't go any further, so while we have this room we will stay until things settle down. We have been able to survive because we brought some money as golden coins back with us that we had been saving over the years from the business.

"We can't make any detailed plans until we find out if Ludwig is alive. When he comes back, we can make a new start."

During the night, I was woken up by a loud rumbling and voices shouting in the distance. I looked around. The room was dark, and Mum and Grandma were whispering together with worried looks on their faces. The voices were Russian. They were soldiers calling out to each other. They appeared to be searching homes in the small hamlet, going from house to house, and they were knocking on doors, demanding to search inside. The voices were getting closer and louder. The rumbling of the armored vehicles and tanks running up and down the streets was deafening, and the ground shook with the proximity of the armed vehicles. We heard Russian voices demanding if there were any Ukrainians in the houses.

We were terrified. The color drained from Mum's face, and she became agitated.

"God help us, God help us," she prayed, crossing herself. We realized that it was us they were looking for, since we were the only Ukrainians likely to be in the area. The chance remark made by my mother to the old cart driver must have leaked across the border to the Russians. They might have expected a larger group with some intent of attacking them, not just a woman and two young children. Nevertheless, if we fell into their hands, we could expect little mercy.

Grandma took charge, more or less. "This is what we are going to do, everybody. We will stay in the dark, so as not to draw any attention to us. Now, we are all Germans. I speak perfect German. Kate and the children can speak perfect German, and Lydia, you can also speak German. I know that Ludmilla and Vala cannot speak German. If they come in, they can lie down and pretend to sleep. We'll put them to bed, and we will all speak German, stating that we are German citizens living here. A group of women and children are probably not of much interest to them, so they won't spend much time."

This was quickly agreed. We all got into our beds. The light was off, and we children were put to bed to go to sleep.

Very soon we heard knocking and shouting very close to us, and the house in front of the shed was being invaded and searched. The owners tried to speak in German, but the Russians did not understand them. They shouted at them demanding to know, "Where are the Ukrainians, where are the Ukrainians?" The door to the shed was forced open and a soldier entered. It was terrifying. He was dressed in black leather gear with a leather safety helmet. He held a snub-nosed machine gun in his hand, which he trained on us as he shone the torch. We looked at him silently, our eyes being screwed up directly from the light, and we pretended we were being woken up by the commotion. He just checked us over, shining the torch in everybody's face, and noting that there were only some women and children in the room, he left. He didn't even bother to close the door.

"Ah, there's nobody in there," we heard him say to his comrade. "Just an old woman and two younger ones with their brood of kids. There is not one man in there. Wherever these Ukrainians are, they are certainly hiding well, if they ever existed at all."

We breathed a sigh of relief but didn't say a word. Mum got up and closed the door again, and we just huddled in our beds.

After a few hours, all the commotion stopped and there was silence again, with only an occasional dog barking and yelping in the distance, but the rumbling of the tanks and the shouting and the demands by the Russian soldiers had abated. We saw them cross the border again into the Russian zone. Our joy was completely shattered. The reunion between Mother and Grandma was destroyed with the fearful experience. Mum was still anxious that they might come back and demand to see papers. We had only our refugee papers now, so if we were caught, it would be obvious who we were.

"We can't stay here, we really have to go. It is just too dangerous for us to stay here. We might end up being shot, or worse," said Mum.

Grandma was visibly upset. She just sat quietly crying, not saying anything. She knew this would be another wretched departure with her daughter and her grandchildren torn away from her, another loss.

"When will this ever stop?" she murmured. "When will my children be left to me without being torn away by evil people?" But she agreed that it was too dangerous to stay.

We rested for a few hours, I dropped off to sleep, and then much later, around two or three o'clock, Mum decided to make a move. She said good-bye to Grandma, with a lot of hugs and kisses, as Grandma said good-bye to us. It was the last time we saw Grandma and the last time Mum saw her mother.

Mum then went outside very quietly, checking if there were any tanks still around. Everything was quiet. We sneaked quietly out of the shed into the garden, and made our way along the street, keeping close to the fence and trees in the shadows of the night until we reached a small stream. Mum led us into the stream, and we walked along the stony bottom, with our feet up to the ankles in water.

We paced along quietly without talking, and when she thought it was safe, we made our way across some fields to a track, and followed that until we reached the narrow dusty road we had travelled on the day before in the cart. Now we were some kilometers away from the hamlet and the border, so we thought it safe.

We slowly made it to the station and huddled together on a seat until we could catch the morning train back to the main line. Mother didn't speak much on the trip home, but from time to time, I could see her wiping some tears away from her eyes with her handkerchief.

At last we got back to Ellwangen Refugee Camp and our one room, and in contrast to what had just happened, it felt so lovely to have it. When Mum told Dad the story of our near arrest, he nodded his head and said, "Well, I'm glad I didn't go, because I would have been caught and they would have demanded my identity papers. They would have suspected that I was a Ukrainian saboteur."

I could see that Mum was also glad now he hadn't gone, although she had been a bit angry at him for not doing so initially.

At the time it seemed a fortunate escape, and, of course, it was. Yet looking back now as an adult, I'm inclined to suspect it was also a crucial turning point. It was an experience that somehow cemented my mother's recognition of her *Volksdeutsch* legacy. From that, a much unanticipated result would follow.

* * * *

Chapter 17

Camp Life

Returning to Ellwangen was effectively going back to Ukraine. Even at the time, I could feel my mother flinch. Over the next few days, we drifted back into the indolent life of the camp. Because the United Nations Refugee Organization (UNRO) provided basic food and sustenance, no one had any need to do anything useful to survive. The refugees progressed from slave labor in concentration camps to a complete life of ease in refugee camps. It was not difficult to enjoy this state for a short time before boredom set in.

People took the opportunity to allow their previously oppressed cultural and nationalistic feelings to flower. This was probably the first time in thirty or forty years that they had the chance to enjoy their own songs, history, and myths, and even their own poetry and language, which had always been repressed under the Russian regime, even before Stalin took over.

The camp committees organized Ukrainian schools and an associated scouting movement from cubs to the senior ranks, with uniforms provided by a sewing group. A theater group was set up as well, which was Dad's main interest. After he finished the church, he went to work building the theater and designing the special stage effects. He spent his days and nights there.

Mum, however, would not get involved. Now she was in Germany, she wanted to be involved in German activities, but at Ellwangen they were non-existent. Because she couldn't fit in, she had to fill in her time just talking to some of the other women about their backgrounds and their personal stories, or on bartering trips to the countryside, which she performed regularly. She did not deal in vodka, but soap and toothpaste we sometimes received in Red Cross parcels. I suppose it gave her some meaningful activity. She had no need to continue her bartering activities as we were well provided with all essentials.

My father, on the other hand, started reading as many Ukrainian books as he could. He even played the balalaika, the ultimate Ukrainian instrument. I saw less and less of him.

I did see some of the plays he was involved in, and they were exciting. I had never seen anything more splendid. There were stories of recent experiences. One was a story of a partisan group who was fighting the Germans in the war. The scenery, painted by my father, was very realistic, with the snow and the fir trees of the forest. The finale when the battle was being fought with machine guns was represented by the flickering of lights. The smoke was issuing around the combatants, and the noise was so realistic that you felt you were in the middle of the whole battle.

I couldn't understand, though, why they chose to have plays about partisan fights and battles with the Germans. They had just lived through all this, and I thought they would have wanted to get away from it, but as soon as they were away, they started acting it out again. I suppose it added excitement to their lives.

Ludmilla was now going to school, and I enrolled in kindergarten. There were about seven or eight of us, and we were more or less entertained during the whole of the day by young teachers. At other times, I and my friends would explore around the camp, which had its risks. Once we found a piece of round wood, partly covered by leaves and debris, which was so heavy that when we pulled it out we could hardly lift it up. At the end of the wooden handle was a metal canister. We started swinging it around and throwing it, not knowing what it was until a man walked by and saw us. He screamed, "STOP, drop that thing straight away, it's a hand grenade!" It was a German-style hand grenade, with the explosive in the end canister. The remains of war were common then. We often found little clumps of copper cartridges that had been left behind by soldiers in some firefight. No one bothered to pick them up. We used to collect them and play with them, pretending they were soldiers.

The next question for my parents to decide was the matter of my education. My mother wanted me to go to a German school. "We are in Germany, and we will probably stay in Germany. It is foolish not to learn German and not to join in the national education system. We won't be in this camp forever, and a Ukrainian education will not get him a job or profession in Germany. And we won't be going back to Ukraine, the only country where Ukrainian is spoken."

My father took the other side, of course. "Yes, but we live in the Ukrainian society here. We and the children are part of it, and Ludmilla is doing well at school now, learning to read and write. She missed a lot of schooling, but she is catching up, and Vala should probably also start in first class like everybody else," he argued.

"You and your Ukrainians are living in a fool's paradise. You are just sitting on your backsides, pretending to be a great cultural center, but you produce nothing, you are just a burden on others. How long will that last, tell me?"

This issue would always end up in a fight.

Once the new school year began, Mum took me into the town of Ellwangen, half an hour's walk from the camp, and asked directions to a small school at the *Rathaus* (council chambers). When we eventually found it, I was enrolled as the only Ukrainian in it. It caused some resentment when the news got out at the camp. The hatred of anything German was vibrant, with the atrocities suffered by everyone at the camp burned into their consciousness. To think that a young Ukrainian boy was being put into a German school outside the camp was unthinkable. Some people stopped talking to Mum, and some of my friends were not even allowed to play with me. I couldn't see what all the fuss was about, but I soon realized. It was another world.

The school was very small and built out of stone in a quiet part of the town, tree-lined, with large trees even in the playground. It was a pleasant area, cool and green, with a large playground where we played, although it was untidy at that time. There were a few classes only, on each side of the long central corridor. Around the front of the door were holes in the stonework like pock marks, the results of bullets striking the front. This had been the site of a battle at some stage at the end of the war.

The teacher was a sad-looking man, very thin, and to me he seemed very old, with a small moustache similar to Hitler. He was a man of few words, and very strict. He did not welcome me with open arms, but still tolerated me, and put me near the back of the class. All the work was, of course, in German, and I couldn't understand it, since I had been going to the Ukrainian kindergarten. Also a name like Kirychenko would not be popular in a German school. I even wore a Ukrainian shirt embroidered with the black and red design common on all Ukrainian goods.

I was met with instant aggression, distrust, and hatred. Most of the children had a father, brother, or some friend or relative killed injured or captured in the war. I was a real-life embodiment of the enemy in their midst. Three of the boys made it their business to make my life a misery. One was a tall, thin fellow, surly and threatening, who reminded me of a snake. Another one was fleshy and round with very fair hair and rosy cheeks. He wore the usual green shirt and the traditional German leather shorts supported by fancy leather H-shaped braces, and he reminded me of a pig. The third was a big, strong, muscular fellow who did most of the fighting. He was the gorilla in my mind.

They picked on me from the start, even during the first lunch time. They started jostling me and throwing stones at me when I moved out of their way.

After school I tried to be the first one out of class and run as fast as I could towards the camp before they had a chance to catch me. If I took the route through the cemetery, entering in one gate and out the other end towards the camp, the graves deterred them from coming in. I think they were still superstitious, and any proximity to dead bodies and associated ghosts and spirits was scary to young boys, including me. I was scared more of them than of dead bodies, and I ran as quickly as I could. Arriving at the camp always gave me a feeling of safety.

I dared not tell my mother, in case she lost her temper and made a scene, making things worse. So I made no friends at that school, but after a while, the novelty of my presence wore off, and they accepted me as part of the furniture, tolerated but ignored.

I still attended the Ukrainian scout meetings, being one of the two or three members in the cubs group who were regular and always attended in the winter, when there was little activity and little fun. Come the spring of 1947, the activity in the scouts increased, and plans were made for more outdoor activities, now that the snow was melting away. I was looking forward to this.

But the day I attended the meeting, the big hall was filled with people who had hardly attended through the winter. There were about twenty, my age and older, wearing new cub uniforms with colorful badges and ribbons on their lapels or side of their shoulders; their troops and leaders were already established.

"When did all this happen?" I asked one of the boys I knew. "You didn't attend any meetings or train during the winter months?"

"No, we didn't have to. This was all done at the school. All the people in the first class were divided into troops and the leaders were picked. We got our uniforms weeks ago. Didn't you get one?"

"No, I didn't," I said tersely and walked away. When I tried to get in line, I was pushed out of the way and told, "You are not part of this troop, and besides, you haven't got a uniform. You'd better go."

Fuming, I raced out of the hall, just managing not to burst into tears. It was so unjust at that age: I had attended every cub meeting through the autumn and winter months and had been looking forward to the summer activities of camping, swimming, and hiking. Now, as soon as spring arrived, my interest and attendance were of no value. I was not part of the Ukrainian school, so I was not part of the scouting group. I didn't fit anywhere. I wasn't part of the German school, nor invited into their activities. I was also not part of the Ukrainian cubs or any of their activities. I was in no-man's land.

I swore to myself that I really didn't need them. I could look after myself. I had a pocket knife. Using that and rubber from old pushbike inner tubes and a piece of leather from an old shoe tongue, I was able to make a very good catapult. I would go off in a quiet part of the camp with a good selection of stones, and ping away at various targets as part of an imaginary war game where I was the leader attacking fortifications. I became a very good shot as I had a lot of practice, and now and again, I would have a pot shot at some kids that might come within range.

Ludmilla, on the other hand, had a lot of friends her age at her Ukrainian school, and we hardly saw her. After school she went to play with her friends, learned to dance Ukrainian dances, and took part in the scouting movement. She was always away for weekend camping.

By this time Mother and Father were continually fighting. She resented his participation in the theater groups, because she felt she was excluded, and he taunted her about her German background. She would lose her temper and start hitting him. She was fairly formidable, with big arms and shoulders, and poor Dad was very thin and did not have a chance. He would just retreat from the room and stay out all night.

Often the fights were about me going to the German school, and I felt somehow responsible for that as the fights got more frequent and more violent. Finally Father packed a warm eiderdown and a large feather pillow and removed himself to the theater, where he made a temporary home in a small room under the stage, which was used as a workshop by him to make the theater props.

After a week or so, Mum could not stand it any longer.

"Come on, Vala, we will go and see your father right now and see what he's up to." It was late, everybody was asleep, and I didn't feel like going out in the cold night to watch another fight between my mother and father. It was already very embarrassing because everybody knew what was happening, and with her German background and me going to the German school, the family was earning an unsavory reputation.

Mother walked resolutely to the theater, holding my hand, knowing Dad was there. She knocked on the door of the little storeroom, and Dad opened it.

"Well, what do you want?" he asked Mother tersely. The room was bare. He was sleeping on a wooden bench and there were few comforts present. I felt sorry for him—he really had no comforts, and I wished he would come home and stay in our room and be part of the family again. Mother, however, was fuming, and in no mood for compromise or reconciliation.

"I'll tell you what I want!" she shouted. "I want what I earned with my hard work while you were frittering away your time. Give me those eiderdowns and pillows, they don't belong to you. I bartered for the feathers and I made the covers myself, and you are the only one using them."

She folded the eiderdown in a large bundle. "Grab that pillow, Vala. We are not leaving any luxuries that he doesn't deserve," she called out.

I had no option but to grab the large pillow and was pushed out of the room with her behind me.

Poor Dad just stood there quietly watching us go. I felt so sorry for him. He had nothing now, just a cold bare room with a wooden bench, no company, no support of the family, or an eiderdown to keep him warm.

"Please, Mum, please, Mum, can I just give a pillow to

Dad?" I pleaded.

"No, he doesn't deserve a thing," she retorted angrily.

I kept on pleading and begging as we went on, hoping that she would change her mind. The further away we went, the more determined she was against my pleadings, but eventually she said, "Alright, go and take him a pillow, but that's all, and come straight back, as we have to go home." At that I rejoiced and ran back, eagerly calling out, "Dad, Dad, here's your pillow, here's your pillow, you can at least be comfortable." I looked up at his quiet face that looked much older than his forty-odd years.

He looked down as he accepted the pillow and whispered softly, "Thanks, son. Look after Mum and Ludmilla."

I skipped back happily, thinking that perhaps this was a change in the relationship, and Dad would return to our quarters.

I was wrong. Dad never returned. Mum was probably just being vindictive that night, thinking that things would settle down and be the same as usual. When he still had not returned after another week, she said to me, "You had better go and see where your father is. He should have been back by now. He can't live in that pokey little room by himself."

I ran back to the theater, but there was no one there, and I noticed that all his personal items were gone. I raced out and asked a few people nearby if they had seen my dad, but they said, "No, he's been gone about a week or so." I was quite panicky now. I didn't know where he was or what he was doing, so I ran back home and told my mother I couldn't find him, and that all his things were gone.

I could see she was panicking now, too. She hadn't expected him to disappear. She thought that like all previous fights, they would make up and things would be the same. She did not see that the strong bond that held them together to survive the horrors of war was no longer required. Their cultural differences and the pressures of the situation prevented them from forging a spiritual and emotional bond necessary to sustain their relationship—nobody knew this.

We rushed over to find Nicola, Dad's best friend. Nicola

lived in the single quarters and shared a room with another man. He talked to Mother very gently. "No, Ivan is not in the camp anymore. He left about a week ago and went to Stuttgart to try to get some work in the American Army camp. He knows some people in the American Army that he met shortly after the war ended. I can't really be sure as I haven't heard what he's actually done, but he was talking about that, as he didn't really want to stay here anymore."

Mum was seriously upset. "You mean to say he left us, and didn't even say good-bye to me or the children without telling us where he went?" She was incredulous.

"Well, he really felt he had no more to say as you obviously didn't want him and threw him out with nothing, and he was too sad to see the kids again, and he just left by himself," Nicola told her.

With that we turned around and walked slowly to our rooms.

This was tragedy. What had kept my family together and protected us from all the horrors created by Europe's age-old morass of racial hatred, the curse of xenophobia that rages through history, was their refusal to let it enter their own lives. Now my mother's growing identification, after all this while, with her distant *Volksdeutsch* background had destroyed that shield.

And it didn't end there; the management committee of the camp was determined to punish Mum. Everybody knew what happened as the gossip spread. Very soon we got a letter from the management committee to tell us that we were no longer considered to be a family. The husband was no longer living in the family quarters, and we were to vacate them forthwith. We were evicted. We got a small room in the single quarters, no more than a tiny bedroom where we virtually had to stand sideways to get dressed.

Our misfortune was not to end there. Mum's German background made her very unpopular in the camp, where people felt everyone should be a fervent Ukrainian patriot. They had tolerated Mum only because my father was held in such high regard, and while he was around to act as our protector, we were not disturbed. Now he was gone, it was decided to have a "screening process" in the camp: anyone seen as tainted with German sympathies was not considered worthy of the care and protection provided by the camp and the UNRO. That applied to us. We were not refugees anymore but Germans in Germany. Scarce facilities and resources should not be wasted on us.

* * * *

Kindergarten class at Ellwangen Refugee Camp, Germany. Vala is 8th from left in 3rd row.

German school at Ellwangen, 1947. Vala is 4th from left in 2nd row.

Chapter 18

Life Outside the Camp

Mum was a perfect candidate for expulsion from the care and protection of the Ellwangen Camp. Of course, when Dad left us to go to work with the American Army, we were left as sitting ducks to be "screened out."

We duly received an invitation to attend the camp management committee to discuss our future at the camp. I attended the meeting with Mum. She was just as abrasive and unrepentant as ever.

"And, what is your specific personal background?" asked the chairman of the committee.

Mum did not hesitate to give him a full outline. "I'm of German background. I had German parents and I'm certainly pleased to be in Germany now."

"Well, you are in Germany now, but you are living in a Ukrainian camp," replied the chairman testily.

"My husband is Ukrainian, so I have a right to be in this camp."

"Where is your husband now?" he asked, knowing full well that he no longer lived with us.

"Well, he has left the camp for a little while. I think he is at Stuttgart," she answered.

"Are you saying that he no longer lives with you and the family?" asked the chairman.

"Not exactly. He is not living with us at the moment," she trailed off.

"We can then conclude that your Ukrainian husband is no longer living with you.

Now the second issue is that we believe you are sending your son to a German school. What is the reason for this action? Aren't we good enough to teach your son Ukrainian history and to read and write in his native tongue? Do you think we have an inferior culture not worth learning and preserving as Ukrainians?" he accused.

This really infuriated my mother and set her off into one of her black moods.

"Don't you dare talk to me like that! We are in Germany, and he goes to a German school. We have to live here and work here, and if we can't speak German or read German, he won't be able to get a job or become assimilated. You people are living in a fool's paradise, thinking you can make a Ukrainian enclave of two thousand to three thousand and live here like lords and ladies. This won't last long, mark my words. You are only fooling yourselves." With a thump of her fist on the desk that nearly shattered it, she grabbed my hand and dragged me out of the room. "Do what you want, you scoundrels, I don't really care."

And they did what they wanted: they finally got rid of Mum and me. We received a letter saying that as Mum was of German origin and as this was Germany, she could not be considered to be a refugee. The fact was that she was not born in Germany, never lived in Germany, and had grown up in Ukraine. That she was dragged by Hitler's troops through Ukraine, to Germany, to work camps, did not matter at all. The fact that I went to a German school would also render me a German and therefore not under the protection of UNRO.

The case of my sister, Ludmilla, on the other hand, was a different matter. She actually went to a Ukrainian school, she spoke and wrote in Ukrainian, and she participated fully in the Ukrainian cultural activities. She would be allowed to stay in the camp and finish her Ukrainian schooling. She was thirteen years old.

Mum was angry with the decision and somewhat frightened at the prospect of leaving the camp and having to forage and survive in war-torn Germany shortly after the end of the war. There was very little to eat, there was no work, and conditions were extreme. Nobody felt sorry for the Germans, having been occupied by the victors, and, as their brutality in the conquered nations and their atrocities to the Jews in the concentration camps were being revealed, they were considered to be less than human, and anger was building up against them. Because of Mum's temper and her aggressive stance and utterances, we were now being thrown out.

It was like being thrown out of the Garden of Eden, where one had been provided with all the basics of life and everyone participated in interests and cultural activities as they wished. We were now going into the real world, the world of thorns, hard, dry earth, where everything had to be obtained by the "sweat of their labor," and there was very little to go around.

We finally received official documentation that by a certain date we had to leave the camp. We were being transferred to official German citizenship, and we were now at last Germans, something that Mum had always wanted—but she didn't actually appreciate the consequences at that time of her life.

We packed our few belongings. Mum packed the eiderdowns and the large pillows in the galvanized metal baby bath that had been with us through the whole of the war. This was then enclosed in the canvas container with the handles sewn on to make it into a bundle, which could be carried. Another bag was packed with a few extra clothes we had, which were no more than a jumper, a coat, a change of underwear, some socks, and shoes. We also had a wooden box that Father had made, which acted as a small larder, where we kept a lot of the non-perishable food that we obtained from bartering or from the Red Cross parcels that we received on rare occasions.

We could not carry our luggage ourselves, and there was no transport available, but some old friends, particularly my god-father and another man, helped us carry our belongings to the railway station in Ellwangen.

We walked through the main gate of the camp, and I looked around for the last time. There was a high brick wall forming one side of the main gate, with a small pedestrian gate in the middle. Behind could be seen the main buildings of the camp, two stories in height with large steep roofs with dormer windows, and behind that a high tower with a clock and a round roof, which looked like a hat sitting on top of the tower.

We walked to Ellwangen, which was not a very long walk, but with our luggage, goods, and chattels, it was heavy going. We then walked through the center of the town, which to me was a huge place. It was a long street, and the buildings were very large Gothic structures, some three stories high before the roof line. The roofs were very steep to handle the snow, with one to three stories in the attic areas. They were all old, perhaps hundreds of years. Some were beautifully decorated and painted with scenes of religious motifs of Christ and saints. Other buildings were painted with wolves and other animals in forest settings. Some were only decorated in bright colors, such as red or blue. They were all different, individual, and, to me, quite imposing.

The whole town was in a valley surrounded by hills with a large imposing building, a monastery, overlooking the town. This was a stone building with round towers at each corner and a bright red tile roof. Most parts of town had a view of the monastery, with the large imposing structure keeping a stern vigil on the citizens below. We gradually made our way to the station; that was also an old square building, but not nearly as old as the townhouses. It was of sandstone construction with a brown tiled roof. It was only two stories in height and had a much more modern appearance than the old medieval structures in the town. There were no empty spaces between the buildings from bomb destruction, as in other towns. Ellwangen had not been bombed at all, as it had no industries, except the large monastery, which would hardly be a strategic target.

I did not know how Mother knew where to go, but she definitely was told where her new home was to be. We boarded the train in Ellwangen and made our way to Goppingen. We disembarked, dragging our luggage behind us, and then Mum asked for directions to Faundau, a small village in the area. We had to catch another train. This was a much shorter trip. On leaving the train, we eventually managed to obtain a small cart pulled by one horse to take us to our final destination. I don't know how Mother got this address, but it was certainly a long way from Ellwangen and the refugee camp, and was in the middle of nowhere.

We finally arrived at our destination. It was a beautiful place. It was just outside the small village of Faundau, and it was on the river flats. The house where we were to stay was made of dark stone-like granite. It was an old farmhouse; one part was of two stories reached by a staircase through an entry foyer, and another wing was a one-story section. It was beautiful and picturesque. It was built in the flat area between a large river and foothills of mountains seen in the far distance with darker areas of forests. The river flats were used for commercial vegetable gardens as far as the eye could see.

There was a lovely garden around the house with some flowers, but mainly vegetables and small fruit and berries, such as gooseberries. It was right next to a millstream, a narrow but fast-running stream meandering its way to the mill, which was about half a kilometer downstream. There was a small footbridge with two handrails on each side crossing the stream, and a short pathway connecting to a country road running towards the village and parallel to the millstream. Just past the road was the start of a big hill, which was used for open fields with a few scattered trees. But on one side, the hill was cultivated and was a different shade of green. At the top of the hill was the start of a thick forest. It was peaceful and secluded, and as soon as I arrived, I loved it.

We introduced ourselves to the lady who apparently owned the house, and we had to climb up the steep staircase to the accommodation upstairs. It consisted of one room, which was used as a kitchen, dining, and all-purpose room. It was untidy, with a large table in the center with all sorts of dishes and equipment cluttered on it. To our left was another room that was a bedroom used by the lady and the man who owned the house. Apparently we were to live in the room next to theirs. It was a tiny room, which was their son's bedroom. She explained that he had been killed on the Eastern Front at Stalingrad.

She looked at us rather suspiciously when we told her our name, but she seemed relieved when Mother explained that she was of German origin, and that we were Ukrainian, and not Russian. When Mum told her that her own brother was captured in Stalingrad, we were accepted warmly nearly as family.

Our room was tiny; we overlooked the millstream, and the hill was towering above us beyond the dirt road. We placed the small wooden box in front of the window, and we used that as a small table, and also it acted as our larder for the food that we had accumulated. Against the wall, facing the door, we made up our bed on the floor with the eiderdowns and pillows that we brought with us. The room was only about two and a half meters wide and about three meters long, a tiny capsule of life where we could exist.

The toilet and small bathroom were off the main room, and we had limited access to it as required. We, however, could not cook in the kitchen unless we asked for special permission.

Our diet, therefore, was very restricted. We mainly existed on dark rye bread with some pork belly fat and occasional German sausages. When we were really short of food and money, we ate the dark rye bread rubbed over with garlic to give it some taste. When you were hungry, it tasted great. For dessert we would moisten the bread with water and sprinkle it with sugar from our store.

On very special occasions and for certain celebrations, such as birthdays, we would make a "torte." It consisted of white bread (a rare commodity in itself), buttered and then some jam spread on top. This was made in two or three layers and eaten with relish; I never left a crumb.

At a later stage, Mum managed to secure a Primus stove using kerosene as fuel and this provided us with a more varied menu. This was mainly based on frying some pork belly fat with onions and mushrooms picked from the forest nearby, as well as potatoes cut into thin sections and fried with the onions and pork. The smell was unbelievable and the taste was even better. Another favorite was soup, especially pea soup, again combined with fried onion and a piece of hambone—this would be hard to beat on a cold winter's night.

We rarely saw the old man who lived there, as he remained in his room. He was a tall gaunt figure. To me he seemed very, very old with a thin, drawn, and furrowed face and a huge, drooping, gray moustache. He was very quiet, and had a faraway look on his face, hardly ever acknowledging us. He was grieving for his son who was killed in Stalingrad, his only child.

Sometimes in the middle of the night, we would be woken by sad violin music. It would last for hours, far into the night, and I would often drift off to sleep with the music still in my ears. It was the old man's way of expressing his sadness and despair for his missing son.

After the first few days, we started to explore the area. Mum was particularly interested in the woods high on our hill.

One day in early summer, as dusk was falling, Mum said we were going for a walk. I wondered about the timing, as it was wet and a fine drizzle of rain was falling, making everything wet and unpleasant outside.

"Never mind about the drizzling—there will be fewer people to see us. We are going to go for a walk in the forest and have a look around."

We struggled our way up the steep hill with our shoes encased in mud. We continued through the slush and mud until we reached the forest edge. We made our way into the underbrush, and followed a few paths. It was rather frightening. It was getting dark, it was drizzly and wet, and I was frightened of getting lost. It was a thick forest with beech trees, fir trees, and thick undergrowth, and it was difficult to see where we were going. Mum followed a few paths and was looking down on the ground.

"Ah, this should be about right," she said. "See these pellets—they are droppings from an animal. They must come along this path quite often." Mum stopped and took some thin wire out of her coat pocket and made a small loop. She attached one end of the wire to a root in the ground. She tested it to see if it would work with her fingers, and it seemed to be fairly tight and secure. This contraption might well catch a small animal. I wasn't very keen to continue at this time, but Mum insisted, and we went along a few different paths and set a few more traps, making our way out of the forest before it became completely dark and we were drenched to our skins.

After that we would frequently go up into the forest and check our snares. Initially full of hope and anticipation, we imagined that we would catch at least a small deer. We would go up every few days for some weeks, but there was never any game caught. In the end, we were hoping even for a small rabbit.

Alas, it was all in vain. It was just wasted effort to go up there to check the traps. Either the animals were smarter than us and were avoiding the traps, or there were no animals in the forest. No matter how many traps we put out or where we put them, we never caught one poor beast in them. After two or three weeks, Mum gave up her hunting expeditions and reverted back to bartering with the farmers and gardeners. We still had some supplies saved from the Red Cross parcels, like cigarettes, soap, and toothpaste. These were still prized commodities for which food could be exchanged.

Soon after settling in, we met the family who lived in the lower wing of the house. They were a young family, a man and his wife, and they also had a small girl called Gertrude. When I first saw her, I fell in love for the first time. She was about five or six years old, with a beautiful pink complexion and long blonde hair, done in a plait on each side with a middle part. When she smiled, she had a dimple on both cheeks. She was not aggressive or threatening or rude or nasty, nor did she seem to care where I came from or the origin of my name. She just wanted to play skip, chase, and hide and seek. I spent the whole afternoon in her company. The sun was bright, the sky was blue, and I was floating in ecstasy without a care in the world.

Later that afternoon, her mother called her in, and she had to go to visit someone in town. As they walked across the small footbridge, crossing the millstream, and down the dusty road, I waved to her as far as I could. As she was disappearing out of sight, I climbed on the railing of the bridge to get a higher view and keep on waving. As I took my hands off the rails to wave, I suddenly fell backwards into the water and sank slowly down. I couldn't swim, but I had this eerie, unreal sensation as if I were an observer in the event and did not have to panic. I slowly sank deeper into the water, and I looked at the stream bed, thinking how untidy it was, littered with broken glass and debris. I reached the bottom with my feet, kicked back, and slowly rose to the surface again. I was near the bank, and was able to grab hold of some overhanging bushes and pull myself out. I don't know how I didn't drown, as I could not swim. I just lay there in the warm sun and dried out. I didn't change my clothing, as I was too frightened to tell Mum what I did, as I knew I would get a belting for my stupidity. I never told my mother and she never guessed what happened to me. I could have drowned, but that concept didn't even enter my head at that young age. However, I was very careful not to repeat that maneuver in the future.

On another occasion, I saw Gertrude asleep in her garden. I thought, I know what I'll do, I'll sneak up quietly to her and give her a kiss, like the prince in Snow White, who woke her up from a deadly sleep. I slowly crawled towards her. When I looked up and to the side, I saw her father looking at me grimly.

"I was going to wake her up," I said in a whisper, rather sheepishly.

He looked sternly at me and moved his head from side to side and said emphatically, "No, you're not, you young rascal. Off with you and don't dare wake her up."

I was deflated, but I slunk off with my young romantic fantasy shattered by the grown-up.

There was another boy who lived in the area in a similar farmhouse shared by a number of families. His name was Karl. He was also sharing a room with his mother and older brother, but it was bigger, and they had a real kitchen with a stove and a tap. His father had been killed in the war, but he didn't seem to hold it against me personally, and we became good friends. He was also as poor as a church mouse, and the rest of the school shunned him. Karl, Gertrude, and I would run around the countryside exploring, playing games, and living off the land. The whole river flats area between the river and the start of the hill was one huge market garden. There were various farmers working in the area. They worked constantly, digging, pruning, clearing, and planting. They would fertilize the area by pulling up buckets full of smelly liquid from the septic sewerage tanks, and then spread this human manure over their gardens.

Although we would often sample the products, we were careful to be discreet. We would not harm any plant, and we would take only one or two fruits, so that there would be no loss to the farmer. Our favorites were tomatoes and cucumbers, which would then be taken to the creek bed, which was usually dry, unless it rained heavily. We made our secret lair in the exposed roots of trees, where the water had washed away the soil, camouflaging it with bushes, leaves, and branches. No one could see us when we were inside, and we felt safe and secure. We took our booty, such as a few tomatoes, cucumbers, or pieces of rhubarb, and munched away. If the tomatoes were green, we would leave them for a week or so in the sun, and by that time, they were red and tasty. We spent the whole summer holidays climbing in the area. It was now towards the end of summer, and the hill in front of us, which was sown with wheat, was getting yellow and ripe. The heads of wheat were nearly up to our heads. They were thick and heavy with grain.

Finally harvest time arrived, and a motorized harvester appeared for the job. It was marvelous. I had never seen a harvester work before: this chugging, puffing machine with blue smoke emitting from the exhaust was moving slowly along, at the same time cutting the wheat, throwing the cut heads inside, and threshing it to break free the grains of wheat. It was not, however, one hundred percent efficient, and we were allowed to follow it and pick up any heads of wheat that it might have missed. There were a few women and children involved in this. Food was so short that not a grain was wasted. We walked along slowly with our heads bent down searching for every grain. We would pounce on a full head, but even some grains were picked up and put in a bag around my neck. We didn't get much, but every seed was precious. This was only the second harvest after the war, and food was very scarce.

At lunch time, we sat with the women, and they shared their drink with us, a cloudy liquid, tasty with a tangy cheesy flavor. This was whey, the liquid expressed when cottage cheese is made. We sat on the hill and looked down below us to the little village hidden among the trees in the valley. We could see the tall steeple of the church, which was a square tower, some three or four stories high with a steep roof of black tiles. Only the roofs of the other buildings were visible through the trees. Further, past the village, were more hills blue in the distance. It felt good to be working and sharing a drink with these women. It felt grown-up. The scene was peaceful with a promise for the future, with the yellow fields around us and below the verdant forest of trees with some of the roofs of the village glistening in the sunlight. I was working, gathering wheat, which would provide nourishment for my mother and me, and I was anticipating the cakes and bread that she would bake.

By the time the harvest was over, it was late afternoon and going towards evening. I dragged myself home exhausted from bending over continually through the day and picking up little heads of wheat that were not picked up by the machinery. But the rewards were great. My bag was nearly filled with the wheat and was quite heavy to carry. Mum took the bag to the miller, and for a percentage of the wheat, he agreed to mill it for us. We ended up with a large bowl of beautiful white flour. For the next few weeks or so, I was treated to the aroma of baking cakes, strudels, and buns. The lady let us use her oven, for which we shared part of our cakes. My labor was richly rewarded.

Food was always a problem and foremost in our minds, and by early afternoon, we were always hungry after playing all day, and looked for something to eat.

On one occasion, Karl said, "Let's go to my home and see what's to eat there. Mum may cook something." We made our way to his house. I had never been to his house before, but when we entered, it was very similar to where I lived, a small farm-house divided into various rooms where people lived. They lived also in the upper part of the house, and we entered a large room with two beds against the wall and a table and chairs with a cooking corner. They had a stove in their room, which we did not. The place was untidy and rough, a bit like ours, but ours was always tidy, as Mum was fastidious. His mother was sitting at the table and appeared to be asleep with her head on her arms. We sneaked in quietly. There was a bottle on the table, and I could smell a sour mixture of alcohol and stale tobacco.

There was no food in the house except for a pot on the stove. This held congealed pea soup, cold and unappetizing. Karl's fa-ther had been killed in the war, and his mother had not got over it. She was often drunk and unconscious, leaving Karl and his brother to fend for themselves. He was dressed poorly, and his hair was long, straggly, and often uncombed. He would often turn up at school with no shoes. I felt sorry for him, as my par-ents always ensured I had proper shoes to wear.

"Well, there is nothing here," I said gently. "Let's go over to my house—we might find some food there." I knew we had a stock in our larder and could probably sneak something out without Mum knowing.

When we arrived at our house, I told him to wait outside and I went upstairs. Mum wasn't in, so I opened the wooden box and took out a packet. I went down.

"Try this, Karlo. I don't know whether you've ever tried some of this American stuff." We tore open the packet and started eating the lovely red crystals with sugar. It would just melt in the mouth with a tang of fruity flavor. We'd fill our mouths.

"That is beautiful," he said. "What is it?"

"Well, I don't know. It's always that sort of powder. I eat it now and again and really love the flavor." We couldn't read the instructions to find out that it was jelly and how to make it—we just ate the crystals and enjoyed the concentrated flavor.

"Can I have some more?" said Karl. "This is great."

"I don't think so, I don't think there is much left," I said, realizing that we could eat up the whole supply in no time and Mum would probably get suspicious and start asking questions next time she opened the larder.

"Come on, Walter (German of my name), just one more. I haven't tasted anything like this before."

I reluctantly agreed to get another packet and share it with Karl. I again walked up the steps leading to our room and went to the larder, and at the bottom of the steps outside the door, we opened a packet again and started indulging ourselves with the crystalline taste sensation. Just at that very moment, my mother came in through the door and saw us in the act. My heart sank. I was done, caught in the act, with not a chance of explaining this one away.

"Alright, Vala, up you go," she said in a stern voice. I just left the packet with Karl and walked upstairs slowly in front of Mum. Once inside our room, I got the belting of my lifetime, and at every hit, Mum called out, "Don't you dare waste the food in such a way."

I learned from that experience that in a survival situation, sharing our meager resources was a very dangerous thing to do, and it was likely to result in quite a beating.

I was not sorry, however, despite the beating I received. I felt sorry for poor Karl. At least my father was still alive, even though I had not heard from him for nearly a year.

Food was always a problem and I always had to keep an eye
open for an opportunity to supplement the diet. I noticed that just
outside the village on the way home was a house with an unruly
garden, overgrown with various trees, shrubs, and bushes. An old
lady lived there, and she didn't care much about the garden and let
everything go. However, in one corner of the garden was a short
tree with thin branches. I noticed some nuts on the ground and on
the tree. Without much effort, I slipped over the fence and gathered up all the nuts off the ground. They were hazelnuts.

I filled my pockets with the hazelnuts and made my way to
our secret lair. Gertrude and Karl joined me, and for the rest of
the afternoon, we had a great time smashing the nuts between
two rocks and eating the nutmeat. This continued for a few
weeks. Every time I passed the house with the hazelnut tree, I
would slip over the fence and pick up the nuts from the ground
like a squirrel until there were no nuts left. It amazed me that in
those days when food was so scarce, people did not use all of the
resources available to them. Obviously the lady who lived in the
house didn't like nuts, or was not hungry.

Other sources of ready snacks were also available in our
area. The farmers, when they harvested the cabbages, Brussels
sprouts, etc., left the stalks and the root in the fields. Whenever
we felt hungry, we would go along and, using our penknives, cut
off the stalks at ground level. The hard cellular skin was stripped
off, leaving the crunchy center. This was not unlike an apple in
consistency, but had the vegetable taste and tang of a cabbage
or Brussels sprout. However, three or four stalks would make a
fine snack if one was really hungry. Other sources, such as apple
or pear trees growing by the side of the road, could yield a fine
harvest in autumn. I often took bags of apples home, and Mum
would cook them with sugar, if there was any available. There
were also berries and mushrooms in the forest, for which we foraged regularly. We were reluctant to venture too far, as the dark
quiet forests were scary.

One afternoon when I came home from school, Mum called
out excitedly, "Come and see what I've got for you today." I

walked into the room, and there was a small cage with two small, fluffy bodies exploring the cage. They were two rabbits, beautiful, fluffy little creatures with long whiskers and noses, which continually quivered. They weren't at all scared, and could be handled, patted, and cuddled.

"These will be your responsibility," said Mum. "You will have to get grass for them every day and make sure the water container is always filled."

We made a small hutch for them just outside the front door of the house with some old wire netting and timber, which was lying around the yard. It was a rough job, but adequate, with a small swinging door to access the cage.

Every morning before going to school, I would go out and spend ten to fifteen minutes gathering armfuls of grass, which I left for the rabbits to eat during the day. The water container was also filled. When I arrived home, I would first look at the rabbits and make sure they had more grass available and have a pat. They were friendly and trusting, continually twitching their noses. They loved to be tickled around the ears and under the chin, and they could stand for a long time just having their ears rubbed at the base. They were my first pets, and I loved them dearly. Weeks and months slipped by, summer was passing into autumn, and the rabbits were getting big and fat. They were just as friendly and trusting, however, and I would never tire of stroking them or tickling their ears. They knew me and always looked forward to seeing me coming, particularly if I managed to get half a carrot, or some other piece of hard vegetable for them.

One afternoon I came home from school, and to my surprise and horror, the rabbit hutch was empty. I raced up the steps calling out, "Mum, Mum, the rabbits are gone. Someone has pinched the rabbits." I burst into the room and saw that there was a man there.

"Hush," she said. "Don't go on so. We have a visitor. Of course, you know Mr. Voderenko. He has come to visit us and tell us what has happened in Ellwangen."

I certainly did know Mr. Voderenko. He had stayed in our room once when we were transferred from the private quarters when Dad left. He stayed with us for about a month, and he used to make me clean his shoes for him. He said that the young members of the family should do all the work for the older people. I disliked him intensely. I certainly hoped he was not going to stay with us in this room, as I would probably leave if he stayed.

The dinner was cooking merrily on the stove, and the pot was bubbling. A lovely aroma was coming from the cooking, and I was just a little bit suspicious and had an uneasy feeling.

We made some small talk; obviously the subject they had been talking about before I came in was changed.

When Mum dished out the dinner, it was a lovely-smelling meat stew. We sat around the small wooden chest that we used as a table. I looked at her rather suspiciously, not really wanting to eat it. Mr. Voderenko took a few big mouthfuls and ate it with relish.

"Mmmmm, what a lovely stew. What sort of meat is that?"

"Rabbit," Mum answered softly. At this, I gagged and nearly vomited. I was angry and felt like bursting into tears. I controlled myself, as I did not want to cry and be upset in front of him. He would probably make some funny remark about it. I didn't eat any of the food. I just played around, thinking continually of my poor little rabbits, who were sacrificed for the satisfaction of this fat fool. As soon as I could, I raced out to my secret lair and burst out crying.

For the next few weeks, I was rather cool with Mum and, although she was extra nice with me, I answered her direct questions only in short sentences. But my anger and sadness also passed. I knew that food was an essential item of life, and getting fond of rabbits was a risky business in postwar Germany when food, particularly meat, was very scarce and everything was destined for the pot if it was at all edible.

The school in the village was small, and there were only about sixty or so children. In the first class, the class that I was enrolled in, there were only about fifteen children. Some of them were children from the local farms, and a lot of them were from families who lived in the actual village. They ran the butcher shop, the bakery, and other businesses found in these places. Some were like Karl and me, hungry and unkempt, with no fathers and inadequate mothers. We tended to be ignored and allowed to languish at the back of the class. We were the riff-raff with no future. The tradition in the place was that the sons would take over the profession or trade of the father, as they grew older. There was even a special children's day that was celebrated. All the boys dressed up in the uniforms or clothing of their future trades and occupations, which usually meant that the butcher's son would be dressed up as a butcher, the baker's son would be dressed as a baker, etc. There was even a parade where all these young people were marching in their dressed-up uniforms led by a small brass band, which was part of the school activities.

The "riff-raff" boys did not bother to march in the parade, as we had no future occupations to inherit, with no fathers working in the area. The town was neat and clean with cobbled streets and a cobbled square, which was the main center of activity for the village, where the market was held once a week. All celebrations and marchers congregated in this area. On the occasion of the Apprenticeship March, there was a fair held in the square. There was a large pole, unfortunately greased, and at the top was a bunch of sausages. Anyone who could climb up the pole could claim the sausages. I, of course, tried and tried, but did not have a chance. I don't think there was any risk of the sausages being won. I went off home after the celebrations, rather sad that I had no future career, not really knowing what I would be when I grew up.

The school was not friendly. I was always regarded and referred to as the *"Ausländer,"* or the foreigner, or in a more aggressive manner, as a "Russian brat." I hated the situation but with a name like Kirychenko, it would be difficult to pretend otherwise. My German was also poor, and I really was the *Ausländer*. I didn't really care. I had good friends in Karl and Gertrude, and we had great fun together away from school and the other children.

I learned very little at the school, as we, the riff-raff, mainly congregated at the back of the class. We had a black slate to write on, as there was no paper, and all of our practice of sums and writing was written on the slate, but there was no record kept, as after filling the slate, it had to be cleaned off before we could write any more.

The main reading textbook was not available to anyone who could not provide an equivalent amount of paper, cardboard, or rags. I had to hunt around for any paper and rags. It took me a few weeks to obtain enough weight of paper to then exchange for the book. Commodities were so scarce that even paper for school books was restricted. The textbook was printed in gothic, Germanic lettering, and it was difficult to read, so I did not get very far in reading and writing German in my first year at the German school.

One day in late autumn, Mum was rather excited and said, "Guess what, Dad's coming over to visit us soon. I received a letter from him and he wants to see us."

Well, that was a surprise. It was nearly a year since I had last seen him, and we really hadn't heard from him at all. I would think of him sometimes and wonder what he was doing and where he was living. Mother might have known, but she didn't tell me anything about him. I felt sad that the family was split. The intense, warm relationship during the war years was broken during the years after the war, when safety had at last arrived. There could have been so many things that Dad and I could have done together.

He duly arrived, walking the considerable distance from the railway station on foot. He waved as he saw us near the house, and I ran towards him over the little footbridge as he turned off from the road into our yard area.

"Hello, my little Cossack," he said, as he gave me a hug.

I was a bit embarrassed with this, as I was nearly six years old, and I thought it was too effeminate to cuddle your father. We took him up the dingy, dark stairway and into our room.

"Oh, it looks very comfortable. You made it nice and homey, Lydia. It's very small, though, and there wouldn't be much room for anyone else."

"We don't need anyone else," Mum said pointedly. "Ludmilla comes occasionally on the weekends and during her school holidays, and we make up a bed for her on the floor with the eiderdowns."

Mum made a special effort cooking. We had borsch, the famous beetroot soup made in Ukraine and Russia, and we also had a stew with meat and vegetables. Thankfully it was not rabbit meat this time. I ate it all and heartily enjoyed it.

Dad brought some chocolate and American sweets that he had managed to obtain from the American store where he was working. He worked in an army camp, and his job was to service the cars and trucks in the camp area. He loved the work. It was the sort of work that he enjoyed, tinkering around cars, solving little problems and making repairs.

From the conversation, I gleaned that Father wanted to emigrate from Germany, perhaps go to Canada, America, or even Australia, and he was discussing this with Mum. As always, she was adamant and fixed in her stance that she wanted to stay in Germany and would not budge.

"Run along now, Vala, and play outside while the sun is still shining, while we discuss a few things here," she said. I got the hint. They obviously wanted to talk things out without me, so I wandered off and played outside. I found Karl, and we sat there shooting at an old log with our catapults. We had perfected the art of making catapults. We used a fork of a tree. It had to be just the right thickness and the right angle to give the best results. We then used the rubber from a bike inner tube cut to an even thickness, about one centimeter in width. The bit that held the rock was made from a thin piece of leather, possibly from an old shoe or an old handbag that we managed to scrounge up. Everything was secured together with fine wire and tightened. We pretended we were soldiers shooting the enemy and made the appropriate noises.

After a while, I decided to go up and see what they were doing.

"I'd better go and see what my parents are doing. I hope they are not fighting, but I don't think so. They haven't seen each other for such a long time there wouldn't be much to fight about," I said to Karl.

I made my way up slowly and entered the room. They both looked harried, and Father looked rather tense and irritated. They were obviously fighting about something, even after not seeing each other for nearly a year. I wondered what could be so important.

"Why don't you take Dad for a walk into the forest, Vala, and show him how we set our traps. Not that we have caught anything yet, but you never know."

"That's a good idea," said Dad. "I would love to have a look through the forest and see where you do your 'hunting.' That would be fun."

We walked across the little bridge, up the hill, and to the top where the dense forest started. We stuck to the main path as Dad had on his good clothes and shoes and we didn't want to get them dirty or tear them.

Dad was quiet and didn't talk much. He asked a few questions about me, how I liked school and if I had friends, but I could see that he was deeply preoccupied and rather tense. Whatever they were talking about in the room must have upset him.

I had found a long stick, which I knew would make a fine spear, so I was carrying it with me and waving it around. Suddenly I accidentally shoved it between Dad's legs, and he went hurtling down beside me, tripping over the stick. He got up with part of his trousers dirty and slightly torn. He was very angry.

"What a stupid thing to do!" he cried out. "Give me that stick." He grabbed the stick and broke it in half and threw it away. Then he gave me a few good whacks. I started crying, and at that he stopped and appeared sorry. I wasn't crying because he broke the stick and whacked me—Mum hit twice as hard. I was upset that after not seeing him for one year, the day was spoiled by an accident. I thought he hated me.

"Let's go back home," he said gruffly, and off he went with his hands in his pockets, not looking behind him where I was following him, sobbing away. I wasn't too keen to see him again soon, and I didn't. It was nearly two years before I saw him again.

By the time we entered the room, I had managed to stop crying and wiped away most of my tears. Mum, however, noticed that something was wrong.

"You seem to have been crying," she said.

"No, nothing at all really, Mum. I fell over," I lied. I couldn't tell Mum that Dad belted me; that would really start a ruckus, and Mum would probably throw him out again. Shortly after that, Dad had to leave to catch his train connection back to Stuttgart. It was a complicated trip requiring a number of interconnections between the various train lines.

Dad's visit was upsetting. It brought back the memories of the life at the camp and during the war, which I was slowly forgetting living in that place. I had the river, the fields, the mountains, and the forest to roam in. School wasn't so bad, and I had a good friend, and, of course, I had Gertrude, my lovely neighbor. We had a great time together exploring the creek beds and fields, and pinching fruits and vegetables from the farmers.

It was getting colder now. Going to school was more difficult, and I had to wear every jumper that I owned and even a coat. I had good shoes, though, as Mother always made sure that I was well shod. Probably her experience in Siberia taught her that frostbite of the toes could be lethal. Some of the boys, such as Karl, didn't have good shoes, and they found the cold weather uncomfortable.

The short trousers were also cold, and the richer boys, who wore expensive leather shorts, changed to thick woolen pants quickly. Of course, there was no uniform at the school—we just wore the clothes we had and were lucky to have any clothes at all.

One day I woke feeling cold and cramped. I slept in the same bed as Mum, so it was fairly warm in bed, but that day my face was cold and my ears were tingling. I got up slowly and looked out the window, and there it was: the whole area was covered with snow. It was a wonderful sight. The millstream was still running quickly, but the hill in front of us, which was usually green or yellow with wheat, was a lovely clean white. All the trees were covered with snow. There were icicles hanging from the eaves, and the window pane was covered in frost. We ran off to school, skating on the frozen puddles as we went along. It was great fun, and some of the thinner ones cracked as soon as we jumped on them. At school everybody was playing snowballs, and, of course, a gang of the German boys decided to pick on Karl and me. We gave them a good account, throwing snowballs as quickly as possible, pretending they were machine guns, and then when overwhelmed by the enemy, we made a strategic withdrawal by turning around and running for our lives into the classroom. No snowballs were allowed in the classroom. The snow allowed new activities and possibilities for playing and having some fun. We were skating on the big mud puddles, which turned into ice. There were snowball fights at school, and when we got home, we were involved in building a snowman and forts from the snow, and then pretending to defend them with snowballs.

Towards the middle of winter, Karl somehow obtained a sled. Now *that* was fun. We would go up the steep hill in front of our house and slide down as far as the road. We would take it in turns. I would slide down and then take the sled up to the top again, and then Karl would slide down. We would do this for hours, exhilarated by the speed and the wind blowing in our face and hair, and the cold biting on the skin until it tingled.

One afternoon we were sledding down the hill close to a few trees near the bottom. I was careful to avoid them and had no trouble. On one occasion, I noticed that Karl was getting too close to the trees. He must have lost control or concentration— he couldn't avoid one of them and hit it sideways, striking his left leg on the tree with terrific force. It was near the bottom of the hill, and he was moving at top speed.

The sled tipped over with Karl underneath. I was waiting for him to get up and come back up again, but he just stayed there. I quickly ran to him and saw his left leg. It was a horrible sight. The glancing blow had torn his pants away and I could see his left leg in a strange angle underneath him. He was bleeding, with a round bright red ring soaking into the white snow. The contrast made it so much worse, and through the skin was a white sharp protrusion, which I realized was the cracked bone of his leg.

I was sick. I felt like vomiting, but I knew that I had to bring some help as quickly as possible. I leaned over to Karl, and he was not crying, but groaning in a dazed semi-conscious state.

"Don't worry, Karl. I'll get someone here as quickly as possible. You'll be alright. Just wait there and don't worry about a thing." I didn't want to touch him in case I caused more damage. I quickly ran to his house and banged loudly on his door. His mother eventually opened it with a dazed look on her face, and a cigarette sticking out of her mouth.

"Hang on there, hang on there," she said irritated. "Don't knock the door down, young man. What is it anyway? Karl isn't here, so you better look for him somewhere else."

"It's Karl! Come quick, he's tore his leg off!"

She was jolted as if hit by an electric current. She straightened up and the cigarette dropped out of her mouth. She put her shoes on and ran quickly to her neighbors.

"Quick," she said, "Call the police, call the ambulance, Karl's been hurt. He's up on the hill."

I ran quickly back to where Karl was lying semi-conscious, with her following behind me. She looked blue and cold as the wind caught her. She had only a thin jumper on and didn't have time to put on a coat or other warm clothes. She didn't feel the cold—she kept on calling out, "*Gott im Himmel, Gott im Himmel*" (God in heaven). We reached Karl shortly, and he was now more conscious and crying loudly, especially when he saw his mother.

"My leg, my leg," he said. "I can't move it, and it's hurting." She hurriedly lifted up his head and made him more comfortable. Before long an ambulance did arrive. The driver and his assistant came running with a stretcher, puffing and blowing. They injected Karl with some drug, and I could see his face relax as the pain ebbed away. They then gently put him on a stretcher, which must have been a painful procedure, as Karl's face again became strained, and he called out sharply in between his sobbing.

I stood back watching as they gradually carried him down the hill and put him into the ambulance and took him away. All that was left was a stain of red blood soaking into the snow. It was quite frightening to see the blood there with everyone gone except me. I quietly took the sled, pulled it to Karl's house, and left it with his brother.

The accident was the talk of the school the next day. Everybody was talking about how Karl nearly had his leg torn off when he hit the tree. After that I was not allowed to go on the sled. Of course, that was Mum's official stance, but unofficially I still went sledding, hoping Mother wouldn't catch me, as there would have been a belting in store.

Poor Karl was in the hospital for six to seven weeks. He came out on crutches and was further restricted in walking for another few months. He hardly went to school that winter, and by the time he could walk without the crutches, it was nearly spring. He was never the same again. He walked with a severe limp, had difficulty running, and felt very self-conscious about his disability. There was a hideous scar on the outer part of the leg where the bone tore through the flesh. Every time I thought of him lying there with the blood oozing onto the white snow and the whitish bone splintered and sticking out through his flesh, I would feel a shudder up my spine.

Apart from that accident, I had a great time during winter and always had plenty to do and enjoyed the countryside under snow.

Mum had a hard time, though. There was no heating in the room at all. It was very cold, and the only way to keep warm was to stay in bed. She could not get a job anywhere. There were no factories working, particularly in the countryside. She was on some small pittance of a pension from the German government. It couldn't afford to feed all the widows and orphans resulting from the war, as there was no economy base to employ or manufacture the required goods. The Marshall Plan had not yet started to create its miracle of rejuvenating Germany into an economic super power.

If it were not for the stock of food that we had accumulated over the last few years, and the cigarettes, toothpaste, toothbrushes, and soap that Mum had stored away, which were used with the farmers as bargaining chips for food, we would have been very thin indeed that winter. She was very glad to see the spring at last, with a few flowers and grass forcing their way through the thin part of the snow and the snow melting and forming small rivulets to take all the water into the rivers. I hated this part of the year—it was so slushy, wet, and muddy. Wherever you walked, you got your feet wet in mud. There were no footpaths or made roads in that area, so there was only mud. I tried to stay inside more until the snow had melted. It was nice to see the days getting warmer, and as soon as the snow thawed, Mum and I made a small garden near the house. We planted radishes, shallots, and tomatoes—it was too small a plot for many potatoes. The shallots and the radishes were tasty with dark rye bread, especially if we had some butter and salt.

We stayed there until Easter and that was a lovely time. The parents hid candy formed into eggs and chickens all around the garden and the house, and the children spent the morning fossicking and looking where the "bunny rabbit" might have hidden the candy. It was great. I got a few rabbits and an egg out of it. Mum also cooked some hard-boiled eggs, and we had a game with all the kids in the neighborhood. There was a competition where the eggs were struck together with each individual holding their own egg. The owner of the egg that broke was declared the loser, and the winner would win the hard-boiled egg from the loser. I collected a few eggs, and we had an egg dinner that night.

Chapter 19

Out of Germany

That spring Mum decided that the German "adventure" was over for us. It was too hard. Living in a small room in a German farmhouse with no money, no food, by herself with no support, was too difficult and lonely. She could see no end to the deprivation, and she could not anticipate the tremendous improvement in years to come. She decided to emigrate.

She discussed this with Ludmilla and me when Ludmilla came to visit us on some weekends. We spent endless nights discussing where we should go. The choices available were all in the "New World." We could have gone to Canada, America, or a whole range of South American countries with exotic names, such as Paraguay, Venezuela, or Brazil. We knew nothing about any of these countries. We knew something about America as we had met American soldiers, who seemed to be exceedingly rich, well fed, and pleasant, and it did sound like a great place to live. There were also a lot of Ukrainians in Canada, and, in fact, Mum's uncle was in Canada and might still be alive. Of course, she had not heard from him since before World War One. We were tossing ideas around continually without resolution. Then she said, "I know what we'll do. We'll find out where your father is."

That took some doing. She had to go to the UNRO offices in Mannheim and make inquiries in person. She could not communicate by letter as she could not write or read, so everything had to be done in person, and I, of course, had to accompany her. We spent hours travelling and changing trains, but they had improved since our visit to see our grandmother. All the lines were now repaired and there were no major hold-ups in the train travel. There were still hours of waiting to catch a connection at the various stations. Mum finally talked to the right official, and managed to find out where Dad had actually emigrated to.

"So where is my husband then?" she asked this clerk impatiently.

He looked bored. He opened pages and sifted through the names and destinations, and he said, "Ah, ah. Kirychenko, Ivan."

"Yes, yes, that's the one, that's my husband. Where did he go?" inquired Mum impatiently.

The clerk looked at her in an irritated way, not believing that a person could emigrate and not tell his family, and finally said, "He went to Australia."

"Australia? Where is Australia, what sort of country is that? I've never heard of Australia. I thought to myself. Australia!" Mum again exclaimed. "What on earth would make him go to Australia? It is the end of the world. There are no white people there. It is just like Siberia."

She was dumbfounded. She walked out of the room in a daze, and we caught the trains back to our little village, and then walked the long trudge home from the railway station.

"Well, we'll have to go to Australia, I suppose," she said, "although I'd rather go to Canada or America, or even the South

American countries, but seeing your father chose Australia, the furthermost place from here, we will have to go to Australia."

To become eligible to immigrate to these countries, we had to regain refugee status. That meant losing our German citizenship, of which my mother was so proud, and reverting back to Ukrainian refugees. She had to go to Ellwangen and see the officials to see how it could all be done. She explained that her husband was now in Australia and she wished to join him there with her two children, who were born in Ukraine, although she was born in Poland. The priest prepared a sworn document emphasizing the place of birth. She was allowed to therefore change her status, as she was really following her husband to Australia, and we made arrangements to go back to Ellwangen.

I was sorry to say good-bye to Faundau. It was a beautiful, peaceful place, a little backwater of civilization, just as it was one hundred years or so ago. Everything was still primitive—the roads, sanitation, and the house we lived in would have been at least one hundred years old. There were a lot of fields, a mill-stream with an old water mill still in working order, and a wide river where we often played, throwing little flat stones into the water to make them bounce and lots and lots of forests. There was the big hill ascending up from the road where we played, sledded, and ran around.

I was sorry to say good-bye to Karl. We did this very formally. I shook his hand and said "Well, good-bye, Karl. I hope to see you sometime soon," and he also returned the farewell in a similar manner, but we both knew that despite the formal farewells, we were fairly close to tears as we said good-bye. We had spent a lovely year in the area, and it was just like one long holiday. I enjoyed the different times of the year, spring, summer, autumn, and winter. This was the first period of peace I had experienced without fear of bombs, persecution, and hatred.

It was sad to say good-bye to Gertrude, too. She was my companion for the whole year, and we did so many things together. I gave her a kiss on the cheek, and her father didn't even disapprove, knowing full well that I was going anyway, and couldn't get into any mischief. I also said good-bye to the old man who played the violin nearly every night and kept us awake for hours. He looked as sad as ever, but he shook my hand and said I was a good boy. The old woman gave Mum a big hug and wished her well in her trip to Australia. She heard about our intentions, as Mum talked about nothing else now.

We packed our baby bath and our eiderdowns in the canvas covering, and our clothes into our one suitcase, and loaded everything into a cart that Mum arranged to take us to the station. I looked back as we clip-clopped along the dirt road, as the house, the millstream, and the big hill slowly disappeared out of my life.

We arrived back at the Ellwangen refugee camp. Things had changed. It was not so well organized, and was now being used as a holding area for people waiting for their turn to emigrate to the various countries that had agreed to take up the refugees. The Refugee Resettlement Program was now fully in progress and people were keen to be resettled and travel to their new homelands. The creation of a "mini homeland" in the camps was of secondary consideration. Everything was now temporary, after four years of tranquility.

Australia was the country least known to practically everybody in the camp. One thing known about it was that it was sparsely populated, so people had images of dense forests and jungles where they would have to settle, and cut out a life and existence out of the wilderness.

Mum remembered her life in Siberia when she was only four, and she imagined it would be very similar: vast tracts of unsettled country with little civilization and a shortage of all facilities, equipment, and even basic tools.

Consequently, she took steps to make sure that she had everything necessary for us to survive in a fairly hostile environment. She bought a large cross-saw to take with us, an axe, various tools, and, of course, such things as pots and pans, cooking utensils, etc. If only we had known we were going to a civilized place, and everything we needed was already there, we would have travelled much more lightly with less trouble.

The procedure was fairly routine. An application was made to the host country, and this was processed by the immigration officials. This was followed by an interview, where questions were asked about why we wanted to go to Australia. It was very simple in our case. Mum just said that her husband was already in Australia as an immigrant, and we wanted to join him. This was a very solid, plausible reason, and we had little trouble to obtain our visas and approvals.

After that we had to go through a rigorous medical examination, including x-rays to cull out any tuberculosis sufferers. That was a problem for some people, as tuberculosis was prevalent in the refugee camps, contracted in the work camps under the Nazi regime, where there was poor hygiene and poor diet, with overwork. The Nazis did not care how quickly the workers died, as there were always more being transported from the occupied countries. My godfather particularly was worried that he might have a mark on his lung that would medically exclude him from any immigration. In our naïveté, we accepted the rumor that eating a lot of fat would camouflage the tuberculosis lesions. People therefore became quite fat while waiting for their medical examinations. We had no problems with ours. We had our x-rays done and they were clear, and the doctor did a perfunctory chest examination, and we passed without any problems.

In a matter of months, all of our papers were completed. We passed our medical examination, and we were only waiting for our transport arrangements. The procedure was that lists of families would be asked to be ready by a certain date. They would then catch a special train at the Ellwangen station, and this would take them to Naples in Italy. They would then stay in a transit camp until their boat was ready for sailing. Every day, therefore, groups of people would congregate at the immigration offices, trying to find their departure times.

The organization of the camp had now collapsed, as people were moving out, and the various activities and organizations, such as scouting, theater, dancing, and singing groups, were all folding up as their members left for their final destination. There was an air of excitement and expectancy as people talked about their various choices and their hopes for the future. Any information was shared, particularly letters from friends who had already arrived at their destinations.

Our turn finally came. I was very excited, as I just could not imagine what the sea looked like. I imagined it to be like a big river where you couldn't see the other bank, but certainly I couldn't imagine the color, the waves, and the dynamic life of its own that I found it to have. I asked Mum, but she also couldn't tell me, as she had never seen the sea. We didn't even have a picture or photograph. Ludmilla, Mum, and I were already packed, and when we received our departure date, we were ready to go.

We again had our baby bath and bedding in a canvas-covered pack. We had a suitcase for Mum and Ludmilla, and we had our old wooden box, which had previously acted as a larder. This time, however, it did not contain food, but our equipment that Mum thought we might need to survive in the dense forests of Australia. This was quite heavy and we had difficulty with our luggage. Fortunately, we had some friends who helped us, particularly Nicola and Natalie, a young couple who were married at the camp. They were good friends of the family and were also on the same train to Italy.

Trucks were provided to load all the people and their gear, and they took us directly to the train waiting at Ellwangen Station. Everybody was excited, a little anxious, and sad. We were saying good-bye, knowing that we may not see each other again. It was now about three and a half years since the end of the war, late summer in 1948. After this period of time of inactivity and uncertainty, pleasant as it was for some people, everybody was keen to make a new start and forge ahead with their lives. Many had married in the camps, and some even had young children, as the majority of them were young people when they left their homes seven or eight years before. Everybody on the train was going to Australia, and we were due to catch the same ship from Naples. The train was fully loaded, but we were comfortable as we all had seats, with only the hand luggage in the carriages, and the heavy suitcases and boxes, instead of people, were stashed in the goods wagons.

The hours passed slowly. We just watched the scenery pass by as we slipped through the towns and villages without stopping anywhere, and then through the countryside. The train continued south, and we noticed that it was getting warmer. We eventually stopped at a place called Banalla, in the northeastern corner of Italy on the Adriatic Sea. The train virtually stopped only a few hundred meters from the beach, and there before us was the sea.

It was the most wonderful view I had ever seen. It was bright blue with waves a foot high rolling in on the clean yellow sand. I have never seen so much sand in my life, and it was so inviting and cool. We were very hot at this stage, as the trains were full. There was no air-conditioning, and it was in late summer. This was where we were to stay the night, and apparently there was a holding camp for us to stay before going on to Naples. Without any hesitation, or asking permission, all the children jumped out of the train, took off their clothing and just raced into the water for their first swim in the sea. There was pandemonium as they all splashed and cavorted in the warm water. The waves were gentle. It was shallow, but we just splashed, pushed, and floated. All the parents were concerned with the luggage, and by the time they retrieved the luggage and tried to retrieve their children and impose some sort of order, the children were cooled and refreshed. I got a bit of a belting for my enthusiasm, but it was worth it. Mum tried to tell me that you could catch all sorts of things from the sea, and I wasn't to swim in it again. In the morning, we embarked on the train, slowly made our way further south, and by the afternoon were in a camp outside Naples, ready for our boats.

We were in a large camp in the hills of Naples, next to a citrus orchard. We were separated by high wire fences, and not allowed to roam outside the camp perimeter. There was a large area that looked like a parade ground. This was probably an old army camp. The people managed to find and arrange forty-four–gallon drums, which were placed around the field, and in the evening they made a fire in these drums, and congregated around the drums. This was a social event, and they sometimes roasted some bread, but it was mainly to socialize, talk, and perhaps sing a few rounds of folk songs. There was nothing to do in the large dormitories, which were absolutely crammed with bunks, three in height, with only space to walk past between the bunks.

The younger children my age congregated together, and, of course, we played our various games to keep ourselves occupied for days. One particular game was to hit a piece of stick about ten centimeters in length, sharpened at both ends. It would be placed on the ground with one of the sharp ends raised slightly. This would be hit by another longer stick like a bat to make it fly up in the air, and while it was in the air we endeavored to hit it with the stick we were holding in our hand, as far as possible. There were also competitions with teams on each side, and we would kick a football between the two teams, and whoever got to the end of the field won the game. We also tried throwing a few stones at the boys working in the orchards. They retaliated by throwing some oranges at us, which we appreciatively received. We passed the time happily.

Chapter 20

Trachoma Ward

Before the final departure, we had to undergo another medical examination. Our names were already on the list to catch the next boat, and a few days before, we had to all line up at the medical center to get a final clearance.

Ludmilla was examined, with the doctor looking under the eyelids, into her eyes, into her throat, her mouth, and her nose, listening to her chest, both back and front, and that completed her examination. My mother was also examined and passed readily with a full clearance stamped on her papers. When I was examined, however, there was some concern on the doctor's face when he looked under my eyelids. He took me aside and did not clear me, much to Mother's consternation. The doctor called someone else in to have a look at my eyelids. Another doctor came along and shined a light into my eyes, onto the lower and upper eyelids, nodded his head and said something to the other doctor. By this time, Mother was getting really worried, as she knew something was wrong, and I was not being cleared for final departure. She couldn't possibly understand what the problem was. I was completely healthy when examined at the Ellwangen camp, although I do remember that they did not examine under the eyelids. The doctor then called Mum over and through a translator he said, "I'm very sorry, but we cannot clear your son to go to Australia. He has trachoma."

Mum had no idea what trachoma was, and she glared at me, saying, "See, I told you. You shouldn't have gone for a swim in that sea, now you've caused something in your eye and won't be able to go to Australia." She was very worried. She didn't know whether this was permanent, or what treatment was required.

"Well, I'm very sorry, but this is an infectious disease, and you have to be completely clear before you will be allowed to travel on to Australia."

"But how long will it take? What do we have to do? What sort of treatment is it?" asked Mum, completely confused by this sudden change of events.

"Well, you'll have to go into hospital where they'll treat the trachoma, and it might take some weeks, or even a month to treat it, but we're not sure because it depends how it will respond to the treatment."

Our little family was therefore set aside. We saw all the other people pass the final medical, and we said good-bye to some of the friends that we had made on the trip down from Germany, and also some of the people we knew in the camps. We were worried and confused and did not really know what was going to happen to us, as we were now in Italy. We could not understand Italian, and I had to go to some hospital and stay for some weeks.

We were taken to the infectious diseases hospital. This was situated in the countryside, high in the hills, with a good view of Mt. Vesuvius. It was barren countryside, hilly, rocky, with no trees and sparse, dry vegetation. I suppose it was the end of summer, and the area was dry and hot. Mum and Ludmilla stayed in a small camp, which was set up for the relatives of people who were in the hospital. They lived in corrugated iron huts, in dormitories divided for men and women to live separately. Usually one member of the family was taken to the hospital, hoping to recover quickly.

I was taken to the trachoma ward with Mum, and she had to leave me there. I really didn't want her to leave and had to be persuaded. They were all strangers and grown-up men, some elderly, in their fifties and sixties, but most were in their thirties and forties. There were about ten or twelve men in a large dormitory, and only one other boy, whom I was to meet later. They were all different nationalities, and included Latvians, Lithuanians, some Czechs, and some I didn't even know, but there were no Ukrainians, so I had no one to talk to.

The hospital was very small. It consisted of only a single story, built on a rectangular design and an open space in the middle. This contained an old gazebo-type structure made of wooden poles covered by bamboo with some seats and a table. The service section of the hospital occupied one wing of the rectangle.

I was allotted one of the beds with the standard hospital bedside table made of steel. We were all physically well, except for our eye infections, and therefore we were expected to look after ourselves and make our own beds, wash ourselves, etc. There was no nursing care as such in this ward. The matron would, however, make a daily inspection, and we had to ensure that our beds were made to her standards. She would insist that they were tucked in and tight, and any unevenness or wrinkles would result in a strict reprimand. She spoke Italian, and although I could not understand what she was saying, there was no doubt that she was able to get the message across, and you tried much harder the next time to avoid the verbal tongue-lashing. I was aged seven and a half, and I was an expert bed-maker by the time I completed my stint at the hospital.

I met the other boy later—he was Latvian, and he was about thirteen or fourteen years old, considerably older than I. There was also a Latvian girl in the women's quarters—she was slightly younger and they were very friendly with each other. I was always on the periphery of their activities. The rest were all men and were not very interested in amusing small boys.

Again, I had to amuse myself. I quickly explored the grounds, and it did show some possibilities. The bamboo, I decided, would make a good bow and some of the thinner bamboo pieces would make excellent arrows. The laundry was situated in the service wing, and early in the morning until about just after lunch, about five or six Italian ladies were busily washing all the hospital sheets, towels, etc. by hand. There were no washing machines in that hospital. Everything was boiled in coppers, washed by hand, and then hung up to dry on lines in the middle quadrangle. It was interesting to watch them. They were constantly talking in loud but rather melodious tones with lot of laughter. There was very little that I could understand, but gradually I started to learn a few words, such as the word *mangiare*, to eat. However, I could always ask for food when I was hungry.

The food at the hospital was absolutely wonderful compared to what we were used to. There were such delicacies as stuffed green peppers, with a mixture of mincemeat and rice, seasoned with all sorts of herbs and baked in ovens with cheese on top. The cheese was golden and crisp and tasty. There were a lot of salads, pasta of all varieties. After most meals, there was a good supply of fresh fruit and watermelon.

The men there found it exceedingly boring. They just hated sitting around the beds, walking around with nothing really to do. There was no reading material, no radio music, and they could only talk and walk around. One night they decided to break out. Two of them climbed over the wire mesh fence and hopped on to the other side. They walked to the nearby village and came back with a few large flasks of red wine. They climbed back in, and that night I was kept awake by loud chatter and laughter as they enjoyed the rare privilege of having a drinking party. By morning everything was cleaned up and the bottles disposed of so that the matron had no idea what was happening. There was no nurse on night duty as we were all healthy individuals and required no nursing care.

The treatment for trachoma at that time was diabolical. Trachoma is an infection of the eyelids by chlamydia trachomatis, causing chronic conjunctivitis. The lining of the eyelids forms small granules and tubercles, and scar tissue gradually distorts the eyelid to the extent that the eyelid will be inverted and hairs would rub on the eye, gradually injuring the cornea, resulting in scar formation and eventual blindness. It is the result of living in poverty with overcrowded conditions and poor hygiene, the sort of condition I was virtually born in and had lived in for all of my life. It was not surprising that I got trachoma—what was surprising is that more people didn't get it.

We all had to join the treatment line in the morning. The matron came in with the doctor, pushing a medication trolley. Each patient had his individual small tray, and in the tray were some tissue paper and a crystalline blue-colored stone. It was actually called "blue-stone," and the treatment was simple: opening up the eyelid and rubbing the blue-stone over the surface of the eyelid, both on the bottom and the top. The pain was excruciating. It was a burning pain, as if acid were being rubbed into the eyelids. I thought I was being tortured and screamed out in pain. The nurse had to hold my hands with my face pointing upwards, while pulling back on my hair. This allowed the doctor to perform the "torture treatment." I went off crying to my bed and threw myself down on the pillow crying, covering my eyes with the tissues. It continued to burn, and it took about half an hour to an hour for the pain to completely subside, with some residual stinging. We also had some ointment applied, which eased the pain. This was a daily event, and every morning our day would start with blue-stone "torture." I would then be on my bed for about an hour until the pain settled down. I could see that the men were also in pain; they were all grumpy and surly after the treatment. One man, who was aged about sixty, was so keen to get better that he stole a piece of blue-stone and he would apply it to his eyes three or four times a day, thinking that the more he applied it the quicker he would get better. Unfortunately, more was not better, and instead of curing the trachoma more quickly, he developed an ulcer in his eyelid, and this took some weeks to heal—all treatment was stopped for that period when the doctor discovered the ulcer. That poor man must have been in pain all day applying his blue-stone on his own eyelids.

The rest of the day was spent any way we wished. I made myself a bow and arrows from the bamboo, and would go out into the courtyard and play with it for hours. The other young boy and the girl were sometimes friendly, but most of the time they would go off by themselves. There was obviously a romantic connection between them, and they preferred to be by themselves without a third young person to interfere with them. I had a comic with me, an old copy of *Katzenjammer Kids,* a German comic about a group of children and all the antics they would get up to playing tricks on the adults, etc. I would read that every day. I would make up my own stories as I looked at the pictures, and that was my most treasured possession in that isolation ward. I did not see my mother or my sister at all, as this was an isolation ward and only the nurses were allowed in with some degree of infection control. Because it was a communicable disease, the rules of isolation were very strict, as antibiotics were rare and very expensive, and infection control was only by isolation.

One morning I woke up with funny spots on my arms and legs. I was wondering what that was. I thought it might have been some dirt, so I tried to have a shower to wash it off, but it wouldn't come off. I started to worry a bit. Would I get into trouble again and be blamed for this disease also?

The matron on her treatment rounds noticed the spots as I had some on my face as well.

"Well, what have we here, young man?" she asked sternly. She looked closely and pointed out the spots to the doctor. He agreed with her, nodding his head. I heard something about chicken pox being mentioned.

Without much ado, I was transferred to an isolation room,

to isolate me further as I had another communicable disease in addition to my trachoma. I was put into a room all by myself without any contact with anyone, except for the provision of meals by a nurse. It was rather ridiculous. It was like being put in a solitary confinement cell in a prison. I was already restricted, and then placed completely into solitary confinement. I stayed there for about ten days, and as the spots faded and scabbed, I was allowed to return to the relative companionship of the trachoma isolation ward. I was glad to get back to at least some other human faces again.

On Christmas Day, the place was decorated for the occasion. The dinner was specially cooked, and we had roast chicken with all the trimmings and vegetables and a sweet pudding afterwards. There were a lot of cordials, but, of course, no alcohol was allowed in the hospital, except what was smuggled in by the grown-ups. There was no Santa Claus, however, and no presents, but a Latvian Catholic priest arrived with some presents for the two Latvian children. I was envious when I saw the beautiful wrapped bundles and the thrill they experienced when they opened up and saw the toys and the books they received. I wished I could have had a present too.

The days slowly slipped by. One day was exactly the same as the one before, and the one following was exactly the same: getting up in the morning, making the beds, having breakfast, having treatment with the blue-stone, which would burn the eyes for an hour or so, and then playing in the quadrangle. To pass some of the time, I would read and reread the one comic that I owned, making up my own story as I went along so that it would be a different story every time. There were no radios, televisions, books, or toys, so I had to make the best of the situation.

One evening about six months after I entered the ward, one of the nurses told me to follow her. I went outside and I was instructed to get into an old pre-war ambulance. It was getting dark now and I was wondering what this was all about, as this was a complete change to the normal routine. No one explained anything as they spoke only Italian, and I couldn't understand

Italian. We drove for about an hour or longer. I was not certain of the time, but it seemed a long way, and we entered the winding streets of Naples. At last we stopped in one of the narrow streets, and I was taken out of the ambulance and taken up a flight of stairs. I was placed in a reclining chair, similar to a dentist's chair. Bright lights were focused on my face, and someone put some drops in my eyes, and I could see some instruments coming towards me and tissue being removed from my eyelids. I couldn't feel anything, but I was frightened and screaming for help, as I wasn't sure what they were doing with me. After both my eyelids were treated, my eyes were dressed with eye pads taped on, and I was taken back to the hospital. I was not placed back into the ward, but was put into a room by myself and kept there for a day. The next day, the doctor checked my eyes again. I was told by the nurse that I was now cured. Mum was called, and I was reunited with my family after six months of isolation and daily torture.

We had to attend the hospital to pick up my few belongings, and we were told that everything had to go through the sterilizing procedure so that no trachoma infection would remain on the articles. I picked up my shoes and clothes, but alas my treasured comic book was ruined in the process.

We were then taken back to the transit camp and waited our turn to join the next available boat of refugees going to Australia.

Chapter 21

Australia

We searched daily for our names on the embarkation lists for three weeks, but each day we walked away disappointed when we failed to find our names on the list for a boat to Australia. All our visas and travelling documents were finalized, and we were waiting impatiently for our berth on the ship. One day we made our way to the notice board and pushed closer to find our names. There must have been about a thousand names on the list, and crowds of people were all around the notice board trying to find their names. We fought our way out of the crowd, elated at last—our name was there. Our long journey was about to resume.

"I'm so glad to be on the way again," said Mother. "But it's sad that all the friends from Ellwangen won't be with us and we'll be among a group of strangers."

"We'll probably catch up with them in Australia," answered Ludmilla. She too was desperate to get moving again. We had been in Italy for eight months. I was in hospital in the trachoma ward, while Mum and Ludmilla were just waiting around the transit camps seeing all their friends leave and boatload after boatload of people bypass them. They felt their lives were on hold.

We collected our few bags and the wooden case containing all the hardware and tools. Everything was loaded onto the truck. All of the heavy luggage was loaded separately into the ship's holds. We were allowed only one small suitcase to be taken on board by hand, consisting of our clothing and other personal belongings required for the trip.

When the buses arrived at the docks, we dutifully lined up one behind the other with our identification ticket attached to our coats as if we ourselves were only a piece of luggage. We had to show our visas and travelling documents as we boarded the ship in single file.

There was complete segregation between the sexes on the ship, as the conditions were poor with limited facilities. It was an old troop ship, and the men were herded into a huge dormitory-type cabin, which looked like a cave. There were no portholes for light or ventilation. It was stuffy and all the air had to be pumped in, so there was a steady hum of machinery noise, and there was a smell of diesel or some oil pervading the ship.

The bedding arrangements were cramped with bunks three high, and in rows separated by about one meter all throughout the room. There were hundreds of men and boys in the room. I, at the age of eight, was considered to be a man, and was separated from Mum and Ludmilla. I had one of the lower bunks, as I had difficulty getting into the higher bunks without any ladders. There were no cupboards or lockers, and all personal things were just placed under the pillow of the bunk or in suitcases in the narrow passageway between the bunks.

I was fearful of losing my only valuable possession, a small brass telescope Mum bought me in Naples after I was discharged from the hospital. It was my pride and joy. As soon as I was allocated my bunk, I ran out onto the deck and was observing the area around us with the telescope. I looked at the other ships berthed in the port, smaller boats scurrying busily around the harbor and some of the hills surrounding the harbor side, with winding steep streets and crowded houses. I was happy to just sit there for hours and observe the activities with my telescope.

I played with some of the boys, but they were unfriendly, and I felt they were jealous of my telescope.

The women were more comfortable. They were bunked in cabins, four to six women per cabin. Although they were crowded, they had a lot more privacy and quietness, and not the same press of humanity as in the men's quarters.

The first day was fun exploring the ship. It was huge. I never imagined a ship could be so big. It was like a multi-story building on its side. Our quarters were the lowest level, and there was another level above us, also containing men, but the women were in the cabins above with portholes for windows, which made the rooms light and breezy as the windows could be opened to allow in fresh sea air. In the quarters below, there was no fresh air and it had to be pumped in, making the dormitory stuffy and smelly.

I soon found Mum's and Ludmilla's cabin. They shared it with three other women who were strangers. I visited them, and we went around the ship exploring and discovering where all the services and facilities were situated: the closest toilets and bathrooms, and, of course, the cafeteria, where we all had meals in shifts, as there were too many of us to have a meal in one sitting.

By the next afternoon, the loading was complete, both the luggage and the human cargo. There were loud whistles and steam pouring out of the two funnels. The ship started to slowly move out of its berth with the help of two tugboats, and slowly the Italian coastline was receding and the buildings getting smaller in the distance as we made our way into the Mediterranean Sea. It was fine weather, although cold in mid November and the wind called the Minstral had quite a chill on deck. Most of the people were inside. Mum, Ludmilla, and I remained on deck, watching the shore disappear slowly with the distance and the receding light of the evening.

Life in the huge dormitory occupied by the men was daunting. It was very overcrowded, and every time I moved, I bumped into somebody or their luggage placed in the passageways or someone getting either dressed or undressed. I was in the lowest bunk, and had two bigger boys above me. I was by myself in the dormitory, but all the other children had their fathers with them to look after them.

Most of the boys around were envious of my brass telescope, and constantly wanted to borrow it to look at the sea or any other features, such as passing boats. I usually lent them this valuable instrument, even though it was my prized possession. I was observing everything in detail. I would find a vantage point, as high as possible on the decks. I would sit and look at the passengers, any passing ships, or just at the birds.

My stay in the male dormitory came to a nasty end only a few days after we left Naples.

At night before going to bed, I would go and have a shower in the communal washing facilities. I would always place my belongings under the pillow. These consisted only of my telescope and pocket knife. I did the same thing that night, and that night when I came back about half an hour later ready to go to bed, I looked under the pillow and my telescope was gone. I was frantic.

I started running around trying to find it. It was not on the ground, so I started asking around to see if anyone else had seen it. Near the door of the dormitory, I saw three or four boys sitting around in a circle, unusually occupied with something in the middle. They were laughing and giggling between themselves. When I got closer my heart sank. There were brass pieces, fine circles with threads on them and four or five glass lenses on the floor. The telescope was in bits, taken apart by these young hooligans. My anger swelled up inside me and I went racing up shouting, "What have you done with my telescope?" I grabbed the nearest boy by the scruff of his neck. I started shaking him. Before long the other boys joined in, and we were in a heap, pulling and punching. I had the advantage of surprise and anger, and was doing considerable damage. One of the other boys ran back and called his father, and in a few minutes, I felt myself being lifted up by my collar and pants by a big man.

"And what do you think you are doing, you young ruffian?" he growled, while holding me about a meter off the ground.

I called out in desperation, "They have stolen my telescope and broken it. Look, it is all in pieces." I pointed in the direction of the brass parts.

"All this fuss about a telescope. How dare you cause all this?" He let me down onto the ground with a cuff over the ear.

"You stole my telescope and you broke it. You owe me another one," I called out.

"No we didn't, it was just rolling around on the floor. We didn't know who it belonged to," replied one of the boys.

I knew that he was lying. There was no way it could have dropped out of the bed, as I had it well packed under the pillows, as I always did. However, there was no use arguing against them—they were a group of four and they had their brothers and fathers with them. I was by myself and had no chance of obtaining justice.

I sadly gathered all the pieces and tried to put them together. It was, however, hopeless, as there were bits missing and some of the lenses were broken, so there was no way it could be reassembled and work in the precise way that it had previously.

I immediately went to Mum's cabin and told her the whole sorry episode, crying in disappointment.

"Well, there is no way you are going back to that hole. Rule or no rule, you are going to stay in this cabin with us. You are only a child, and you can't be put among that lot."

I was pleased with Mum's decision, as I didn't feel safe going back to that group. I knew they would gang up on me in the future and take every chance to pick on me. I think I gave a few of them a black eye, and they had some scratches and bruises, and they would be keen to even up the score.

There was no school on board, but a few mornings a week, we had the option of going to the English classes. These were run by a young lady who was a teacher.

Alas, she tried hard to teach us English, but it was a lost cause. We weren't good students, and we didn't pay much attention, much to our disadvantage. We learned very little during this time, and I came away in the end knowing only a few words, such as "hello," "good-bye," "thank you," etc. We didn't learn really important things, like "Could you show me to the toilets, please," and I found this lack of knowledge a great disadvantage when I eventually did start school in Australia. We, however, learned some songs, and although we did not understand them, we sang the words from memory with a great deal of enthusiasm, but very little musical talent. Our favorite song was "You are my sunshine, my only sunshine."

In spite of the initial fracas, and the loss of my telescope, the remainder of the trip was enjoyable. Children my age played chase and hide and seek among the ship's various decks and cabins. There were also war games, where two teams would try to fortify positions among the deck chairs. We used to impro-vise and use toys such as homemade swords, with which we had sword fights, or wads of wet toilet paper squeezed out into pel-lets and used as hand grenades or artillery shells. A direct hit on the face wouldn't hurt, but certainly would produce a satisfying "splatter" sound. Best of all were the pillow fights. We would divide into two camps and attack each other with pillows, or even pretend we were riding on horses with one fighter on the shoulders of another boy. We would wield the pillows until we would knock each other off the shoulders, or knock over the rider and horse, to the ground. The time was pleasantly spent in these frolics or just resting, looking up at the bright blue sky in the hot sun. It was getting warmer. We were approaching the equator, as we left the winter cold of Europe behind us.

We had a stop for a very short time at Port Said, at the head of the Suez Canal. I watched the different small boats crowd around our ship, as they tried to sell their fruit or handicrafts to the passengers, but none of us had any money, so they usually went away disappointed. It was interesting to see the different colors of fruits that I hadn't seen before. I would have loved to have a taste of them, but I had no money to buy any.

After about four weeks, it felt as if the journey would never end. One day was like any other day. There was no school or responsibility. We just occupied ourselves with play. It was now getting wearisome, and we were all looking forward to the end of the journey. There was excitement in the air as we anticipated the first sight of land heralding the arrival to our destination. People were always looking and studying the horizon to see if they could see any land; grown-ups and the children too were keen to complete the journey.

Land was eventually sighted, a little speck on the horizon that slowly grew bigger and bigger, and was a pink line looking hazy and unreal, as if a mirage. We were having English training when we heard the news, and were so excited we burst forth spontaneously into song, singing "You are my sunshine, my only sunshine." The mood on the ship changed. There was an air of excitement, and people talked about what they were going to do on the land, speculating what type of country it might be. We had no idea of life in Australia. The prevailing concept was that it was a vast continent of wilderness, and that we had to virtually cut out an existence from the bush to survive without any modern tools of civilization.

We followed the coastline of the Great Australian Bight for days, tantalizing in the far distance.

The ship eventually came closer and closer to the shore. The faint shoreline slowly grew until we were quite close. We could observe the breakers breaking onto the cliffs. These were sheer sandstone cliffs, some twenty to thirty meters in height. There was a white lighthouse visible and some buildings at the very top of the cliffs. We then turned in a westerly direction, and steamed through a passage between high headlands. The passage was only about one and a half kilometers in width. As we passed through these "gates," we entered Sydney Harbour. The view was enchanting. After leaving war-ravaged Europe and devastation with bombed-out buildings and streets, and being on the sea for five weeks, we entered, what seemed to me, an enchanted harbor. There were myriads of little bays and beaches as we sailed down the middle, and headlands covered with a thick growth of trees, particularly on the right side. There were also elegant homes fronting some of the bays, with red roofs. There were many parks and trees along the harbor front. The little bays were filled with boats of all sizes, from big sailing boats to little cabin cruisers. Some of the sailing boats were out sailing with their white sails billowing with the wind and tilting over with the wind in a leisurely, languid way.

The sun was setting in the west as we were steaming towards it, producing the most beautiful display of colored cloud formation, bright orange, pink, and blue. The water had a purplish hue reflecting from the sunset. Before long the enormous, steel structure of the Harbour Bridge came into view. It was a huge metal structure with a circular top and horizontal road section supported by two huge sandstone pylons of square construction on the two sides of the harbor. To the left, we passed a circular bay containing a number of planes floating on the water. These were flying boats, huge, which somehow reminded me of pelicans. We steamed closer to the bridge. On the left was another small harbor, circular in shape, with six or seven wharves, very busy with ferries taking on passengers from the wharves, and some ferries already leaving full of passengers. The passengers from our ship were all on deck close to the handrails and on other vantage points, trying to observe their new home. There were friendly waves from the boats and ferries as we passed them. We all waved back eagerly. Just as we passed the bridge, on the right hand side, was a huge structure resembling a face with a big smile. It was brightly lit with lights, and beyond the smiling face was a large carnival park, with all sorts of Ferris wheels and other rides. It was filled with people, and there was gay music drifting across from the fun park. The whole place had such a relaxed friendly atmosphere. Fun and happiness seemed to be a feature of this enchanted place, with a large smiling face to welcome us.

Sailing into Sydney Harbour on a warm, balmy, sunny evening at sunset, welcomed by the friendly gestures of the people in the boats, was my most unforgettable experience. At that time, I decided that I wanted to be part of these people. I was wrenched from being Ukrainian, I failed to be a German, and the Italian experience was nothing but torture. I decided at that point that I would do my utmost to become an Australian. I felt that I was home at last, with all the travelling and dislocation of my previous life only part of a long journey to come home to Sydney.

After passing under the bridge, we turned left and docked, in what I later discovered to be Darling Harbour. We disembarked and went straight onto trains waiting to take us to the transit camps in Bathurst.

Chapter 22

Life in Australia

By the time we disembarked and transferred to the waiting train at the Darling Harbour docks, it was very late. I was exhausted and fell asleep as soon as I made myself comfortable on the train. When I woke up, we were already in Bathurst. I saw nothing of Sydney and missed the whole trip to Bathurst. We were transferred onto a fleet of old buses and made our way to a large camp, where all the new arrivals were processed.

The landscape was different than anything I saw before. As far as I could see, there were undulating hills covered with sparse, brown, sun burnt grass with small clumps of trees. These were gum trees. Sheep were grazing in the huge paddocks in small groups. There were dams half-filled with water and surrounded with a mantle of red earth, dry and cracked on the periphery.

The most striking impression was the sky. It was the most intense blue without a single cloud. It was so bright that I had to squint to protect my eyes. The sun was hot, unrelenting at this time of the day, and I had to seek some shade.

We were transferred to a large building with a high ceiling that looked like a warehouse or factory. The families made themselves comfortable in small cubicles with hard mattress already provided. Toilets and showers were communal, but segregated between the sexes.

The food was cooked for us, and we were served by walking past a serving bar with our plates. The food consisted of the usual carrots, peas and mashed potatoes but the meat was baked lamb, grilled lamb chops, or lamb stew. Lamb was a delicacy I never tasted before. The servings of meat were huge by our experience. The meat was delicious. There was plenty of milk and bread. Desert was often tinned peaches and custard. I loved it.

We washed the dishes ourselves in an outdoor area with rows of sinks, assembled roughly but fitted with hot water. After the meals, the children my age played together. The games were again pillow fights and wrestling while riding on someone's shoulders. Soccer when someone had a ball was also popular. Catching rabbits was a new activity. There were hundreds of them, but Mum but did not need to catch any as we had plenty of food.

All we had to do was eat and play. There was no school at the camp. It was only a short-term stay to sort out the new arrivals before sending them to their employment. The contract was that on arrival to Australia, every person of working age had to accept any employment that was offered, in any area for a period of two years. There were no unemployment benefits, as there was plenty of work available but sometimes in less desirable positions.

Lucy at age sixteen was considered of working age, and she was the first to be assigned a job. She was sent to work as a kitchen assistant in a small holiday hotel in Manly, a popular seaside suburb in Sydney. She had the use of a small room in the basement of the building. She was excited about starting her new life and to actually earn some money. She was confident about leaving us, since she boarded at Ellvangen refugee camp while finishing her schooling.

Finding work for Mum took a little longer. She spoke no English and had no reading skills. Eventually she was placed as a housekeeper in Rose Bay, a harborside suburb close to Bondi, another famous beach in Sydney.

The position was perfect. She was employed by a Jewish family. The woman was originally from Germany and could readily communicate with Mum in German. Mum could understand a little Yiddish, the Jewish language. She also was experienced in the special requirements in a Jewish household as she worked in a number of Jewish homes in Ukraine. She could cook and bake in the Jewish tradition and serve during the Sabbath. She also cleaned the very large, luxurious house. I have never seen such opulence, certainly not in the work or refugee camps.

The man owned a number of butcher shops. He was starting work very early in the morning and came home late at night. We hardly ever saw him. The family had three children, including a boy aged about fourteen. He was tall and gangly, much too superior to associate with me except when he wanted a boxing sparring partner. I complied with his request a few times, but it was no contest. He was a foot higher and years older. After he knocked me out one day, when he hit me on the face and I hit my head on the wall behind me, I refused any further bouts and kept away from him. Mum was furious and nearly walked out when she heard of the incident.

The girl was about thirteen and also started high school. Her main interest was dressage horse riding. She had her horse kept in stables attached to Centennial Park, a huge area of parkland attached to the exclusive Eastern suburbs of Sydney. She must have been very good. Her bedroom had a whole wall covered with ribbons that she won in dressage competitions.

The baby was a delight. He was only fourteen months old and demanded a lot of care and attention. I soon realized that everyone was too busy with their own affairs to provide the constant care he demanded. I started to play with him and take care that he did not run onto the road, picked him up if he fell, amused him if he cried, etc. This made me "useful," and I was included in all the family outings such as to the beach, visiting the horse stables, and even visits to other families. It also kept me out of the way of the son, who tended to be a bully.

I was in the background during all the activities and was absorbing and learning the behavior, etiquette, and even the basic rules of table manners. I was a complete stranger to all the cultural norms and practices in this country. My English language skills were not developed during this time as I was comfortable talking German in the home.

I at last had to start school as the summer holiday drew to a close. I was enrolled in Rose Bay Public School, not far from the beautiful Sydney Harbour. Attending a new school was very daunting. I was now over eight years old and up to the present time had little and only fragmented education, some in Ukrainian, a little in German, even though I could speak only limited German. The last year was spent in a trachoma ward and travelling to Australia, so I forgot everything I ever learned. The only thing I learned on the boat was how to sing the songs "You Are My Sunshine" and "God Save the Queen," although I did not know the meaning of the words and sang out of tune—hardly a scholarly or musical achievement. I could not read or write in any language and had a rudimentary understanding of numbers and what they did. Now I was starting school, again in a new language and in a new country.

The first day was a disaster. At that time, there were no services available for new immigrants, and teachers were not trained to handle the children with language difficulties. When other children talked to me, I nodded or shook my head, not really understanding what they were saying. The critical issue for me was finding the toilets. I could not ask directions and had to wait till lunch time when I observed the "flow" of male students and followed them.

I made no friends at the school, as it was difficult to communicate with anyone. The children laughed at my attempts to talk and when asked to repeat my name, they would burst into laughter and call me "kerosene tin" as they could not understand "Kirychenko."

After school I would frequently wander around the harbor shore by myself and explore the boats and look at the Catalina flying boats landing and taking off. They looked like huge pelicans.

Our protected life in Rose Bay came to a sudden end. Since my mother's head injury during the war, she suffered from occasional epileptic seizures. They were worse if she was under stress. At that time, there was no medication and no way of controlling them. She sustained a number of fits in a cluster. The employer was concerned about the effects this would have on the children, as the fits were frightening and disturbing. She therefore terminated the employment. Mum was also getting tired of the constant work of looking after the needs of the large family and cleaning the huge house. She was ready to go.

We caught a taxi to Manly with our suitcases of meager belongings. With permission from the hotel management, we moved into the small room used by Lucy. It was tiny, with only enough room for two small beds and the suitcases stored under the beds. We were happy to be together again. The room was cozy and warm. It was luxury compared to some of our previous primitive accommodation. Mother obtained work in the hotel kitchen, and we dined well on the leftover food after the hotel residents had their meals.

I was enrolled again in the small Manly Primary School only about a block away from the mighty Manly beach. The children were friendly and curious but interaction was again limited. I just sat at the back of the class and listened to the confusing talk and the procedures of the classroom.

After school, however, I was free to enjoy the wonders of Manly. It was one of the best beaches in Sydney. The surf was constantly pounding the wide expense of yellow sand, and there were huge pine trees along the beach front. The color of the sea and sky was always changing depending on the weather and the position of the sun. Sunsets were always the most colorful. I roamed the area, exploring the rocks and rock pools on the southern edge of the beach, catching and examining the sea creatures left behind by the tide.

On the Sydney Harbour side of the peninsula, it was just as interesting, with the small boats moored in the bay and a large ferry wharf where the Manly ferry docked every half hour. Young boys would swim near the wharf and dive for coins that some generous passengers threw into the water. I admired their skill a lot, as I could not even swim. At this stage, it did not matter as it was winter and the blue water did not attract me to enter the sea.

One day when I arrived home from school, Lucy met me with unrestrained excitement. She had a letter in her hand and was waving it about. "Father is coming. Father is coming." She had a smile on her face from ear to ear.

I was apprehensive, as I had not seen or heard from him since the day in Germany when he left so angry three years ago. I even received a belting that day. At the time I felt abandoned and did not think of him as part of my life anymore. I never thought I would see him again.

We met him at Central Railway Station. He walked to us slowly with a large battered suitcase in his right hand as we waited on the platform. He looked older, smaller, and thinner than I imagined him. His face was burned like dark, old leather by the hot western sun, with cracks and lines on his face that I did not remember. He wore a dark felt hat at a cocked angle and had a cigarette in the corner of his mouth. He looked like a stranger, except for his eyes. They were large and dark brown, with a softness and sadness that I remembered from the last time I saw him. Yes, he was my father.

When he saw us, his face broke into a smile, and he dropped his suitcase and ran towards us. We hugged together and could say very little as tears choked any words. Our family circle was at last complete, in Australia, having survived the ravages of war, bombings, refugee camps, and separation.

We travelled back to Manly to our little room and basked

in the warmth of the moment. We ate the chocolates that Dad brought for us and listened to stories of his life in Western Australia. He worked in the forests of the southwestern corner of Australia, logging the huge, hardwood trees. He described the animals, snakes, and trees that he saw in the bush. He also described the long train trip from Perth, travelling days through the desert on the southern edge of Australia—things I did not even imagine existed.

Over the next few days, Mum and Dad became the old team that enabled them to survive during the war. Father was able to save a considerable amount of money since coming to Australia, and he was now keen to stabilize the family and build a home again. Mother was keen to have a plot of ground and grow her own vegetable garden and run some chickens.

While Lucy and Mum worked, Dad was looking for a suitable block of land. It had to be within the price range of their available capital, as the concept of borrowing money was foreign to them.

One Sunday Lucy woke me up early and told me that Dad had bought a block of land and we were going to see it that day. Mum and Dad were already there. I was ecstatic. "Where was it? How big is the house?" I wanted to know everything about it.

"Well, it's not a house but only a block of land. We will have to build the house on it," replied Lucy, trying to quiet me down. "Get dressed and we will go and look at it."

We quickly got dressed and caught the Manly ferry to the city. I loved going on the ferry. It was like going on a mini sea voyage, with a large swell as we passed the heads and were exposed to the sea. The waves would sometimes break over the front of the boat sending spray everywhere. It took about half an hour to get to the city. We then caught a train to Parramatta, a large commercial center west of the city. We left the station and walked west up a steep hill, through a golf course on the right side. On the left was Parramatta High School with its playing fields. (Little did I realize that in the future, I would attend that school. My adult life would be molded in those classrooms and the playing fields, and I would become the school captain.)

We then went down the other side of the hill, and after four blocks, we turned into our street, Broxbourne Street. Our land was the first block on the left.

It was large, about fifty feet wide and two hundred and fifty feet long. It was flat and covered with weedy bushes with one large tree on the right boundary. Right at the end of the block was a small iron shed used as a chicken coop. There were no doors or windows, and one side was open and covered with wire netting to keep the chickens inside. The floor was earth.

"Well, this will be our home and next weekend we will move in," declared Dad. "We will live here and gradually I will build a large house in front. This house will be ours, and no one will take it away from us." He was excited at the prospect of at last building a secure foundation and home for his family. We were all swept along by this vision, and prepared to apply all our efforts to achieve this goal.

We lived in the chicken shed for six months until we built a small two-room cabin. It was like living in a drafty tent. The chicken coop was made much more comfortable when we poured a concrete floor. The weather was getting warm by then, so it was not too uncomfortable.

We lived in the small cabin for nearly four years until we built our house. We had an outside cold water tap and an outside toilet. We cooked on a cooker and bathed once a week in the old baby bath, heating all the water on a Primus cooker. Mum had her free-range chickens and sold the eggs, and we used the whole block as a vegetable garden.

These days we would be regarded as producing a very small carbon footprint, but then we were regarded as very poor, and the neighbors could not understand what we were doing.

However, compared to our previous life, we felt happy. We had at last found our home.

Small cabin built on land in Australia 1951.

Ivan working as a timber cutter in Western Australia during 1949

Lydia and family outside their cabin in 1952.

Father building our house in Australia --1953

Printed in Australia
AUHW020813220322
361200AU00001B/1

9 781609 7647